International Political Economy Series

Series Editor
Timothy M. Shaw, University of Massachusetts Boston, Boston, MA,
USA;
Emeritus Professor, University of London, London, UK

The global political economy is in flux as a series of cumulative crises impacts its organization and governance. The IPE series has tracked its development in both analysis and structure over the last three decades. It has always had a concentration on the global South. Now the South increasingly challenges the North as the centre of development, also reflected in a growing number of submissions and publications on indebted Eurozone economies in Southern Europe. An indispensable resource for scholars and researchers, the series examines a variety of capitalisms and connections by focusing on emerging economies, companies and sectors, debates and policies. It informs diverse policy communities as the established trans-Atlantic North declines and 'the rest', especially the BRICS, rise.

NOW INDEXED ON SCOPUS!

Manuel Neumann

The Political Economy of Green Bonds in Emerging Markets

South Africa's Faltering Transition

Manuel Neumann
Political Science
University of Kassel
Kassel, Germany

ISSN 2662-2483 ISSN 2662-2491 (electronic)
International Political Economy Series
ISBN 978-3-031-30501-6 ISBN 978-3-031-30502-3 (eBook)
https://doi.org/10.1007/978-3-031-30502-3

Cover illustration: © Rob Friedman/iStockphoto.com

This Palgrave Macmillan imprint is published by the registered company Springer Nature
Switzerland AG
The registered company address is: Gewerbestrasse 11, 6330 Cham, Switzerland

Acknowledgments

First and foremost, I owe a big thanks to Franziska Müller, for the work she put into advising me on my journey towards publishing this book. Insisting on sending me into the 'field' early into my research proved exceptionally foresighted given the limitations the Covid-19 pandemic would later place on travel. Thank you also for the constructive one-on-one sessions we had on refining the structure and main ideas of each chapter.

Many thanks are due Christoph Scherrer, who readily welcomed me into his colloquium despite his already innumerable obligations. I am grateful for the feedback I received on the chapters I presented in his brown-bag lunches.

I am exceptionally grateful to Simone Claar, my research project lead. Without the research funding you secured with Franziska, I would not have gotten this fantastic opportunity to pursue this work. Thanks for having my back over the last couple of months I needed to finish this book. Thanks, also, for creating a work environment conducive to open discussions. I appreciate especially your candid advice on vital matters such as work regulations or career choices.

Thanks to Daniel Mertens, for taking me up on my invitation to come to Kassel for the presentation of this book, even though we had only 'met' digitally on the DVPW Political Economy Section, hosted in Braunschweig in 2021. Thanks for your thoughtful questions.

Special mentions are also in order for my publishers, especially Timothy Shaw, Anca Pusca, and Lynnie Sharon at Palgrave's International Political Economy Series. Thanks for your encouragement to pursue publishing my work with this brilliant series.

Of course, none of this research would have been possible without the assistance from colleagues at Wits University in Johannesburg. Special thanks go to Vishwas Satgar for organizing an office space at Wits and granting me the opportunity to present our work at his lecture series as part of the Emancipatory Futures Studies Program. Thanks also to Patrick Bond and Barend Erasmus, not only for their great inputs, but more so for facilitating crucial connections to institutions and stakeholders in the green finance realm.

I am significantly indebted to all my interviewees for making the time to speak with me despite the lack of immediate return an academic book offers to practitioners and civil society actors. Thanks for your revealing insights and for recommending me on to colleagues without any reservations. This work would have been impossible without you.

My research stay in Johannesburg and Cape Town would have taken a different turn had I not met Jon Barnes and Anna Dowrick early on to share the plight and joys of academics working their field of research. Thanks for your company after long days of work. Research stays often mean schedules being packed with interviews and mine was no different. But thanks to an incredibly welcoming frisbee 'pick-up' session, I got some respite by joining the Wits Ultimate Frisbee team for several games. A big shout-out go to the entire squad, especially Tshepo Thaela, Lungile Ngwenya, Hannah Sarakinsky, Ross Bentley, and Nicole Wernberg.

My colleagues and friends at Kassel and Hamburg University earn immeasurable gratitude for their support during and after office hours for matters related to this work and beyond: Carsten Elsner, Ellie Gunesch, Tobias Kalt, Swazi Mthombeni, Nina Glatzer, Anna Pagel, and Anil Shah.

At last, my deepest gratitude for their love and support belongs to my family: My parents Norbert & Ella and my siblings Nicolai & Charlotte.

About This Book

This book is based on my Ph.D. dissertation entitled "Green Bonds in South Africa—The political economy of a stalling market" which I submitted to the University of Kassel (FB05, Social Sciences) on June 30, 2022, and successfully defended on November 2, 2022. I conducted my research as part of the research group 'Glocalpower', which is financed by the German Ministry of Education and Research (BMBF, funding line 01LN1707A).

CONTENTS

About the Author

Manuel Neumann is a Senior Policy Officer at the German Federal Ministry for Economic Cooperation and Development. He did his Ph.D. at Kassel University and was a visiting scholar at Wits University in Johannesburg in 2018 and 2019. Beforehand, he worked in the development context in Geneva, Kathmandu, and Berlin and studied in London (M.Sc.), New Delhi, and Tübingen (B.Sc.). His research revolves around green financial innovation and the political economy of energy transitions in the global South.

ABBREVIATIONS

AfDB   African Development Bank
ANC   African National Congress
ASEAN   Association of Southeast Asian Nations
ASISA   Association for Savings and Investments South Africa
BASA   Banking Association South Africa
BATSETA   The Council of Retirement Funds for South Africa
BEE   Black Economic Empowerment
BRICS   Brazil, Russia, India, China, and South Africa
C40   Cities Climate Leadership Group
CBI   Climate Bonds Initiative
CICERO   Center for International Climate Research
COP   Conference of the Parties
COSATU   Congress of South African Trade Unions
CRISA   The Code for Responsible Investing in South Africa
CSIR   Council for Scientific and Industrial Research
DBSA   Development Bank of Southern Africa
DFIs   Development Finance Institutions
ESG   Environmental, Social, and Governance
FSCA   Financial Sector Conduct Authority
GBP   Green Bond Principles
GDP   Gross Domestic Product
GEAR   Growth, Employment, and Redistribution Program
GEPF   Government Employees Pension Fund
GGKP   Green Growth Knowledge Partnership
GHG   Greenhouse Gases
ICLEI   International Council for Local Environmental Initiatives

ICMA	International Capital Markets Association
IDC	Industrial Development Corporation
IFC	International Finance Corporation
ILO	International Labor Organization
IMF	International Monetary Fund
INR	Indian Rupee
IPCC	Intergovernmental Panel on Climate Change
IPP	Independent Power Producers
IRP	Integrated Resource Plan
JSE	Johannesburg Stock Exchange
KfW	Kreditanstalt für Wiederaufbau
KPIs	Key Performance Indicators
LDC	Less-Developed Country
MDB	Multilateral Development Bank
MEC	Minerals-Energy Complex
NDCs	Nationally Determined Contributions
NGO	Non-Governmental Organizations
NUM	National Union of Mineworkers
OECD	Organization for Economic Co-operation and Development
PIC	Public Investment Corporation
PPP	Public-Private-Partnerships
RDP	Reconstruction and Development Plan
REI4P	Renewable Energy Independent Power Producers Procurement Program
SACP	South African Communist Party
SAWEA	South African Wind Energy Association
SDGs	Sustainable Development Goals
SEB	Skandinaviska Enskilda Banken AB
SOE	State-Owned Enterprise
SPV	Special-Purpose-Vehicle
SSO	Standard-Setting Organization
UNDP	United Nations Development Program
UNEP	United Nations Environment Program
UNFCCC	United Nations Framework Convention on Climate Change
WWF	World Wildlife Fund
ZAR	South African Rand

LIST OF FIGURES

CHAPTER 1

Green Bonds and the Long Way to Paris

After the nations' heads of state convened at the 27th Conference of the Parties (COP27) in the city of Sharm el-Sheik just off the North-Eastern edge of the African continent in November 2022, Paris seemed distant, not only geographically. Also, the climate goals—agreed in Paris in 2015—of staying below 1.5 °C of global warming at the end of this century have remained an almost unsurmountable yet equivocally pressing challenge. Successive special reports by the Intergovernmental Panel on Climate Change (IPCCC) sounded the alarm on thresholds or tipping points drawing closer which could render impossible human and non-human livelihoods in vast parts of the world (see the latest IPCC summary for policy-makers, Pörtner et al., 2022). The ramifications borne out of climate change, however, have asymmetrical effects across the globe. According to the African Development Bank's African Economic Outlook published in May 2022, the continent "is the least climate-resilient region in the world, with high vulnerability to climate change and low readiness for adaptation to climatic shocks" (AfDB, 2022, p. iv). And despite "the world's biggest technical potential for renewable energy " (ibid., p. 79), a renewable energy transition is still in its nascent stages despite a few promising policy mixes across the continent (Müller et al., 2020, 2021).

Arguably one of the biggest hurdles in advancing climate mitigation and adaptation is attracting the necessary funding. The gulf between

M. Neumann, *The Political Economy of Green Bonds in Emerging Markets*, International Political Economy Series, https://doi.org/10.1007/978-3-031-30502-3_1

1

climate finance and the infrastructural demand for the continent is enormous. The AfDB (2022, p. 9) estimates an investment gap to meet the continent's nationally determined contributions (NDCs) to achieving net zero by 2050 to range from US$ 99.9 to 127.2 billion considering current inflows of climate finance. Unfortunately, wealthy countries failed to meet their pledge to developing and emerging countries to provide an annual 100 billion in climate finance until 2020 as agreed upon at COP15 in Copenhagen in 2009. By 2019, merely US$ 79.6 bn in annual support (up just 2% from 2018) has been transferred (Gabbatiss, 2021), not to mention allegations of double-counting which additionally cloud the picture (Timperley, 2021). With scenarios projecting climate finance to reach the targeted US$100 billion only by 2023 (OECD, 2021, p. 6), the pledge has fallen short of expectations.

Propelled by the discourse around the investment gap, private investors have increasingly ventured into the arenas of sustainable development and climate governance, incrementally repositioning finance as a key driver in these endeavors. Though the private sector was invited to participate in development efforts already in the early 2000s (Dodds et al., 2017, p. 144), the universally applicable Sustainable Development Goals (SDGs) carved this trend directly into their agenda in 2015. The UN passed the SDGs with explicit reference to global partnerships (Goal 17) across public and private sectors, thus calling for increased private ownership and buy-in into transnational development agendas (see Perry, 2021, for a critical reading). To implement the SDG agenda, the United Nations Development Program (UNDP) suggests an annual investment need ranging between US$ 5 to 7 trillion, of which a majority shall stem from private actors. The UN, indeed, has not put up a concrete figure that it demands from the private sector, but it joined the chorus of International Monetary Fund (IMF), some regional development banks and the World Bank (2015) who declared the overhaul of development finance by "moving from billions to trillions" (p. n/a)—simply by enticing private sector investments (see Mawdsley, 2018, for a critique). The recently launched World Bank campaign 'maximizing finance for development' aims to "systematically leverage *all* sources of finance, expertise, and solutions to support development countries sustainable growth" (World Bank, 2022, p. n/a, own emphasis).

All these programs prominently feature the financial sector as a major piece in their puzzle. That same financial sector has witnessed astounding growth rates in the last three decades and emerged as a key player in allocating transnational investments through various innovations. Against the backdrop of insufficient (public) official development assistance and the active call to enlist non-conventional actors in the struggle for sustainable transformation, financial innovations that target climate-related investments have started plugging this gap.

Green bonds are one such innovative instrument that has gained particular momentum in the last 15 years. The World Bank defines a green bond as "a debt security that is issued to raise capital specifically to support climate-related environmental projects" (World Bank, 2015, p. 23). Praised as 'innovative finance' by the World Bank's vice president (Arunma Oteh, 2018) for its result-oriented usage, its efficiency, and cost-competitiveness, green bonds have witnessed exponential growth rates since their inception in 2007. In 2020, cumulative issuance volumes surpassed US$ 1 trillion (CBI & Agora Energiewende, 2021, p. 7) with growth trajectories remaining unwaveringly optimistic and new actors from both the private and public spheres entering this bourgeoning market.

As Fig. 1.1 demonstrates, however, the lion's share of climate finance (including green bonds) between 2017 and 2021 was invested in Europe/Central Asia. Hardly any climate finance flowed into Africa. Against the backdrop of its significant climate vulnerability, its limited contribution to global CO2 emission (as captured in the carbon budget to which Africa contributes less than 3% (AfDB, 2022, p. 62)), and vast technical transition potential, it comes as no surprise that the President of the AfDB bemoans the "current lopsided global climate finance architecture" (ibid., p. iv). This book will dwell on some of the reasons for the limited success of green financial innovations, focusing specifically on green bonds.

As a BRICS member (see Monyae & Ndzendze, 2021 for a comparison of its members and stance vis-à-vis the 'West' and Zondi, 2022, for the bloc's weight towards advancing the SDGs), South Africa is an integral green economy among emerging economies. Accounting for 73.8% of cumulative issuances between 2010 and 2021 (ibid., p. 108), South Africa has got the most active green bond market on the continent. As one of the most industrialized economies (third in overall gross domestic product (GDP) only to Nigeria and Egypt (World Population Review, 2022)), South Africa disposes of a vibrant economy and is an

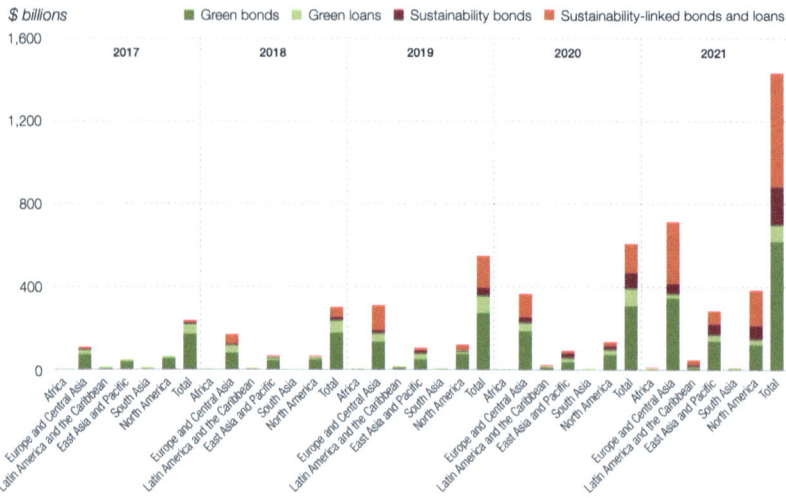

Fig. 1.1 Volumes of sustainable bond investment across regions and bond type (in US$), drawn from AfDB (2022, p. 107)

oft-overlooked 'green state' frontrunner despite tanking pertinent environmental and transition rankings (Death, 2014, 2016). Commanding the most sophisticated capital markets on the continent, the country comfortably leads the chart of capital stock market capitalization as a share of GDP) at 235% (compared to second-placed Mauritius at 56%, see AfDB, 2022, p. 106). But despite scoring relatively high on the Climate Resilience Index score (ibid., p. 54), the floods in KwaZulu-Natal and Durban in April 2022 underscored the country's persisting exposure to climate shocks (Carrington, 2022; Magome, 2022), borne disproportionately by the economically worse off. Climate change trends, equally, sound the alarm. Rainfall is projected to decrease by as much as 400 mm per year (equaling 50% of the baseline normal) in the Northern and central regions and also temperature may go up 2 C to 4 C in the coastal regions and 3 C to 6 C in the inland regions (AfDB, 2018, p. 9), underscoring the urgency of mitigating measures in South Africa and beyond.

To address climate change on a national level, the current government updated its NDCs in 2021. National Greenhouse gas (GHG) emissions are now supposed to peak and plateau around 2025 at 398–510 Mt CO_2-eq and decline to 350–420 Mt CO_2-eq by 2030 (Republic of South

Africa, 2021). To make these ambitions reality, however, the country faces estimated financing needs amounting to US$ 55–59 billion between 2020–30 (AfDB, 2022, p. 171). Heavily steeped in fossil resource extraction, South Africa ranks 12th in the list of highest global emitters (ibid., p. 171) underscoring the need to shift the country into greener futures. This deep-seated fossil path dependency also makes it a fascinating case of inquiry, especially from a political economic point of view. Given the deep entrenchment technological path dependencies and lock-ins (Brown & Sovacool, 2011; Unruh, 2000), transitioning away from unsustainable modes of consumption and production is a challenging task. One emerging demand is that a radical socio-economic transformation is required at this stage, encompassing a revamping of production chains, occupational skills, logistics, public and service sector activities, and not least individual consumer habits (Swilling & Annecke, 2012, p. xix). As the Climate Bonds Initiative (CBI) put it, South Africa has a huge opportunity "to be the first coal-based economy in the global south [sic] to make a successful transition to a low carbon economy" (CBI & Agora Energiewende, 2021, p. 2). Green investment lobby groups like the CBI readily promote green bonds as the vehicle to make the 'green economy' and thus, the reconciliation of economic growth with sustainable modes of living, a reality. However, opportunity does not mean feasibility from a political economic point of view, especially where fossil incumbents hold powerful sway.

THE RESEARCH PUZZLE—SOUTH AFRICA'S GREEN BOND MARKET

The research puzzle, this book seeks to untangle, revolves around the *lack* of green bonds being issued in South Africa. Despite exponential growth rates of the market elsewhere in the world, such as Europe, the USA, or China, issuances of green bonds in South Africa seemed to have stalled recently. According to a comprehensive assessment of South Africa's green bond market by Climate Bonds Initiative (CBI) and Agora Energiewende (2021) in August 2021, just 12 green bonds had made it onto the CBI's green bond database (see Fig. 1.2). Only Nedbank (JSE, 2021) and Standard Bank (Engineering News, 2021) listed another green bond for green residential development and renewable energy, respectively, since this CBI report was launched, thus raising the count to 14. As things stood as of June 2021, only 10 different issuers listed green bonds on the JSE (see Fig. 1.3), with Standard Bank joining later on in December 2021 (Businesslive, 2021; Engineering News, 2021).

Simultaneously, global green bond markets have set consecutive records in volumes issued, with Europe leading the charge (see Figs. 1.1 and 1.4). As per an Environmental Finance (2022) annual round-up

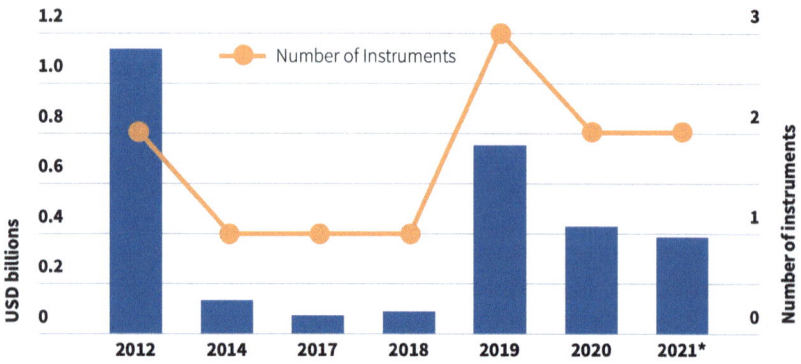

*Some 2021 deals are pending inclusion in the Climate Bonds green bonds database due to a lack of information available but are included here and below for completeness.

Fig. 1.2 South African green bond market issuances (Climate Bonds Initiative and Agora Energiewende, 2021, p. 8)

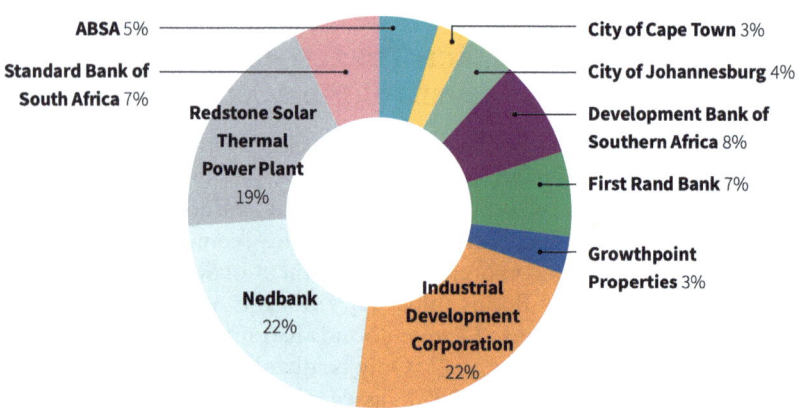

Fig. 1.3 South Africa's green bond issuers (till July 2021) (Climate Bonds Initiative and Agora Energiewende, 2021, p. 8)

for 2021 and CBI's Fig. 1.4, green bonds have almost doubled the previous year's volumes (which had already set a record) at US$ 501 billion, *amidst* the ongoing Covid-19 pandemic. And the feast seems far from over. Current projections paint an exponential growth trajectory for the next couple of years, with US$ 5 trillion in sight for 2025 alone (Climate Bonds Initiative, 2022). Despite the apparent benefits of green bonds that the financial practitioner literature so actively espouses (see Chapter 2), neither South African issuers nor interested investors could thus far harness a similar momentum domestically (see Figs. 1.1 and 1.4). The overarching research question of this book, therefore, is: *Why have green bonds not taken off in South Africa?* In raising this question, this book critically discusses some of the limits of green market innovations in emerging economies. It also provides important counterevidence to those promoting green bonds as the self-fulfilling prophecy of a green economy and, thus, contributes to the literature discussing the political economy of finance-driven transition endeavors (Paterson, 2020b). This book helps close a blind spot in the scholarship of the International Political Economy by dealing with some of the challenges posed by climate change (LeBaron et al., 2020).

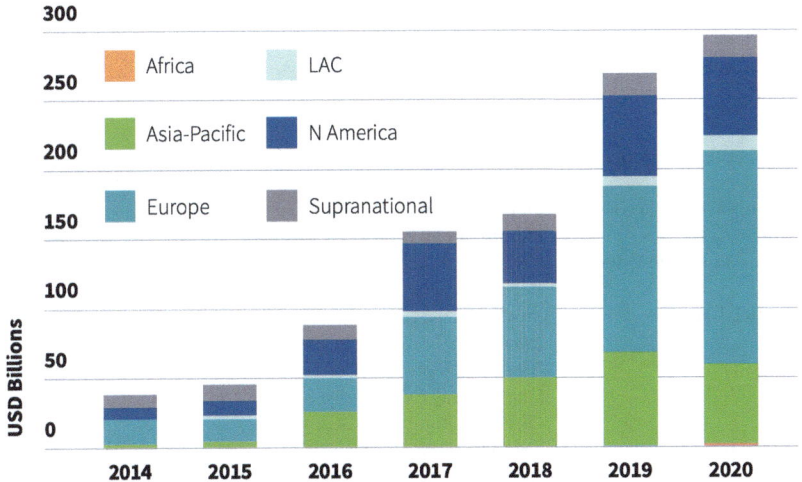

Fig. 1.4 Global green bond market by US$ volumes issued per region, adapted from Climate Bonds Initiative and Agora Energiewende (2021, p. 7)

This book draws on a total of 46 interviews with financial practitioners, government officials, development bankers, and environmental interest groups conducted during and after a research stay in Johannesburg and Cape Town from February to April 2019. Table 1.1 provides an overview of the interviews I conducted and the additional sources I consulted.

These interviews are assessed using qualitative content analysis (Mayring, 2015) informed by an abductive research framework comprising pertinent literature from the strands of Cultural Political Economy, financialization, and Transition Studies. In line with the University's ethical research conduct, the interviewees' remarks were recorded if consent was provided, their comments anonymized and solely used for academic purposes, i.e. the publication of this book. As primary sources, the interviews were analyzed using the software MAXQDA, a coding software. Via a subscription to Environmental Finance, a magazine focused on green bonds globally and to Bloomberg Green (up to the end of 2021, respectively), market developments were thoroughly analyzed, and the interviewees' insights further substantiated. The launch of this taxonomy marked the end of my empirical data gathering in June 2022.

Table 1.1 Anonymized Sampling Overview, sorted by actor category (author's own compilation)

Interview Sample		
Actor category	*Sub-category*	*Interviewees*
Governmental actors	Ministry representatives	3
	Municipal representatives	4
Developmental actors	Development partners	4
	Development bank representatives	4
Domestic stakeholders	Civil society actors	5
	Renewable energy industry	3
Financial actors	Stock Exchange representatives	3
	Institutional Investors	2
	Asset consultants	2
	Fund managers	4
	Domestic commercial bankers	4
External actors	External service providers	3
	Independent experts (university, renewable energy space)	5
	Total	**46**

In combination with pertinent webinars by the Responsible Investor and the Climate Bonds Initiative, among others, they provided additional empirical data that form the basis of this book.

The monography proceeds as follows. In Chapter 2, prevailing green bond literature will be reviewed and pertinent gaps identified. The review notes the siloed approaches towards studying green bonds with little cross-citation between disciplines. It also finds very little qualitative literature on green bonds. Thirdly, lots of findings were flagged as provisional given the nascency of the market, warranting in-depth follow-up. Lastly, the dearth of green bond literature on emerging and developing markets (except for China) provides additional impetus for this case selection. The review calls for a theoretical approach that contributes to closing these gaps.

Chapter 3 draws up three theoretical perspectives that seek to provide adequate lenses to address these gaps. To understand the reasons behind the limited expansion of a nascent and immature market, poststructural political economic approaches with a specific eye for discursive elements offer valuable insights into the creation of new markets. In this vein, Cultural Political Economy (Best & Paterson, 2010; Sum & Jessop, 2013) scrutinizes the dynamics of a market-in-the-making (Asiyanbi, 2018) and unearths the depoliticizing elements (Ferguson, 1994) such a market setup entails. The financialization literature (Bracking, 2015; Chiapello, 2020; Gabor, 2021; Knuth, 2018), in turn, zooms in on potentially adverse effects of a finance-led transition endeavor and examines the financial practices bolstering this market. Lastly, Transition Studies (Kern & Markard, 2016; Köhler et al., 2019; Monk & Perkins, 2020) disposes of the tools to organize the complex and at times messy dynamics characterizing an ongoing transition. Its 'just transition' component (Barnes, 2022; Swilling & Annecke, 2012) grants important political considerations largely ignored in technically governed transitions and adds an important prism to assess the procedural, distributional, and recognitional elements (Svarstad & Benjaminsen, 2020) of a finance-led transition attempt. In combining these three very different literature strands, the manifold reasons for the limited take-up of green bonds can be assessed from different angles. Therefore, the theory chapter closes with a few substantiating research questions, resulting from the insights gained in Chapters 2 and 3.

In Chapter 4, I recap the historical emergence of South Africa's capital markets and highlight pertinent challenges in South Africa's contemporary political economy. Therein, I develop four overarching themes around the country's fossil path dependence, the governing party's legitimacy crisis, the financial sector's emboldened stance ensuring the global financial crisis in 2008 and competing policy priorities, all of which impact the transition to greener futures.

Chapter 5 lays out the empirical findings. Along seven pillars, I trace the reasons for the limited take-up of green bonds in South Africa. I start with discussing the promised opportunities green bonds offer in the context of South Africa as an emerging market. I touch on prevailing success stories and their relevance in lending credibility to nascent markets and dwell on a few conceptual limitations of the financial innovation. In a fourth step, I juxtapose globally prevalent concerns around greenwashing with South Africa's progress in passing its own green finance taxonomy. I, then, zoom in on the peculiarities of South Africa's capital markets, contrast the green bond efforts with just transition concerns, and, finally, elucidate a few attempts to depoliticize the low-carbon transition trajectory more generally, and green bond diffusion more specifically.

The final chapter takes stock of these findings and discusses them in light of ongoing scholarly debates. It recapitulates the merits of deploying an interdisciplinary research framework which helps explain how the instrument's dependence on conventional market metrics prohibits a faster provision of much-needed capital for sustainable transformation. It unearths some depoliticizing elements in the promotion of green bonds and demonstrates the incommensurability with demands for a just transition. It also sheds light on the barriers technical solutions like green bonds face in a deeply contested political landscape like South Africa which qualify the premature hype this instrument has generated elsewhere. The book concludes with wider implications of these findings for the quest to finance sustainable futures and points out avenues for further research.

REFERENCES

AfDB. (2018). South Africa—National Climate Change Profile. *African Development Bank*, October, 28. https://www.afdb.org/sites/default/files/docume nts/publications/afdb_mali_final_2018_english.pdf

AfDB. (2022). *African Economic Outlook 2022.* https://www.afdb.org/filead min/uploads/afdb/Documents/Publications/African_Economic_Outlook_ 2018_-_EN.pdf

Arunma Oteh. (2018). *Leveraging innovative finance for realizing the sustainable development goals.* https://www.worldbank.org/en/news/speech/2018/05/ 15/leveraging-innovative-finance-for-realizing-the-sustainable-development-goals

Asiyanbi, A. P. (2018). Financialisation in the green economy: Material connections, markets-in-the-making and Foucauldian organising actions. *Environment and Planning A, 50*(3), 531–548. https://doi.org/10.1177/030851 8X17708787

Barnes, J. (2022). Divergent desires for the just transition in South Africa: An assemblage analysis. *Political Geography, 97*(April). https://doi.org/10. 1016/j.polgeo.2022.102655

Best, J., & Paterson, M. (Eds.). (2010). *Cultural political economy* (1st ed.), Routledge.

Bracking, S. (2015). Performativity in the green economy: How far does climate finance create a fictive economy? *Third World Quarterly, 36*(12), 2337–2357. https://doi.org/10.1080/01436597.2015.1086263

Brown, M. A., & Sovacool, B. K. (2011). Barriers to the diffusion of climate-friendly technologies. *International Journal of Technology Transfer and Commercialisation, 10*(1), 43. https://doi.org/10.1504/ijttc.2011.038453

Businesslive. (2021, December 10). *Standard Bank issues green bonds for renewable energy and housing.* 1–2. https://www.businesslive.co.za/bd/com panies/financial-services/20...tandard-bank-issues-green-bonds-for-renewa ble-energy-and-housing/

Carrington, D. (2022, May 13). South Africa's April floods made twice as likely by climate crisis, scientists say. *The Guardian.* https://www.theguardian. com/environment/2022/may/13/south-africa-floods-climate-crisis-global-heating?CMP=Share_iOSApp_Other

CBI & Agora Energiewende. (2021). *Green bonds in South Africa: How green bonds can support South Africa's energy transition.* https://www.climatebonds. net/files/reports/cbio_sa_energytrans_03d.pdf

Chiapello, E. (2020). Financialization as a Socio-technical Process. In P. Mader, D. Mertens, & N. van der Zwan (Eds.), *The Routledge international handbook of financialization* (1st ed., pp. 81–91). https://doi.org/10.4324/978131 5142876-7

Climate Bonds Initiative. (2022). *$ 500 billion Green Issuance 2021: social and sustainable acceleration: Annual green $ 1 trillion in sight: Market expansion forecasts for 2022 and 2025* (Issue January 31). https://www.climatebonds.net/2022/01/500bn-green-issuance-2021-social-and-sustainable-acceleration-annual-green-1tn-sight-market

Death, C. (2014). The green economy in South Africa: Global discourses and local politics. *Politikon, 41*(1), 1–22. https://doi.org/10.1080/02589346. 2014.885668

Death, C. (2016). Green states in Africa: Beyond the usual suspects. *Environmental Politics, 25*(1), 116–135. https://doi.org/10.1080/09644016.2015. 1074380

Dodds, F., Donoghue, D., & Roesch, J. L. (2017). *Negotiating the sustainable development goals—a transformational agenda for an insecure world* (1st ed.). Earthscan Routledge.

Engineering News. (2021, December 13). *Standard Bank issues green, social bonds to finance renewable, housing projects in South Africa.* 1–12. https://www.engineeringnews.co.za/article/standard-bank-issues-gr...ren ewable-housing-projects-in-south-africa-2021-12-13/rep_id:4136

Ferguson, J. (1994). *The anti-politics machine. Development, depoliticization, and bureaucratic power in lesotho.* University of Minnesota Press.

Gabbatiss, J. (2021). *Analysis: Why climate finance "flows" are falling short of $ 100 billion pledge.* https://www.carbonbrief.org/analysis-why-climate-fin ance-flows-are-falling-short-of-100bn-pledge/

Gabor, D. (2021). The wall street consensus. *Development and Change, 52*(3), 429–459. https://doi.org/10.1111/dech.12645

International Monetary Fund. (2015). From Billions To Trillions: Transforming Development Finance Post-2015 Financing for Development: Multilateral Development Finance. In *Press Release: Vol. No. 15/170.* https://www.imf. org/en/News/Articles/2015/09/14/01/49/pr15170

JSE. (2021). *Nedbank lists green residential bond.* JSE News. https://www.jse. co.za/news/news/nedbank-lists-green-residential-bond-jse

Kern, F., & Markard, J. (2016). Analysing energy transitions: Combining insights from transition studies and international political economy. In T. Van de Graaf, B. K. Sovacool, A. Ghosh, F. Kern, & M. T. Klare (Eds.), *The Palgrave handbook of the international political economy of energy* (1st ed., pp. 291–318). Palgrave Macmillan UK. https://doi.org/10.1057/978-1-137-55631-8

Knuth, S. (2018). "Breakthroughs" for a green economy? Financialization and clean energy transition. *Energy Research and Social Science, 41*(April), 220–229. https://doi.org/10.1016/j.erss.2018.04.024

Köhler, J., Geels, F. W., Kern, F., Markard, J., Onsongo, E., Wieczorek, A., Alkemade, F., Avelino, F., Bergek, A., Boons, F., Fünfschilling, L., Hess, D., Holtz, G., Hyysalo, S., Jenkins, K., Kivimaa, P., Martiskainen, M., McMeekin, A., Mühlemeier, M. S., & Wells, P. (2019). An agenda for sustainability transitions research: State of the art and future directions. *Environmental Innovation and Societal Transitions, 31*, 1–32. https://doi.org/10.1016/j. eist.2019.01.004

LeBaron, G., Mügge, D., Best, J., & Hay, C. (2020). Blind spots in IPE: Marginalized perspectives and neglected trends in contemporary capitalism. *Review of International Political Economy, 28*(2), 283–294. https://doi.org/10.1080/09692290.2020.1830835

Lester, A. (2022, December 23). Sustainable bonds in 2022—beyond $ 1trn. *Environmental Finance.* https://www.environmental-finance.com/content/analysis/sustainable-bonds-in-2022-beyond-$1trn.html

Magome, M. (2022, April 19). *South Africa launches relief for Durban Flooding; 443 dead.* Bloomberg. https://www.bloomberg.com/news/articles/2022-04-19/south-africa-launches-relief-for-durban-flooding-443-dead

Mawdsley, E. (2018). From billions to trillions': Financing the SDGs in a world 'beyond aid. *Dialogues in Human Geography, 8*(2), 191–195. https://doi.org/10.1177/2043820618780789

Mayring, P. (2015). Qualitative Inhaltsanalyse. In *Qualitative Inhaltsanalyse. Grundlagen und Techniken* (12th ed.). Beltz Verlag. https://doi.org/10.2307/j.ctvhktjdr.31

Monk, A., & Perkins, R. (2020). What explains the emergence and diffusion of green bonds? *Energy Policy, 145*, 111641. https://doi.org/10.1016/j.enpol.2020.111641

Monyae, D., & Ndzendze, B. (2021). The BRICS order. In *International political economy series*. Palgrave Macmillan.

Müller, F., Claar, S., Neumann, M., & Elsner, C. (2020). Is green a Pan-African colour? Mapping African renewable energy policies and transitions in 34 countries. *Energy Research and Social Science, 68*(July 2019), 101551. https://doi.org/10.1016/j.erss.2020.101551

Müller, F., Neumann, M., Elsner, C., & Claar, S. (2021). Assessing african energy transitions: Renewable energy policies, energy justice, and SDG 7. *Politics and Governance, 9*(1), 119–130. https://doi.org/10.17645/pag.v9i1.3615

OECD. (2021). *Forward-looking scenarios of climate finance provided and mobilised by developed countries in 2021–2025 Technical note. 4*(1), 6.

Paterson, M. (2020). SS-03 'The end of the fossil fuel age'? Discourse politics and climate change political economy. *New Political Economy, 1*(14), https://doi.org/10.1080/13563467.2020.1810218

Perry, K. K. (2021). The new 'bond-age', climate crisis and the case for climate reparations: Unpicking old/new colonialities of finance for development within the SDGs. *Geoforum, 126*(February), 361–371. https://doi.org/10.1016/j.geoforum.2021.09.003

Pörtner, H.-O., Roberts, D. C., Poloczanska, E. S., Mintenbeck, K., Tignor, M., Alegría, A., Craig, M., Langsdorf, S., Löschke, S., Möller, V., & Okem, A. (2022). Climate Change 2022 - Impacts, Adaptation and Vulnerability - Summary for Policymakers. In H.-O. Pörtner, D. C. Roberts, E. S.

Poloczanska, K. Mintenbeck, M. Tignor, A. Alegría, M. Craig, S. Langsdorf, S. Löschke, V. Möller, & A. Okem (Eds.), *Climate Change 2022: Impacts, Adaptation, and Vulnerability. Contribution of Working Group II to the Sixth Assessment Report of the Intergovernmental Panel on Climate Change.* Cambridge University Press. https://www.ipcc.ch/report/ar6/wg2/downlo ads/report/IPCC_AR6_WGII_SummaryForPolicymakers.pdf

Republic of South Africa. (2021). *South Africa's first nationally determined contribution under the paris agreement* (Issue September). https://unf ccc.int/sites/default/files/NDC/2022-06/South Africa updated first NDC September 2021.pdf

Sum, N. -L., & Jessop, B. (Eds.). (2013). *Towards a cultural political economy— Putting culture in its place in political economy* (1st ed.). Edward Elgar Publishing Limited.

Svarstad, H., & Benjaminsen, T. A. (2020). Reading radical environmental justice through a political ecology lens. *Geoforum, 108*(March), 1–11. https://doi. org/10.1016/j.geoforum.2019.11.007

Swilling, M., & Annecke, E. (2012). *Just transitions—explorations of sustainability in an unfair world* (1st ed., Vol. 1, Issue 4). United Nations University Press. https://doi.org/10.1080/02652038509373556

Timperley, J. (2021, October 20). The broken $100-billion promise of climate finance - and how to fix it. *Nature*, 1–17. https://doi.org/10.1038/d41586-021-02846-3

Unruh, G. C. (2000). Understanding carbon lock-in. *Energy Policy, 28*(12), 817–830. https://doi.org/10.1016/S0301-4215(00)00070-7

World Bank. (2015). *What are green bonds?* https://documents1.worldbank. org/curated/en/400251468187810398/pdf/99662-REVISED-WB-Green-Bond-Box393208B-PUBLIC.pdf

World Population Review. (2022). Richest African Countries 2022. In *World Population Review.* https://worldpopulationreview.com/country-rankings/ richest-african-countries

World Bank. (2022). *Maximizing finance for development.* https://www.worldb ank.org/en/region/eca/brief/programs

Zondi, S. (Ed.). (2022). *The political economy of intra-BRICS cooperation* (1st ed.). Palgrave Macmillan.

CHAPTER 2

What Do We Already Know About Green Bonds? A Literature Review

"Bonds are boring". (Bigger & Millington, 2019, p. 8)

Though it sounds like a sober characterization of bonds at best and dismissive at worst, Bigger and Millington (2019) capture bonds' unique selling point and key advantage to otherwise more risky financial investment products. Many capital market actors look for safe or low-risk but profitable long-term investment opportunities. Green bonds provide such an avenue. They earmark investments into climate-aligned projects and enable institutional investors such as pension and insurance funds to tap into the monetary gains of low-carbon transitions.

Though green bonds represent a mere drop in the bucket in comparison with global bond market size (when green bonds surpassed the 1-trillion hallmark in the 4th quarter of 2020, global bond markets commanded roughly US$ 128.3 trillion (see ICMA, 2020), they, nonetheless, contribute to closing the investment gap towards climate alignment.

Even though climate-linked bonds were first issued by the European Investment Bank in 2007 and the World Bank in 2008 (Monk & Perkins, 2020), the idea of 'green bonds' has been around longer, with Goldstein (2001) proposing it as a vital prospect in advancing sustainable development for Costa Rica already in 2001. Though preliminary literature reviews on energy finance (Hall et al., 2018), green finance (D. Zhang

© The Author(s), under exclusive license to Springer Nature Switzerland AG 2023
M. Neumann, *The Political Economy of Green Bonds in Emerging Markets*, International Political Economy Series, https://doi.org/10.1007/978-3-031-30502-3_2

et al., 2019) and even green bonds gray literature (Jones et al., 2020) exist, a systemic review of the state of the academic literature on green bonds is still missing. A review of academic literature on green bonds will help to chart out prevailing foci in current research as much as the litera- ture gaps. By running 'green bond' and 'climate bond' through pertinent academic databases like 'sciencedirect', I gathered academic articles on green bonds, trimmed them for topical misnomer and lack of quality, and arrived at just over a hundred papers for more in-depth analysis. Like Hall et al. (2018), who look at energy finance scholarship, one can deduce three broad categories to thematically organize academics contributing to green bond literature. I coin them the *marketeers*, the *reformists,* and the *critics,* respectively. Though they are not entirely mutually exclusive, these labels help sort through the diverse aims and vantage points pursued in each camp and add important insights into prevailing academic under- standing of green bonds. In the following, I introduce each of these strands and trace their respective themes.

THE MARKETEERS

Contributing the biggest share towards green bond knowledge produc- tion, the marketeers generally aim at closing gaps in market under- standing, providing studies geared particularly at practitioners. As is the case in many market-oriented journals (from Finance Research Letter to Energy Economics or Journal of Sustainable Finance), the authors often conclude with concrete advice for practitioners. Russo et al., (2020, p. 1), for example, delve into determinants of green bond pricing on a project, firm and country basis, promising "interesting theoretical and practical implications for green bonds issuers as well as investors and governments interested in green bonds". They hail green bonds as "[a] bridge between corporate finance and corporate sustainability" (ibid., p.1). Whether looking at spillover pricing effects between green bonds and financial markets (Reboredo, 2018; or Tiwari et al., 2022 for a more recent analysis of spillovers during the Covid-19 pandemic), its relation to oil prices and geopolitical risks (Lee et al., 2020) or exploring the market pattern of green and conventional bonds (Pham, 2016; Y. Wang et al., 2020), the general tone is very optimistic, with Pham (2016: 1) concluding that her results offer "meaningful insights into this new, yet very promising market". Methodologically, these studies overwhelmingly rely on quantitative analyses of green bond price developments vis-à-vis other markets through models and approximations of (bond) market dynamics.

The biggest apple of discord, receiving by far the most attention has been the debate around the green premium, also called *greenium*, referring to the price differential between green and regular so-called vanilla bonds (Agliardi & Agliardi, 2019; Hachenberg & Schiereck, 2018; Hammoudeh et al., 2020; Larcker & Watts, 2019; Tang & Zhang, 2018). These debates are held with regard to developed (Baker et al., 2018; Gianfrate & Peri, 2019; Karpf & Mandel, 2018; Tu et al., 2020; Zerbib, 2019) and emerging markets (Chiesa & Barua, 2019; Nanayakkara & Colombage, 2019). Essentially, this discussion circles around the question whether investors are willing to buy green bonds at a lower yield or return. The implicit underlying rationale is to assess the marketability of green bonds and to what extend they can portray a worthwhile choice for both issuers and investment portfolio managers. By systematically reviewing existing literature on the matter, MacAskill and colleagues (2021) provide a preliminary overview on the *greenium*. In their sample, 56% of primary and 70% of secondary market studies conclude that there is a green premium, "particularly for those green bonds that are government issued, investment grade, and that follow defined green bond governance and reporting procedures" (ibid., p. 2). Since their findings generally confirm a green premium, investors purchase them at higher marginal costs or with slightly lower yields in comparison with vanilla bonds, suggesting that pro-environmental and thus non-economic motives feed into investors' decision-making (MacAskill et al., 2021, p. 5; see also Zerbi, 2019). Hyun and co-authors (2020) expand the *greenium* debate by looking specifically at green certification, which, they find, provides a discount on issuance, suggesting that universally accepted greenness measure will help overcome market uncertainty around the greenness of the respective bond and thus contribute to the development and expansion of green bond markets.

Another focus rests on studying investor needs and responses to green products, such as green bonds. In their assessment of investor's needs for driving a green shift, McInerney and Bunn (2019, p. 1240) identify "the lack of appeal in matching projects with conventional market products". Essentially, they argue that the main bottleneck inhibiting investors from driving green bond market expansion are missing bankable projects. Tang and Zhang (2018) find stock prices to positively respond to green bond issuance, benefiting especially domestic shareholders and first-time issuers (Baulkaran, 2019; or J. Wang et al., 2020 for an exclusive assessment of the Chinese bond market). Flammer (2020) seconds these findings and argues the respective company's environmental performance also improves with green bond issuance. This effect is particularly significant when these bonds get a green third-party certification, suggesting this tool to be an effective climate governance mechanism (see also Simeth, 2022 who argues for the successful signaling effect of third-party reviews). Piñeiro-Chousa and colleagues (2021) assess in particular the role of social media in informing investors' decisions. Pham and Huynh (2020) aptly summarize the promise green bonds hold with regard to catching investor attention:

> As there exist feedback effects between green bond and investor attention, policy that informs investors about green bonds can influence incentives to invest in this market, thereby offering an additional channel to fulfill the financing requirements for transitioning to a low-carbon economy. (p. 7)

Launching a green bond at any listed market in media-savvy fashion, these studies find, thus more readily capture the attention of potential investors, leading to over-subscription, cheaper debt for issuers, and increased shareholder values.

Other studies quantitatively assess the impact of certain policies and particular actors on green bond market behavior. Tolliver and his co-authors assess the impact of nationally determined contributions (Tolliver et al., 2020a, 2020b) and the relationship between the Paris Agreement and SDGs (Tolliver et al., 2019) and their effect on green bond markets, observing positive correlations, respectively. Agliardi and Agliardi (2021) discuss the effects of transition risks (i.e. through tightened mitigation policies) on green bond pricing and financial stability more generally. Still others compare green bond market standards and regulations with a general impetus towards homogenization. Stoian and Iorgulescu (2019) argue, that the lack of a common standard on green bonds is one of the key barriers to its expansion. Comparing Chinese regulations with those predominant in the global North, Zhang (2020) detects general consistencies across Chinese and international standards, though a few eligibility criteria for green use of proceeds and on information disclosure slightly differ, thus possibly affecting a lender's assessment of the respective issuer. A similar comparative endeavor on China, France, India, and the USA highlights respective peculiarities of their bond markets, with China's key distinctive feature being the strong role of the central bank in market development (Faske, 2018). Huang and Yue (2020) build on this observation, arguing for the Chinese central bank to expand its role to address regulatory arbitrage, as they term the current regulatory decentralization across green bond markets (see also L. Y. Zhang, 2019 and more recently Baer et al., 2021, grapple with the Chinese state promoting green bond expansion).

Lastly, this camp also skillfully deploys arguments around ethical questions and the financial sector's legitimacy in driving sustainable change. The first is inter-generational equity. Flaherty et al. (2016) propose green bonds as suitable instruments to finance climate policies for intertemporal burden sharing (see also Andersen et al., 2020 for an updated take). According to their logic, green bonds could be used to "reimburse the current generation's mitigation and adaptation costs [that] are repaid by future generations through taxation" (Flaherty et al., 2016, p. 1). The narrow focus on pareto-efficient, and thus, economic metrics stands at significant odds with political economy concepts, such as the polluter-pays principle, to name one of the distributional questions at hand. The second contestable term is the claimed 'bottom-up' approach. Affiliated to Cicero, a Norway-based main third-party-opinion provider on greenness, Glomsrød and Wei (2018), paints green bonds as a 'bottom-up approach' to climate action within the business community, thereby upending prevailing notions in the heterodox political sciences that usually view financial actors as elites.

In all, the impetus of this strand is to not only build market knowledge on green bonds, but to also actively promote its expansion. Several authors praise it as an opportunity to diversify the investors base through green financial products (Maltais & Nykvist, 2020; Nanayakkara & Colombage, 2019), which presents particular appeal to ethical investors (Paranque & Revelli, 2019). Green bonds are celebrated as a new asset class, or "blended value" (Chiesa & Barua, 2019), meaning business models that combine profitability with social benefit.

The Reformists

The second group, the reformists, trace the challenges emerging during green bond market developments, assessing regulatory weaknesses or political bottlenecks in a descriptive manner. Their goal is to *understand* how green bonds work and to widen *academic access to* this financial tool for other social science disciplines. Thus, it is not the market practitioner, but the political regulator and academic, who represents their targeted audience. Publications in this cluster predominantly appear in Energy Policy, less so in Energy Research & Social Science, and more generally in journals of sustainability, and sustainable economics and finance. In the following, we touch upon the core themes in the reformist agenda: Untapping capital for sustainable development and its key actors, regulation and standards related to green labels, and various diffusion mechanisms. In contrast to the marketeers' section, I will outline a few contributions in depth here, as they will be pertinent sources for my own theoretical framework.

A large part of this literature strands seeks ways to reform the system to fill the investment gap and better untap private investment for sustainable development and low-carbon transitions. Green bonds are evaluated as a means or proposed as a vehicle to reach this goal, whether through studies in developing countries generally (Clark et al., 2018), single case studies on Chile (Goldstein, 2001), South Africa (Ngwenya & Simatele, 2020a), or Japan (Schumacher et al., 2020), emerging Asia (Burger et al., 2015), Asia in general (Ng & Tao, 2016), Southern Africa (Ngwenya & Simatele, 2020b), or developed regions such as the EU (Polzin & Sanders, 2020). These studies discuss green bonds mainly as a way to close the investment gap towards sustainable development, without raising fundamental concerns.

In the literature on the investment gap, Burger et al. (2015), for example, highlight high inflation volatility as the major obstacle and strengthening legal rights of borrowers as a key enabler of the green bond market in Asia. Beyond the diversification of the investor base with trillions at the ready, Ng and Tao (2016, p. 3f) point out that bond financing offers dispersed ownership through debt financing (as opposed to loans or equity ownership) and promotes liquidity through secondary markets. This strand also focuses on particular actors and discusses ways to reform their role in advancing the ambitious climate targets, as in the case of Rempel and Gupta's critique of pension funds (2020), which, as per their argument, have not done enough and need additional policy incentive to fully commit to these targets. Another study looks particularly at the municipality level and their untapped potential in driving transformation through market means, arguing that better understanding about their respective creditworthiness may give them leverage to finance more sustainable infrastructural overhauls through capital markets (Rashidi et al., 2019). All cities in this study's sample adopted climate mitigation policies as part of their global sustainability agenda, even if benefits accrue globally rather than locally. This is because, "these policies, despite their net costs, have at least one key benefit to cities. Visibility and attracting socially conscious investors" (Rashidi et al., 2019, p. 136), i.e. through platforms and networks such as ICLEI and the C40.[1] Geddes et al. (2018) look at the role of state-investment banks as potential catalyzers in this drive towards sustainability, through capital provision, de-risking, but also through financial sector learning and by building trust in low-carbon sectors in taking up the role of first mover or early adopter. Unfortunately, their paper does not delve deeply enough into the green bond markets to merit additional insights. All these examples underscore the research impetus on reform towards gathering more investments for sustainability.

Very recently, Nykvist and Maltais (2022) called for a more ambitious narrative to be needed on how public and private sectors can work together to share the risks of investing in sustainability transitions. Quite in contrast to the critiques below, they place the burden on government to take a more active role in de-risking private sector investments, revamping regulations, and charting out taxonomies for investors in order to enable them to invest along clearly standardized sustainability criteria. On top of this broad research agenda, there are some hotly debates topics within this reformist vault that are outlined next.

Generally, regulation is a big bone of contention, chewed by political scientists, economists, and lawyers alike. Among the latter, Wang (2018) argues for mandatory regulatory support to be imposed on bond issuers in the USA, including obligatory quarterly reporting and stricter penalties in the case of issuers misusing bond money. Talbot (2017, p. 135), further, argues that unless mandatory regulations and standards are put in place, "there is nothing to prevent a corporation from using its 'green bonds' in a way that does not truly benefit the environment". This is also echoed by Mihàlovits and Tapaszti (2018, p. 311), who advocate for a legal framework making penalties in cases of misconduct obligatory, for example by

---

[1] The International Council for Local Environmental Initiatives (ICLEI) is an NGO headquartered in Oakland (USA) that organizes a network of more than 2500 local and regional governments committed towards sustainable urban development (ICLEI, 2022). C40 Cities Climate Leadership Group is a network of 97 cities committed to tackling the climate crisis (C40, 2022).

ordering the bond issuer to repurchase the green bonds, redacting their tax benefit, or withdrawing the green classification of all their green bonds issued. They, further, bemoan the lack of key performance indicators tied to green bonds, and particularly the lack of quantification of the environmental benefits, resulting in emphasis being placed on metrics familiar to investors, such as yield to maturity, spread, and duration of the investment (ibid., confer with Bracking's critique (2015) of green bonds as separating financial from environmental value below). At the bottom of this lays the fear of greenwashing and its adverse effects it may have on the sustainable credentials of the respective investments.

Beyond regulation, another core concern in the reform vault revolves around additionality, or in other words, whether green bonds actually muster *additional* capital that aide low-carbon transitions around the world. Azhgaliyeva and colleagues (2020) review issuance of green bonds in ASEAN and conclude that though grants and subsidies for first-time issuers promote green bond issuance, "this does not mean that green bond grants led to decarbonization in countries where these bonds were issued", as "proceedings were also used for financings [sic] green projects abroad or for re-financing" past projects (Azhgaliyeva et al., 2020, p. 135f; see also Maltais & Nykvist, 2020; and Schneeweiß (2019) for a German-language civil society publication on the matter of additionality). Reformists tend to chip in quick fixes for this problem. One such idea is called green striping, which Banga (2019) briefly alludes to by building on a legal finance scholar (Franklin, 2016). Franklin (2016, p. 2) describes it as companies, or any other entity investing in green projects for that matter, "[committing] to use a stated fraction of the total principal amount of a series of bonds for environmental purposes". Other academics float the same idea in a policy and working paper (Bongaerts & Schoenmaker, 2020a, 2020b), arguing that this new design not only sets incentives for new projects rather than mere refinancing and simultaneously enhances the securities liquidity and improve market price information on environmental performance. A few employees of the Bank of International Settlement explore a different reform quest with similar underlying rationale that tries to link green bonds to overall firm performance. They suggest a complementary firm-level rating along with the project-based green labels as a means to encourage firms to lower their carbon footprint (Ehlers et al., 2020).

Beyond these incremental reform proposals, this camp also contains publications unearthing details around the emergence and diffusion of green bonds. Monk and Perkins (2020) are such a key example here, and so are Elliott and Zhang (2019). Both pairs of authors draw on Transition Studies literature to trace the ascent of green bonds as an environmentally conscious asset class, with a global focus in the former and with special attention on China in the latter. Drawing in particular on transnational transition management and social network analysis, some studies reproduce China's green bond market evolution (Elliott & Zhang, 2019; Fu et al., 2020, see Chapter 3). Just as two papers from the marketers' section (Faske, 2018; Huang & Yue, 2020), Elliot and Zhang (2019) identify the People's Bank of China as the steering leader. But they focus on processes rather than market streamlining and are, hence, clustered in this section. Therein, they name coalitions with policy-makers and organizations in transnational spaces were important catalyzers in the diffusion, benefiting in particular from consensus building, coordinated experimentation and distributed monitoring and evaluation.

Monk and Perkins (2020), in turn, also draw on literature strands of the Transition Studies scholarship. They identify learning, standardization, and positive feedback loops as key to the early diffusion of green bonds, foreshadowing the importance of the Green Bond Principles and the opportunities green bonds presented as providing financial market actors with "opportunities for re-legitimization" (Monk & Perkins, 2020, p. 9).

In all, the reformist camp offers interesting insights into describing how green bonds diffuse and what levers to pull to gear them more effectively towards sustainable and inclusive outcomes. What has been left unaddressed in the two strands so far are the inconsistencies, contradictions in interests, socio-economic and environmental ramifications of the finance sector repositioning itself as a key entity in governing transition endeavors more generally, and green bond deployment as a pertinent tool in mustering the changes, in particular. The critics fill this gap in large part.

THE CRITICS

The last segment of the literature review heavily draws on geographers' insights derived from financialization and political economy literature, published predominantly in critical geography journals, such as Geoforum, Economy and Space, and Progress in Human Geography. This section deals with these concerns and presents them, if relevant for my theory chapter, in more detail.

A big chunk in this strand deals with the financialization of public infrastructure, financed through green bonds oftentimes at the municipal level. Loo et al. (2018), for example, compare Hong Kong's mass transit Railway and London's underground to trace land value capture along tendencies of financialization. They point out an omission in the debate of financialization on infrastructure that revolves around institutional investors reframing physical structures into risk-return profiles, as overlooking what exactly is being financialized, namely not just the mere ownership of infrastructure, but also its direct and indirect services. It, thus, delves into the political economy of public versus private service distribution. Bigger and Millington (2019) operate at the same geographic scales with similar concerns. They compare the green bond issues by the New York Metropolitan Transit Authority and the City of Cape Town and argue that "the use of green debt for climate change adaptation in cities that are already feeling its impact threatens to deepen racialized geographies of financial and environmental risk" (Bigger & Millington, 2019, p. 2). More specifically on South Africa, the authors further argue, that bond issuance needs to be contextualized with federal austerity, economic slowdown, and rifts across political parties, all of which befell South Africa. "Finance", they further ascertain (Bigger & Millington, 2019, p. 2), "does not alter existing geographies and dynamics" pointing to a Western Cape Representative they interviewed, who shrugged: "If you don't need the money [because of sound capital management], you can get it. If you need it you can't" (Bigger & Millington, 2019, p. 3). This statement, thus, calls into question as to whether green bonds can help transform existing social-environmental-economic conditions as their inherently rely on market logics of creditworthiness.

Beyond green bonds' limited accessibility for issuers with limited creditworthiness, another major market drawback relates to increased inequality due to financialized access to services. Bigger and Millington's (2019) focus on water services in South Africa is insightful here. In tying the green bond to technical responses to water scarcity—emblematic in widespread installations of water management devices—water service provision has been increasingly commercialized. They argue that this detrimentally impacts particularly poor households where water bills have not been served and, thus, exacerbates existing economic, social, and racial inequalities. In the authors' own words:

> We emphasize that new forms of finance or municipal governance are not producing entirely new socio-environmental outcomes, but are intensifying existing inequities of service provision and associated economic and environmental risks for marginalized communities. (Bigger & Millington, 2019, p. 16)

Incorporating environmental concerns into financial practices is a trend widely discussed and further deepened in this camp. Bracking (2019) traces four stages of financialization of nature from carbon markets, the financialization of ecosystem services, i.e. through REDD+, to green bonds, and, finally, insurance-linked securities and tradable derivatives. In this process of financializing in each phase, she argues, "nature has been framed, abstracted and pacified as providing "services" or even merely "experiences" or "mitigations", free to circulate as liquid paper" (Bracking, 2019, p. 3). In an older piece, Bracking (2015) looks at the Clean Development Mechanism in South Africa and compares that to the global private green bond market. One lesson Bracking (2015) draws from the South African CDM is that carbon credits can be produced, sold, and traded with only weak evidence of environmental improvement. Her critique, however, ventures deeper than a mere regulation to avoid greenwashing. She concludes:

> Carbon markets have no strong institutional reason for trade to reflect the quality of the underlying assets beyond the issue of reputational risk. This risk was ostensibly addressed by certification, but with the secondary effect of distancing the environmental projects from the tradeable asset they produce. [...] In the case of carbon trading [...] the value of the underlying asset, the dirty industry 'cleaning up' or sequestrating part of 'nature', is of little temporal interest after the initial rating or certification, or scientific confirmation of carbon to be 'saved', has been made. (Bracking, 2015, p. 2341)

Economic aspects and environmental aspects of the asset are thus unambiguously separated. While she makes this statement with regard to the CDM, she suspects similar patterns to emerge in an evolving green bond market. This separation offers companies in dirty industries to greenwash investments. Aided by a "green economy spectacle" promising improvements and solutions, this process "occludes the materiality of a fossil fuels-based global political economy, and highly chemical-intensive global production system", working to the benefit of big corporates, such as the likes of Sasol, PetroSA and Denham Capital (Bracking, 2015, pp. 2343, 2352). The chief concern is the gap these variable evaluation regimes can open between the value circulating in exchange and the value fixed in production. As Jones et al. (2020) paraphrase,

> investors will receive their income from coupons, traders will profit from arbitrage, and fees will flow to financial service providers even if green bonds are issued for dubious projects with weak cases of additionality. Green bonds could therefore favor financial incomes over environmental outcomes. The environmental value of the underlying projects could remain quite modest, even while the monetary value of the green bond market rises rapidly. (p. 55)

These concerns exemplify that critique raised here goes beyond the reformist call for adequate reflection of environmental effects in the performance indicators of green bonds (confer (Mihàlovits & Tapaszti, 2018) to more structural issues, namely the *separation* of environmental and financial value, as much as the prioritization of income over outcome.

Similarly, the *greenium*, the hottest topic in the marketeers' sphere, is viewed from a different angle. If, indeed, there is no discount in 'green' borrowing mechanisms, the added costs of verifying environmental criteria of the bond would increase borrowing costs for issuers—which in the case of public actors—negatively affect taxpayers (Bigger & Millington, 2019, p. 9; Christophers, 2018a, 2018b).

Beyond concerns for inequality and limited positive climate outcome, risk debates feature starkly, though in quite distinctive ways.

Christophers' contribution (2018b) centers on the techniques such as risk and credit ratings that are used to render financial assets fungible and to commensurate and commodify all bonds, green or not. Christophers and his co-authors argue in another publication that green financial mechanisms like green bonds reverse historical neoliberal trends of compression of *spatialities* and temporalities and individualization of risk (Christophers et al., 2020). Rather than heralding a return to welfare states, however, risk is stretched over wider *socialities* without adequate redistribution of vulnerability. By focusing not on the distribution but on the constitution of risk, they refer in the case of green bonds to the question "whose risk the use of bond proceeds is intended to mitigate" (Christophers et al., 2020, p. 92). The question of risk, here, thus goes beyond narrow risk perceptions of investors or the need to internalize environmental externalities correctly (as is the purview of marketeers and reformists alike), but to widen the scope to ask risk mitigation at whose expense.

Bigger (2017, p. 2) examines how environmental and financial risks are quantified, communicated, combined, and distributed through the green bond value chain. He focuses on the instances when these risks deviate from one another or must be stitched together, as these, so his argument goes, represent "opportunities to commodify these increasingly inseparable risks in a financial form" (Bigger, 2017, p. 2). They also complicate matters for buyers who are unused to evaluating environmental criteria or who face regulatory definitions of fiduciary responsibility that render challenging the incorporation of environmental, social, and governance (ESG) criteria into investment decisions. Dwelling in particular on fiduciary responsibility as seeking out the highest return at the highest certainty possible, Bigger (2017) argues, oftentimes forecloses investments in global South countries, given their lower credit ratings, despite increasingly robust data capacities on green bonds in the global South.

Having worked at a green bond standard-setting organization in London, Tripathy (2017) takes an anthropological approach towards understanding how climate finance practitioners *translate* environmental, climate, and engineering expertise into concepts legible for investors. The key vehicle, accordingly, is risk. This translation of climate concerns into risks necessitates the production of market devices, such as standards and indices providing benchmarks. Tripathy (2017) argues that it is exactly this newly introduced risk ambiguity that legitimizes innovations such as green bonds. The concept of green is, thus, yet another form of risk in translation, which green bond standards and its very production help mitigate. As Tripathy (2017) observes,

In this context, both industry and academic perceptions of sustainability converge through the term risk in determining sustainability standards for green bonds. These standards legitimize a market response to climate change and environmental degradation by translating different types of knowledge into risks to be managed. (p. 240)

In the separation of environmental and financial value (as pointed out by Bracking (2015), above), the quantification and objectification of both risk and nature occur. Nature, therein, is homogenized as green, which incidentally is the only separate feature of an otherwise regular bond, well known to institutional investors and asset managers. The green bond market is, thus, another 'missing market' (see Kvangraven et al., 2020) to be penetrated.

Beyond the production and translation of risk, generally, Tripathy (2017) also goes into detail on the various tools, next to the main-streaming of standards, that were deployed by his organization to raise confidence and, thus, investments into this new market. He mentions policy reports and analyses of existing green bond markets, geared towards rendering the market legible for investors and other market actors. Reports combine quasi-academic and quasi-business language, thus yielding both scientific authority and—by refraining from dense unintelligible writing styles—more accessible outputs. Tripathy (2017, p. 248), finally, looks at the green bond standard-setting organization he worked for itself, which, he says, functions as a "collateral institu-tion, interpreting green bond market data before the green bond indices make a final decision". Organizations such as the Climate Bond Initia-tive (CBI) fulfill several roles as advocators, advisors, and custodians of integrity of the green bond market (see also Hilbrandt & Grubbauer, 2020; Mihàlovits & Tapaszti, 2018; L. Y. Zhang, 2019 for a similar assessment of CBI's role).

Quite similar to Tripathy's in-depth study of creating green bond markets through risk translation, Hilbrandt and Grubbauer (2020) discuss the seemingly epiphenomenal processes accompanying green standard-setting in Mexico's green municipal bond market. Their find-ings indicate that standards hardly affect green bond-financed project implementation, as most existing projects already fit the criteria. Instead, "standards worked as vehicles through which infrastructures of markets and political support are built, legitimized, and secured, with SSOs [standard setting organizations] performing important political work" (Hilbrandt & Grubbauer, 2020, p. 1417). Beyond the translation of stan-dards and financial market norms into the work of municipal bureaucracy, "standards foster financial thinking, accountings metrics and the logics of calculating and quantifying green benefits", thus expanding markets globally and deepening financialization locally (Hilbrandt & Grubbauer, 2020, p. 1417). While these findings nourish the general critical impetus around financialization, Hilbrandt and Grubbauer (2020) also observe this expansion to be inherently fragile and laden with conflicting interests, that depend on continuous maintenance and individual support. By visiting Mexico City a couple of times to meet with municipal representatives and thus adding credence to Monk and Perkins's observation (2020), Sean Kidney, the head of CBI, is a key market enabler, catalyzer, and facilitator. The very upkeep of a network that develops through standard-setting activities hinges on concrete actors who may perceive themselves as innovation champions (see also Monk & Perkins, 2020)—so long as they perceive their actions to create such effect. As Hilbrandt and Grubbauer (2020) conclude that the success of green bond-financed infrastructure heavily depends on this network's makeup:

> [With] a change in the local administration and the re- appointment of vital staff members, much of the knowledge infrastructures that had been built were no longer in place, thereby reverting the process to the point at which we began: hurdles in the process of implementing GMBs [green municipal bonds]. (p. 1426)

Depending on the actors, processes of financialization could thus as be reversed (see also Karwowski, 2019 on de-financialization).

Lastly, and very insightful for my theory chapter, discursive studies on green bonds recently emerged (Caprotti et al., 2020; Jones et al., 2020). Though both papers deal with controversial elements of the socio-economic complexity inherent to green bond-driven change, Caprotti and colleagues (2020) focus predominantly on energy policy practice and cover green bonds only briefly. Still, in discussing poor households in green bond-financed energy projects in South Africa from a geography-informed actor-network theory of transitions, they add new layers of inequality to the debate, namely inequality of (energy) access and inequality through exclusion from discourses of power. Discussing various scales from global all the way to community level, they argue that particularly communities are sidelined from policy decision-making processes as these raise issues of equitable access, and, thus, table deeply political struggles that have accompanied South Africa's (post-)Apartheid history. Caprotti et al. (2020) identify municipalities, some of which successfully issued green bonds, as potential democratizing forces in this contested field.

Jones and his colleagues (2020), in turn, map the discursive architecture of green bonds globally. By accessing prevailing literature ranging from some academic, but mainly gray literature and news articles on green bonds, they trace how this instrument is engaged as an ostensible fix for the ecological deficit. Jones et al., (2020, p. 50) refer to the marketeers' claims of green bonds simultaneously benefiting companies, investors, and the planet as a "triple-bottom line for post-Paris finance". Though lofty in thought, this bottom line ignores three contradictions deriving from the respective interests of involved parties that according to the authors have been underemphasized so far. First, the trade-offs in pricing: Lowering capital costs by reducing interest rates on green bonds would benefit issuers and achieve the additionality found wanting in many cases (see reformist camp), yet stands at odds with institutional investors' interests for returns comparable to regular bonds. Second, Jones and colleagues (2020) find the demand for cheap borrowing costs to clash with the unique selling point of green bonds, namely their guarantee of proceeds being funneled into green projects. Safeguarding green bonds' very integrity—from external verification, to monitoring of use-of-proceeds and post-issuance reporting—incurs extra costs, all of which potentially amount to US$ 100,000 (Jones et al., 2020, p. 53). These costs are more readily offset in pricing benefits of very large investment projects that municipalities alone hardly muster, resulting in issuers such as municipalities to face higher transaction costs and potentially even higher borrowing costs. The marketeers' debate on the *greenium*, which focuses on the willingness to accept lower yields and highlights non-pecuniary motives increasingly guiding investor decisions, can, therefore, also be interpreted as a thrust to overcome this contradiction. Two other ways to overcome this problem are enhancing green bond market liquidity by deepening the market through large-size and sovereign issues as well as improving environmental evaluation. In their review, Jones et al. (2020) find key metrics for evaluation to misalign with long-term environmental objectives and risks, translating into little penetration of environmentally conscious indices into mainstream investor portfolios. Pricing in environmental risks remains the key hurdle here, as ESG criteria were initially developed for equity and, thus, is not perfectly fit for purpose in bond markets. The third contradiction echoes Bigger's observation (2017) that fiduciary responsibilities oftentimes foreclose investments in lower-rated developing countries, thus contradicting demands to globalize green bond markets. The aforementioned issues of transaction costs, minimum size, and environmental investment infrastructure are additional compounding factors in preventing green bond diffusion in developing countries (see also Banga, 2019; Bigger & Millington, 2019). The review by Jones and his colleagues (2020) sorts through the cacophony of green bond contributions and helps carve out contradiction in need of further scrutiny.

THE GAPS IN GREEN BOND LITERATURE

Overall, the literature review disclosed four research gaps I want to target with my contribution. Firstly, the strands demonstrated a very siloed approaches to studying green bonds particularly comparing the critical with the market strand, possibly due to vastly different entry points and approaches to the phenomenon at hand. Indeed, the positivist and quantitatively informed research on green bonds in the marketeers' section discusses different questions than the qualitative approach of many critics (see Marsh & Furlong, 2002 for a discussion of these divides). Thus, a broader approach, not necessarily reconciling, but linking and partly integrating these divergent strands, is missing. This does not entail mixing positivist and post-positivist research methods, but rather finding a framework accounting for these voices. A second methodological observation identifies the dominance of quantitative analyses in academic discourses on green bonds—at least measured by published output. Qualitative analyses, particularly those with discursive lenses, are lacking (with Jones et al., 2020, being one of the noted exceptions). Hardly any green bond-linked publication critically assesses the investment gap from a political economy perspective (Bridge et al., 2020, problematize it as part of their critical assessment of carbon finance; and Warren & Seal, 2018 do so merely with regard to a specific cash flow model and a narrow focus on the subsector of electricity generation in Great Britain). Thirdly, some critical authors that published on green bonds flag their assessments as preliminary (Bigger, 2017; Bracking, 2015; Christophers et al., 2020) against the slowly emerging political implications only becoming clearer with maturing markets. Christophers and colleagues (2020), for example, state, that.

our argument is, perforce, somewhat speculative: the two mechanisms [green bonds and sovereign catastrophe insurance pools] we examine are both relatively new, which means conclusiveness about their implications is, at this stage, impossible. (p. 90-91)

Linked to that is the defining difference between green finance instruments such as green bonds and regular finance. At least in its nascent stages, a transition towards climate alignment is policy—rather than market-driven (Kern & Markard, 2016; D. Zhang et al., 2019). Adding in-depth research to an emerging phenomenon like green bonds is, thus, very much in order. Lastly, while Monk and Perkins' deployment of Transition Studies tools to understand green bond emergence is very comprehensive (Monk & Perkins, 2020), it begs revisiting in more concrete country cases to deepen the understanding of green bond governance along processes and actors constellations. Though the geographic spread of literature with interest in destinations such as China has grown, the particular challenges of developing and emerging economies, such as growing financial markets and strengthening institutional frameworks, have hardly been explored (Yamahaki et al., 2020; D. Zhang et al., 2019). Justifying Brazil as their case selection, Yamahaki and colleagues (ibid., p.1f) insist that, "there is still a gap in the literature on identifying such challenges in these countries", which they attempt to close "by analyzing which barriers must be tackled to increase climate finance". In critically assessing the diffusion of green bonds in South Africa with a particular focus on its discursive promotion, discussing the barriers to its expansion, its underlying conflicts, and outlining political governance implications, this book contributes to filling these four gaps in the nascent green bond literature.

REFERENCES

Agliardi, E., & Agliardi, R. (2019). Financing environmentally-sustainable projects with green bonds. *Environment and Development Economics, 24*(6), 608–623. https://doi.org/10.1017/S1355770X19000020

Agliardi, E., & Agliardi, R. (2021). Pricing climate-related risks in the bond market. *Journal of Financial Stability, 54*, 100868. https://doi.org/10.1016/j.jfs.2021.100868

Andersen, T. M., Bhattacharya, J., & Liu, P. (2020). Resolving intergenerational conflict over the environment under the pareto criterion. *Journal of Environmental Economics and Management, 100*, 102290. https://doi.org/10.1016/j.jeem.2019.102290

Azhgaliyeva, D., Kapoor, A., & Liu, Y. (2020). Green bonds for financing renewable energy and energy efficiency in South-East Asia: A review of policies. *Journal of Sustainable Finance and Investment, 10*(2), 113–140. https://doi.org/10.1080/20430795.2019.1704160

Baer, M., Campiglio, E., & Deyris, J. (2021). It takes two to dance: Institutional dynamics and climate-related financial policies. *Ecological Economics, 190.* https://doi.org/10.1016/j.ecolecon.2021.107210

Baker, M., Bergstresser, D., Serafeim, G., & Wurgler, J. (2018). Financing the response to climate change. *Working Paper.* https://doi.org/10.5089/978 1462386864.004

Banga, J. (2019). The green bond market: A potential source of climate finance for developing countries. *Journal of Sustainable Finance and Investment, 9*(1), 17–32. https://doi.org/10.1080/20430795.2018.1498617

Baulkaran, V. (2019). Stock market reaction to green bond issuance. *Journal of Asset Management, 20*(5), 331–340. https://doi.org/10.1057/s41260-018-00105-1

Bernard, L., & Semmler, W. (2015). Oxford handbook of the macroeconomics of global warming. In L. Bernard & W. Semmler (Eds.), *Choice Reviews Online, 52*(10). Oxford University Press. https://doi.org/10.5860/choice.190221

Bigger, P. (2017). Measurement and the circulation of risk in green bonds. *Journal of Environmental Investing, 8*(1), 273–287.

Bigger, P., & Millington, N. (2019). Getting soaked? Climate crisis, adaptation finance, and racialized austerity. *Environment and Planning E: Nature and Space, 3*(3), 601–623. https://doi.org/10.1177/2514848619876539

Bongaerts, D., & Schoenmaker, D. (2020a, November). Green certificates: A better version of green bonds. In *Policy Contribution* (Issue 20).

Bongaerts, D., & Schoenmaker, D. (2020b). The next step in green bond financing. *SSRN Electronic Journal.* https://doi.org/10.2139/ssrn.3389762

Bracking, S. (2015). Performativity in the green economy: How far does climate finance create a fictive economy? *Third World Quarterly, 36*(12), 2337–2357. https://doi.org/10.1080/01436597.2015.1086263

Bracking, S. (2019). Financialisation, climate finance, and the calculative challenges of managing environmental change. *Antipode, 51*(3), 709–729. https://doi.org/10.1111/anti.12510

Bridge, G., Bulkeley, H., Langley, P., & van Veelen, B. (2020). Pluralizing and problematizing carbon finance. *Progress in Human Geography, 44*(4), 724–742. https://doi.org/10.1177/0309132519856260

Burger, J. D., Warnock, F. E., & Warnock, V. C. (2015). Bond market development in developing Asia. *ADB Economics Working Paper Series, 448*, 27.

C40. (2022). *C40 Cities—A global network of mayors taking urgent action to confront the climate crisis and create a future where everyone can thrive.* https://www.c40.org/

Caprotti, F., Essex, S., Phillips, J., de Groot, J., & Baker, L. (2020, April). Scales of governance: Translating multiscalar transitional pathways in South Africa's energy landscape. *Energy Research and Social Science, 70*, 101700. https://doi.org/10.1016/j.erss.2020.101700

Chiesa, M., & Barua, S. (2019). The surge of impact borrowing: The magnitude and determinants of green bond supply and its heterogeneity across markets. *Journal of Sustainable Finance and Investment, 9*(2), 138–161. https://doi.org/10.1080/20430795.2018.1550993

Christophers, B. (2018a). Risk capital: Urban political ecology and entanglements of financial and environmental risk. *Environment and Planning E: Nature and Space, 1*(1–2), 144–164. https://doi.org/10.1177/2514848618770369

Christophers, B. (2018b). Risking value theory in the political economy of finance and nature. *Progress in Human Geography, 42*(3), 330–349. https://doi.org/10.1177/0309132516679268

Christophers, B., Bigger, P., & Johnson, L. (2020). Stretching scales? Risk and sociality in climate finance. *Environment and Planning A, 52*(1), 88–110. https://doi.org/10.1177/0308518X18819004

Clark, R., Reed, J., & Sunderland, T. (2018). Bridging funding gaps for climate and sustainable development: Pitfalls, progress and potential of private finance. *Land Use Policy, 71*(August 2017), 335–346. https://doi.org/10.1016/j.landusepol.2017.12.013

Ehlers, T., Mojon, B., & Packer, F. (2020, September). Green bonds and carbon emissions: Exploring the case for a rating system at the firm-level. *BIS Quarterly Review*, 31–47. https://www.bis.org/publ/qtrpdf/r_qt2009c.htm

Elliott, C., & Zhang, L. Y. (2019). Diffusion and innovation for transition: Transnational governance in China's green bond market development. *Journal of Environmental Policy and Planning, 21*(4), 391–406. https://doi.org/10.1080/1523908X.2019.1623655

Faske, B. (2018). Tuning Billions into (Green) Trillions: Tracking the growth and development of the green bond market in China, France, India, and the United States. *Tulane Environmental Law Journal, 31*(2), 293–325.

Flaherty, M., Gevorkyan, A., Radpour, S., & Semmler, W. (2016). Financing climate policies through climate bonds—A three stage model and empirics. *Research in International Business and Finance, 42*, 468–479. https://doi.org/10.1016/j.ribaf.2016.06.001

Flammer, C. (2020). Green bonds: Effectiveness and Implications for public policy. In *Environmental and energy policy and the economy* (Vol. 1). https://doi.org/10.1086/706794

Franklin, A. (2016). Just add stripes. *IFLR/September 2016*, 1–2. www.iflr.com

Fu, J., & Ng, A. W. (2020). Sustainable energy and green finance for a low-carbon economy. In *Sustainable energy and green finance for a low-carbon economy*. https://doi.org/10.1007/978-3-030-35411-4

Geddes, A., Schmidt, T. S., & Steffen, B. (2018). The multiple roles of state investment banks in low-carbon energy finance: An analysis of Australia, the UK and Germany. *Energy Policy, 115*, 158–170. https://doi.org/10.1016/j.enpol.2018.01.009

Gianfrate, G., & Peri, M. (2019). The green advantage: Exploring the convenience of issuing green bonds. *Journal of Cleaner Production, 219*, 127–135. https://doi.org/10.1016/j.jclepro.2019.02.022

Glomsrød, S., & Wei, T. (2018). Business as unusual: The implications of fossil divestment and green bonds for financial flows, economic growth and energy market. *Energy for Sustainable Development, 44*, 1–10. https://doi.org/10.1016/j.esd.2018.02.005

Goldstein, D. (2001). Financial sector reform and sustainable development: The case of Costa Rica. *Ecological Economics, 37*(2), 199–215. https://doi.org/10.1016/S0921-8009(00)00278-0

Hachenberg, B., & Schiereck, D. (2018). Are green bonds priced differently from conventional bonds? *Journal of Asset Management, 19*(6), 371–383. https://doi.org/10.1057/s41260-018-0088-5

Hall, S., Roelich, K. E., Davis, M. E., & Holstenkamp, L. (2018, April). Finance and justice in low-carbon energy transitions. *Applied Energy, 222*, 772–780. https://doi.org/10.1016/j.apenergy.2018.04.007

Hammoudeh, S., Ajmi, A. N., & Mokni, K. (2020). Relationship between green bonds and financial and environmental variables: A novel time-varying causality. *Energy Economics, 92*, 104941. https://doi.org/10.1016/j.eneco.2020.104941

Hilbrandt, H., & Grubbauer, M. (2020). Standards and SSOs in the contested widening and deepening of financial markets: The arrival of green municipal bonds in Mexico City. *Environment and Planning A, 52*(7), 1415–1433. https://doi.org/10.1177/0308518X20909391

Huang, T., & Yue, Q. (2020). How the game changer was generated? An analysis on the legal rules and development of China's green bond market. *International Environmental Agreements: Politics, Law and Economics, 20*(1), 85–102. https://doi.org/10.1007/s10784-019-09460-9

Hyun, S., Park, D., & Tian, S. (2020). The price of going green: The role of greenness in green bond markets. *Accounting and Finance, 60*(1), 73–95. https://doi.org/10.1111/acfi.12515

ICLEI. (2022). *ICLEI - Local governments for sustainability.* https://iclei.org
ICMA. (2020). *Bond market size.* International capital market association. https://www.icmagroup.org/market-practice-and-regulatory-policy/sec ondary-markets/bond-market-size/
Jones, R., Baker, T., Huet, K., Murphy, L., & Lewis, N. (2020, June). Treating ecological deficit with debt: The practical and political concerns with green bonds. *Geoforum, 114*, 49–58. https://doi.org/10.1016/j.geoforum.2020. 05.014
Karpf, A., & Mandel, A. (2018). The changing value of the "green" label on the US municipal bond market. *Nature Climate Change, 8*(2), 161–165. https://doi.org/10.1038/s41558-017-0062-0
Karwowski, E. (2019). Towards (de-)financialisation: The role of the state. *Cambridge Journal of Economics, 43*(4), 1001–1027. https://doi.org/10. 1093/cje/bez023
Kern, F., & Markard, J. (2016). Analysing energy transitions: Combining insights from transition studies and international political economy. In T. Van de Graaf, B. K. Sovacool, A. Ghosh, F. Kern, & M. T. Klare (Eds.), *The Palgrave Handbook of the International Political Economy of Energy* (1st ed., pp. 291–318). Palgrave Macmillan. https://doi.org/10.1057/978-1-137-55631-8
Kvangraven, I. H., Koddenbrock, K., & Sylla, N. S. (2020). Financial subordination and uneven financialization in 21st century Africa. *Community Development Journal*, 1–22. https://doi.org/10.1093/cdj/bsaa047
Larcker, D. F., & Watts, E. (2019). Where's the Greenium? *SSRN Electronic Journal.* https://doi.org/10.2139/ssrn.3333847
Lee, C.-C., Lee, C.-C., & Li, Y.-Y. (2020). Oil price shocks, geopolitical risks, and green bond market dynamics. *The North American Journal of Economics and Finance*, 101309. https://doi.org/10.1016/j.najef.2020.101309
Loo, B. P. Y., Bryson, J. R., Song, M., & Harris, C. (2018, January). Risking multi-billion decisions on underground railways: Land value capture, differential rent and financialization in London and Hong Kong. *Tunnelling and Underground Space Technology, 81*, 403–412. https://doi.org/10.1016/j. tust.2018.07.011
MacAskill, S., Roca, E., Liu, B., Stewart, R. A., & Sahin, O. (2021). Is there a green premium in the green bond market? Systematic literature review revealing premium determinants. *Journal of Cleaner Production, 280*, 124491. https://doi.org/10.1016/j.jclepro.2020.124491
Maltais, A., & Nykvist, B. (2020). Understanding the role of green bonds in advancing sustainability. *Journal of Sustainable Finance and Investment*, 1–20. https://doi.org/10.1080/20430795.2020.1724864
Marsh, D., & Furlong, P. (2002). A skin, not a sweater—Ontology and epistemology in political science. In V. Lowndes & G. S. David Marsh (Eds.),

Theory and Methods in Political Science, (1st ed.), *1*(69), 17–41. Palgrave Macmillan.

McInerney, C., & Bunn, D. W. (2019, March). Expansion of the investor base for the energy transition. *Energy Policy, 129*, 1240–1244. https://doi.org/10.1016/j.enpol.2019.03.035

Mihàlovits, Z., & Tapaszti, A. (2018). A new financial tool for renewable energy investments: Green bonds. *Public Finance Quarterly, 63*(3), 303–318.

Monk, A., & Perkins, R. (2020). What explains the emergence and diffusion of green bonds? *Energy Policy, 145*, 111641. https://doi.org/10.1016/j.enpol.2020.111641

Nanayakkara, M., & Colombage, S. (2019). Do investors in green bond market pay a premium? *Global Evidence. Applied Economics, 51*(40), 4425–4437. https://doi.org/10.1080/00036846.2019.1591611

Ng, T. H., & Tao, J. Y. (2016). Bond financing for renewable energy in Asia. *Energy Policy, 95*, 509–517. https://doi.org/10.1016/j.enpol.2016.03.015

Ngwenya, N., & Simatele, M. D. (2020a). The emergence of green bonds as an integral component of climate finance in South Africa. *South African Journal of Science, 116*(1–2). https://doi.org/10.17159/sajs.2020/6522

Ngwenya, N., & Simatele, M. D. (2020b). Unbundling of the green bond market in the economic hubs of Africa: Case study of Kenya, Nigeria and South Africa. *Development Southern Africa*, 1–16. https://doi.org/10.1080/0376835X.2020.1725446

Nykvist, B., & Maltais, A. (2022). Too risky—The role of finance as a driver of sustainability transitions. *Environmental Innovation and Societal Transitions, 42*(December 2020), 219–231. https://doi.org/10.1016/j.eist.2022.01.001

Paranque, B., & Revelli, C. (2019, December). Ethico-economic analysis of impact finance: The case of green bonds. *Research in International Business and Finance, 47*, 57–66. https://doi.org/10.1016/j.ribaf.2017.12.003

Pham, L. (2016). Is it risky to go green? A volatility analysis of the green bond market. *Journal of Sustainable Finance and Investment, 6*(4), 263–291. https://doi.org/10.1080/20430795.2016.1237244

Pham, L., Huynh, L. D., & T. (2020, May). How does investor attention influence the green bond market? *Finance Research Letters, 35*, 101533. https://doi.org/10.1016/j.frl.2020.101533

Piñeiro-Chousa, J., López-Cabarcos, M. Á., Caby, J., & Šević, A. (2021). The influence of investor sentiment on the green bond market. *Technological Forecasting and Social Change, 162*, 1–7. https://doi.org/10.1016/j.techfore.2020.120351

Polzin, F., & Sanders, M. (2020, July). How to finance the transition to low-carbon energy in Europe? *Energy Policy, 147*, 1–16. https://doi.org/10.1016/j.enpol.2020.111863

Rashidi, K., Stadelmann, M., & Patt, A. (2019). Creditworthiness and climate: Identifying a hidden financial co-benefit of municipal climate adaptation and mitigation policies. *Energy Research and Social Science, 48*(October 2018), 131–138. https://doi.org/10.1016/j.erss.2018.09.021

Reboredo, J. C. (2018). Green bond and financial markets: Co-movement, diversification and price spillover effects. *Energy Economics, 74*, 38–50. https://doi.org/10.1016/j.eneco.2018.05.030

Rempel, A., & Gupta, J. (2020, August). Conflicting commitments? Examining pension funds, fossil fuel assets and climate policy in the organisation for economic co-operation and development (OECD). *Energy Research and Social Science, 69*, 101736. https://doi.org/10.1016/j.erss.2020.101736

Russo, A., Mariani, M., & Caragnano, A. (2020, July). Exploring the determinants of green bond issuance: Going beyond the long-lasting debate on performance consequences. *Business Strategy and the Environment, 30*(1), 1–22. https://doi.org/10.1002/bse.2608

Schneeweiß, A. (2019). *Große Erwartungen—Glaubwürdigkeit und Zusätzlichkeit von Green Bonds.* https://suedwind-institut.de/files/Suedwind/Publikationen/2018/2018-39 Große Erwartungen—Glaubwuerdigkeit und Zusaetzlichkeit von Green Bonds.pdf

Schumacher, K., Chenet, H., & Volz, U. (2020). Sustainable finance in Japan. *Journal of Sustainable Finance and Investment, 10*(2), 213–246. https://doi.org/10.1080/20430795.2020.1735219

Simeth, N. (2022). The value of external reviews in the secondary green bond market. *Finance Research Letters, 46*(PA), 102306. https://doi.org/10.1016/j.frl.2021.102306

Stoian, A., & Iorgulescu, F. (2019). Sustainable capital market. In M. Zioło & B. S. Sergi (Eds.), *Financing sustainable development—Key challenges and prospects* (pp. 193–226). Palgrave Macmillan. https://doi.org/10.1007/978-3-030-16522-2%0A

Talbot, K. M. (2017). What does green really mean: How increased transparency and standardization can grow the green bond market. *Villanova Environmental Law Journal, 28*(1), 127–146. https://tel.archives-ouvertes.fr/tel-01514176

Tang, D. Y., & Zhang, Y. (2018, November). Do shareholders benefit from green bonds? *Journal of Corporate Finance, 61*, 1–18. https://doi.org/10.1016/j.jcorpfin.2018.12.001

Tiwari, A. K., Aikins Abakah, E. J., Gabauer, D., & Dwumfour, R. A. (2022). Dynamic spillover effects among green bond, renewable energy stocks and carbon markets during COVID-19 pandemic: Implications for hedging and investments strategies. *Global Finance Journal, 51*(November 2021), 100692. https://doi.org/10.1016/j.gfj.2021.100692

Tolliver, C., Keeley, A. R., & Managi, S. (2019). Green bonds for the Paris agreement and sustainable development goals. *Environmental Research Letters*, *14*(6). https://doi.org/10.1088/1748-9326/ab1118

Tolliver, C., Keeley, A. R., & Managi, S. (2020a). Drivers of green bond market growth: The importance of Nationally Determined Contributions to the Paris Agreement and implications for sustainability. *Journal of Cleaner Production*, *244*, 1–36. https://doi.org/10.1016/j.jclepro.2019.118643

Tolliver, C., Keeley, A. R., & Managi, S. (2020b, October). Policy targets behind green bonds for renewable energy: Do climate commitments matter? *Technological Forecasting and Social Change*, *157*, 120051. https://doi.org/10.1016/j.techfore.2020.120051

Tripathy, A. (2017). Translating to risk: The legibility of climate change and nature in the green bond market. *Economic Anthropology*, *4*(2), 239–250. https://doi.org/10.1002/sea2.12091

Tu, C. A., Rasoulinezhad, E., Sarker, T., Ng, A. W., Tripathy, A., Harrison, C., Partridge, C., Tripathy, A., Reed, P., Cort, T., Yonavjak, L., Piontek, K., Kandır, S. Y., Yakar, S., McInerney, C., Bunn, D. W., Paranque, B., Revelli, C., Reboredo, J. C., ... Patt, A. (2020). A new financial tool for renewable energy investments: Green bonds. *Journal of Sustainable Finance and Investment*, *0*(1), 1–22. https://doi.org/10.1016/j.oneear.2019.08.009

Wang, E. K. (2018). Financing green: Reforming green bond regulation in the United States. *Brooklyn Journal of Corporate, Financial & Commercial Law*, *12*(2), 9.

Wang, J., Chen, X., Li, X., Yu, J., & Zhong, R. (2020, February). The market reaction to green bond issuance: Evidence from China. *Pacific Basin Finance Journal*, *60*, 101294. https://doi.org/10.1016/j.pacfin.2020.101294

Warren, L., & Seal, W. (2018). Using investment appraisal models in strategic negotiation: The cultural political economy of electricity generation. *Accounting, Organizations and Society*, *70*, 16–32. https://doi.org/10.1016/j.aos.2018.04.001

Yamahaki, C., Felsberg, A. V., Köberle, A. C., Gurgel, A. C., & Stewart-Richardson, J. (2020). Structural and specific barriers to the development of a green bond market in Brazil. *Journal of Sustainable Finance and Investment*, 1–18. https://doi.org/10.1080/20430795.2020.1769985

Zerbib, O. D. (2019). The effect of pro-environmental preferences on bond prices: Evidence from green bonds. *Journal of Banking and Finance*, *98*, 39–60. https://doi.org/10.1016/j.jbankfin.2018.10.012

Zhang, D., Zhang, Z., & Managi, S. (2019, February). A bibliometric analysis on green finance: Current status, development, and future directions. *Finance Research Letters*, *29*, 425–430. https://doi.org/10.1016/j.frl.2019.02.003

Zhang, H. (2020). Regulating green bond in China: Definition divergence and implications for policy making. *Journal of Sustainable Finance and Investment*, *10*(2), 141–156. https://doi.org/10.1080/20430795.2019.1706310

Zhang, L. Y. (2019). Green bonds in China and the Sino-British collaboration: More a partnership of learning than commerce. *British Journal of Politics and International Relations*, *21*(1), 207–225. https://doi.org/10.1177/136914 8118807854

CHAPTER 3

Towards New Approaches of Understanding the Greening of Capital Markets

The previous chapter identified a range of literature gaps that can best be addressed by combining ideas that capture the dynamics of a new green financial innovation like green bonds in an interdisciplinary fashion. It should cover the discursive, financial(ized), and political economic aspects of green bond take-up in South Africa. To ground these questions theoretically and mirror their setup, I will rely on Cultural Political Economy (CPE), financialization, and Transition Studies. Each strand carries certain analytical capacities needed to gain a fuller picture of the phenomena at hand. CPE adds an oftentimes ignored semiotic component, which will prove highly relevant in the context of financial innovation, both in terms of creating legitimizing narratives and depoliticizing transition endeavors. I will rely mostly on Ngai-Ling Sum, Bob Jessop, Jacqueline Best, Matthew Paterson, and James Ferguson in this part. Financialization, in turn, provides the broad strokes of the financial sectors' repositioning in fighting climate change, but also offers tools to understand the rationales underlying financial innovation. Daniela Gabor, Eve Chiapello, and Sarah Knuth grant insights here. Transition Studies, lastly, offers an analytical grid for describing ongoing transition endeavors (Frank Geels) and helps to expose political economic bottlenecks. While Richard Perkins and Alexander Monk provide details on green bond diffusion worldwide, Jochen Markard and Florian Kern shed light on the political character of transitions. Mark Swilling, Eve Annecke, and Lucy Baker add important

© The Author(s) 2023
M. Neumann, *The Political Economy of Green Bonds in Emerging Markets*, International Political Economy Series,
https://doi.org/10.1007/978-3-031-30502-3_3

characteristics of 'Just Transition' endeavors in South Africa. I will spell out each theoretical component more thoroughly below.

DISCOURSE ANALYSIS INTERVENING
IN INTERNATIONAL POLITICAL ECONOMY

Modern international political economy, or IPE, reconverged as a scholarly discipline only in the 1970s (Cohen, 2008). Many attribute this rekindled interest with Susan Strange's powerful intervention into political science and international economics mutually ignoring each other in academic discourses at the time (Strange, 1970). Since then, IPE has emerged into a vibrant field of scholarly inquiry into global political and economic mega trends shaping our world, whether that is the effects of globalization (Krasner, 1994; Scherrer & Kunze, 2011) or accompanying challenges for development 'latecomers' (Amsden, 2008; Chang, 2003). IPE can also be credited for bringing up the 'complex interdependence' between state rivals in international security (Keohane & Nye, 1977, 1998).[1] IPE also dwelled on the causes and effects of the global financial crisis of 2007–2008 (Palan, 2009) and, off late, also the climate crisis (Katz-Rosene et al., 2021; LeBaron et al., 2020). According to Castree (2010), one of the core questions in political economy "enquires into the origins, character and distribution of wealth" by asking "who gets what, why and with what consequences?" (pp. 1734–1735). Critical international political economists take this approach to unbundle the mechanism of capital and capitalism and raise questions of structural transformation (Bieling, 2011).

The preoccupation of IPE with material distribution has prompted ontological criticism. Jessop (2010) points out the tendencies of IPE as a discipline,

> to naturalize or reify its basic categories (such as land, machines, the division of labor, money, commodities, the information economy), to offer impoverished accounts of how subjects and subjectivities are formed, and to neglect the question of how different modes of calculation emerge, come to be institutionalized, and get modified. (p. 343)

---

[1] Arguably as relevant today as during the cold war (Deitelhoff, 2022).

Building on this criticism, a diverse set of scholars embarked on a cultural intervention into the study of IPE, they coined Cultural Political Economy (hereafter CPE). Pioneered predominantly by Bob Jessop and Ngai-Ling Sum (Sum & Jessop, 2013), CPE introduces a 'cultural turn' to political economy scholarship. While not "abandoning the key concepts and insights" (Sum, 2009, p. 184) of IPE, the approach nonetheless, upends prevailing political economy orthodoxy.

So, what was new in introducing a cultural turn into IPE? As Jessop (2010, p. 37) has it, "the cultural turn includes approaches oriented to argumentation, narrativity, rhetoric, hermeneutics, identity, mentalities, conceptual history, reflexivity, historicity, and discourse". Initial impetus for this turn was given by Raymond Williams' "Culture and Society" (Williams, 1960), which historicizes and theorizes British working-class culture. In Chapter 5 on Marxism and culture (Williams, 1960) delineates the contradicting positions concerning the role of culture in driving transformation, as either "passively dependent on social reality" (p. 292), or, in line with the Romantic tradition, of "the arts, as the creators of consciousness, [determining] social reality" (p. 293), or a mutually reinforcing mixture. By insisting on the ordinariness of culture, namely that of every-day working class, Williams offered a cultural critique of the economic determinism dominating Marxist debates at the time and, thus, created space for cultural interventions (see also Matt Davies, 2010).

Cultural Political Economies—Squaring the Debate

The strength of the cultural turn in political economy lays in its ability to avoid economic determinism, to include extra-economic factors into the dynamics underlying political economies, and to enable critical inspection of prevailing economic practices (see Sau, 2021 for a recent reiteration). Scholars of CPE fulfill these demands in diverse ways on an array of societal phenomena. Jessop (2010), one of the concept's progenitors welcomes this diversity, arguing against a prescriptive version of CPE. As this brief reiteration of discursive interventions demonstrates, the literature to build a case for CPE is quite broad, resulting in different thematic emphases that respective CPE scholars posit. Yet, what exactly is the major vault line within the CPE debate?

The major thematic division I dwell on here cuts across critical neo-Gramscian approaches (Jessop/Sum) and more sociologically inclined approaches (Paterson/Best),[2] though these two accounts share two core elements. Firstly, they both insist that history and institutions matter, thus opposing transhistorical knowledge claims and their lack of contextuality, which prevail in orthodox political economic research conduct (Best & Paterson, 2010; Jessop & Oosterlynck, 2008; Sum & Jessop, 2013). Secondly, they place emphasis on a cultural turn that highlights the complex relationship between meaning and practices. The production of intersubjective meaning thereby garners particular attention as a crucial and underemphasized trait of political economic conduct (ibid.). They do, however, divert in their third trait. Sum and Jessop put particular emphasis on the co-evolution of semiotic and extra-semiotic processes and ability in explaining "the logic of capital accumulation and its relation to the social formations in which it is embedded" (Sum & Jessop, 2013, p. viii). Through CPE, they pursue a normative trajectory, which "involve[s] the critique of ideology and the ways in which morality and ethics are enrolled in reproducing domination" (ibid., p. 8). This trajectory goes beyond *Ideologiekritik* (critique of ideology) by raising questions around *Herrschaftskritik* (critique of domination). Oftentimes linked to discussion around hegemony, Jessop and Sum's approach operates well on the macro-level range to discuss the very capitalist formations overcoming crises moments (see chapter 11 in Sum & Jessop, 2013). Ogman (2018), for example, critically assesses 'ethical capitalism' drawing on a combination of Jessop and Sum's CPE and hegemony projects (see here, i.e. Buckel, 2011). Reconstructing two cases of Social Impact Bond investments, Ogman (2018) argues that the social investment market is part of an attempt to reproduce and remake hegemony since the financial crisis of 2008.

While these contributions are fascinating and would yield apt precedence for an inquiry into green bonds, this kind of approach faces four major drawbacks: the proliferation of existing research on South African capitalism, ontological irreconcilability, tall methodological orders, and class reductionism.

Fine and Rustomjee (2018) have initiated plenty of research dissecting the basic tenets of South Africa's political economy (see since, i.e. Ashman

---

[2] Though I do not mean to infer that there are not any other fault lines along the understanding of culture, i.e. between constructivists in IPE, like (McNamara, 1999) who understands 'culture' in very narrow terms as 'ideas' and 'norms' and those that include habits and practices (Lisle, 2010; Walters, 2010).

et al., 2011b; Baker, 2015; Claar, 2018; Karwowski et al., 2018; van der Merwe, 2016). Rather than adding to this body of literature, I seek to complement a narrower investigation of green bonds in particular. Ontologically, CPE as proposed by Jessop and Sum, is indebted to Critical Realism and the Regulationist School, focused on explaining the 'deep structures' and 'mechanisms' underpinning capitalism. My research neither seeks to venture this deep, nor do I position myself in the critical realist vault. Much rather, I draw on the poststructural turn that informed some CPE strands (more on that below). Analogies and commonalities readily exist between Jessop and Sum's CPE as medium-range theory and financial subordination (Kvangraven et al., 2020) or the broader elements of real versus fictitious economy (Epstein, 2005; Stockhammer, 2012). Still, my research—as will later become clear—does not deploy financialization along the totalities of capitalism, but along slightly smaller scales such as inter-regional comparisons. And, also, the Transition Studies literature I'll draw upon speaks more conducively to Best and Paterson's approach, particularly when accounting for niche dynamics penetrating mainstream practices.

Secondly, Jessop and Sum's approach presents a few methodological hurdles. The emphasis on sequencing crisis dynamics requires assessing a longer sequence of the discourse development in order to meaningfully ascertain the variation, selection, and retention of imaginaries. Simultaneously, a vast breadth of competing actors needs to be consulted to juxtapose competing imaginaries. Given my focus on financial actor arguments, whether through (globally accessible) financial magazines or financial actors in South Africa and my short time span between interviews (2018–2020), I would be unable to adequately reflect these requirements in my research design. Instead, a focus on "what CPE does" (Best & Paterson 2010, p. 12) fits as a method of inquiry. Lastly, Jessop and Sum are subject to criticism of reducing questions of CPE along issues of class. Green bonds are capitalist market instruments which would lend themselves readily for criticism of the global financial elite. Instead of focusing on a class analysis, however, my goal is to widen my research framework to enable a CPE's assessment beyond class concerns. This decision builds on van Heur's assertion "that the very explanatory logic of [Jessop and Sum's] CPE links these economic imaginaries to broader dynamics of capital accumulation and regulation in an unnecessarily reductionist manner" (van Heur, 2010b, p. 454). Further, these "notions of accumulation and regulation all too often become 'composite variables' that obscure more than they explain" (ibid., p. 454). He goes on to conclude that Jessop

> consistently privileges accumulation and regulation in the analysis of concrete knowledge-based economies without, however, paying much – if any – attention to the specific organization and dynamic of the phenomenon under investigation. This leads to biased accounts of actually existing practices in which the description and explanation of alternative modes of regulation remains extraordinarily underdeveloped and de facto to the production of narratives that remain stuck in the arbitrariness and circularity of external criteria of knowledge. (van Heur, 2010b, p. 454)[3]

Against the backdrop of these three caveats, Best and Paterson (2010) provide a suitable alternative. Similar to other CPE scholars, they aver with regard to conventional political economy, that "[it] fails to fully explain its object because it abstracts political economy from its cultural constitution" (Best & Paterson, 2010, pp. 2–3).

Best and Paterson (2010) draw on insights from the poststructural turn in IPE (Amoore & de Goede, 2010; Huysmans, 2006; Peterson, 2006; Wullweber & Scherrer, 2010). They clarify their understanding of the role of 'culture' as constitutive of the political economy by disagreeing with the renowned economic historian Karl Polanyi. Retorting on his widely shared contribution on the 'disembedding of markets' (Polanyi, n.d.), which has marked the demarcation and, henceforth, careful distinction between economic, social, cultural, and political spheres, Best and Patterson (2010) argue that the

> 'disembedding' of markets never in fact detached markets from culture, they rather reconstituted what the content of that culture was. [Hence, t]he idea of a 'free market economy' may serve certain ideological purposes, but it is never in fact able to realize its utopia of a culture-free economy. (pp. 4–5)

They further insist on political economy having always been cultural, whether deployed as a means to stabilize the status quo or to bolster legitimation (Best & Paterson, 2010, p. 36). Several examples support this assertion. The embedding of culture within markets is evident in the

---

[3] See also van Heur (2010a), wherein he calls for CPE to move beyond its Regulationist roots towards a political economy of complexity and emergence.

current endeavors to construct of carbon markets in response to climate change (MacKenzie, 2009; Paterson & Stripple, 2010) or MacKenzie's work on the role of financial models in *driving* financial rather than *displaying* markets (MacKenzie, 2006).

As indicated before, Best and Paterson (2010), however, differ from Jessop and Sum in what trajectories they see CPE pursue. While the latter authors uncover the cultural conditions of capitalism through a debate of hegemony and class in global politics, Best and Paterson point out that "their continued emphasis on class has tended to reduce the question of culture to one of the means by which capitalist domination is reproduced and resisted" (2010, p. 5). Marrying culturally inflected IR and critically attuned IPE with CPE literature, Best and Paterson consider this line of research to be *one of many* within cultural political economy, insisting that they "would want to leave open the possibility of more open-ended interrogations of the phenomenon" (ibid., p. 5).

More recent studies deploying the CPE approach build on this body of knowledge. Some dwell on the constitution of models driving markets, quite along MacKenzie's work (2006). Watts and Scales (2020), for example, draw on CPE to assess social impact investment in Sub-Saharan African agriculture. They focus on who engages in this practice and with what motivation, but also how the notion of social impact is defined and operationalized. They also ask what practices and narratives specifically frame Africa's agricultural sectors as site of investment and what the respective political economic implications are of the assemblages of actors, metrics, and motivations. Warren and Seal (2018), similarly, assess discounted cash flow models to deduce how investment gaps are framed and with what implication for the electricity generation subsector in the UK.

Others zoom in on new 'green' markets. Lehmann (2019) assesses the framing of 'clean cooking' as charismatic carbon, which drives market development. Levy and Spicer (2013) discuss competing imaginaries to better understand the contested discourse and policy field in the US energy space between 1990 and 2013. They shift the analytical concept of imaginaries both thematically from economic to climate-related issues and from a grand application on capitalism to a sector-specific context, namely climate change, thus helping "to understand the intersection of economic, political and ecological issues" (Levy & Spicer, 2013, 660). Taking geoengineering as an example (Markusson et al., 2017), in turn, explain the persistence of technical fixes and the trust markets and societies place in technology for solving contemporary ills.

Certainly, Best and Paterson's approach to CPE has not been void of criticism. Two sets of critique shall be featured here. For one, Jessop and Oosterlynck (2008) view Best and Paterson' version of CPE as 'soft economic sociology'. They aver that CPE needs to be combined with critical political economy, broadly defined,

> to resist the temptation of 'soft' economic or political geographies characteristic of the new economic sociology […] We use the term 'soft' here to describe the subsumption of economic or political categories under general sociological (or cultural) analysis so that the analysis loses sight of the historical specificity and materiality of economics and the dynamics of state power. (Jessop & Oosterlynck, 2008, p. 1168)

To them, 'soft' economic sociology of the likes of Paterson and Best, further "tends to limit the cultural turn to the role of cultural factors as business assets in underpinning regional growth strategies and regional competitiveness and to ignore issues of power" (Jessop & Oosterlynck, 2008, p. 1161). Essentially, they find wanting the critical impetus so important for political economy inquiries.

Kranke (2014) builds on this critique. In his review of their book, he observes—quite in line with the critical vantage point of Jessop and other critical IPE scholars like Robert Cox—that "Best and Paterson set out neither to establish an emancipatory project nor to overrule transatlantic stock-taking" (p. 899). He laments a "disinterest in disciplinary historiographies" (ibid., p. 899) and that "[their] primary target is far more diffuse" (p. 901) in comparison to critical IPE scholars, reaching beyond a clearly defined segment of the discipline. Kranke (2014, p. 906) deplores the book's failure to overcome Eurocentric ontologies and epistemologies, concluding that the "the heterodox recasting remains incomplete for the lack of committed ethno-relativist recasting", which unintentionally upholds "the trope of Eastern passivity and Western hyper-agency". Still, in contrast to Jessop and Oosterlynck's charge of the lack of critical inquiry (2008), Kranke (2014) concedes that "[many] chapters in Best and Paterson's volume would indeed lend themselves to a transformative scholarly agenda" (pp. 902–903) and "raise important questions" (p. 900). With the exception of one chapter (Helleiner, 2010), most chapters in Best and Paterson's book seem, indeed, attuned to emancipatory projects of critical IPE. What Kranke fails to find are epistemological boundaries of CPE and its overlaps with more critical strands.

In their response to this criticism, Best and Paterson (2015) hold that a debate about the definition of the International Political Economy as a field,

> is precisely the kind of reifying move that our volume was trying to avoid. The goal of our projects was precisely not to create a new theory, school or approach that could then be put into contention with other such perspectives within something called 'IPE'. (p. 739, emphasis original)

but to rather emphasize the diverse ways 'culture' constitutes political economic practices. Best and Paterson (2015) acknowledge Kranke's charge of Eurocentrism charge regarding the contributors to their book, but not so much regarding the themes covered, which, they argue, put Southern actors and Southern agency at the centre.

As becomes evident when reading Best and Paterson's book (2010) as well as like-minded scholars, discourses, broadly defined, serve different political economic ends. Beyond constituting and excluding elements of the political economy, they uphold contradictions and paradoxes through equivalence. Walters (2010) draws similar conclusions with a view to migration. Studying map depiction of migration flows, he refers to this as the anti-political economy. Whether through map practices or religious intonations, culture is a central component in providing collective meaning. In their words:

> Culture is what gives meaning to a variety of phenomena, including practices, devices, techniques, bodies, conduct, experiences, and relationships. A focus on culture thus presumes and attempts to demonstrate that these phenomena cannot be usefully understood separately from the meanings that people collectively give to them. The phrase 'collectively' here is important: culture cannot be reduced to ideas and values that can be adopted or espoused individually, but rather implies that the means by which individuals come to espouse such values or ideas are themselves culturally constituted by broader webs of significance. (Best & Paterson, 2010, p. 15)

The political economy, in general, is thus perceived as an assemblage, significant not only in what it includes but also in what it implicitly *excludes* as economic and non-economic, respectively. In Best and Paterson's words (ibid.), culture,

> can thus work to conceal the political and economic character of particular phenomena. [...] The political effects of this process are to constrain the scope of debate by defining certain subjects as apolitical; ironically, appeals to culture can therefore work much the same was as appeals to technical expertise—as a way of depoliticizing certain crucial questions. (pp. 33–34)

In summary, Best and Paterson's book (2010) has two essential arguments: They view culture as a force for reinforcing relations of identity and difference. Therein, "[culture] is thus constitutive of political economy, it plays an important part in constituting what the practices we recognise as within that 'domain' are" (p. 14). Beyond constituting what counts as part of an economy, culture "also works to define the things that it excludes as non-economic" (ibid., p. 14), thus representing a powerful negative force as well. Here, the commonalities to the post-structural interventions and their critical impetus are well reflected. The chapters in their edited volume shed light on various practices, discourses, and depictions that de-economize, de-politicize, and de-culturalize inherently conflictual actions. These traits will help decipher the arguments and practices underpinning the attempted expansion of the green bond market in South Africa.

Insights from Ferguson's Anti-Politics Machine

Efforts to depoliticize and render technical inherently political interventions take different forms. Though specifically focusing on development cooperation, Ferguson's anti-politics machine (1994) provides key insights into attempts to disguise inherently political interventions. Based on his field research of the World Bank's development interventions in Lesotho in the mid-80s, his contribution traces the mechanisms that depoliticize these interventions and, thus, bolster the bureaucratic state power of a government without popular support. Ferguson argues that by constructing Lesotho as a 'typical' less-developed country (LDC), the World Bank creates a register that warrants—in a second step—its "technical, apolitical, 'development' intervention" (Ferguson, 1994, p. 28). He finds that the Bank's country report of 1975 draws on empirical errors and inaccuracies to misrepresent the country in a way to cast development practitioners as the able-bodied to produce and plug in their expertise to achieve the 'needed' outcomes. This exemplifies the relevance of problem or crisis interpretation for the proposal of fitting remedies. Ferguson (1994) concludes that the goal of development discourse is to "make Lesotho out to be an enormously promising candidate for the only sort of intervention a development agency is capable of launching: the apolitical, technical, 'development' intervention" (p. 69).

In light of my research on the transition endeavors in South Africa, Ferguson (1994), offers four powerful takeaways for my own research. Firstly, the *depoliticization of interventions*: The practice of depoliticizing that Ferguson so assiduously delineates, might also be applicable in transition discourses that tend to focus on socio-technical aspects of transitions while ignoring political consequences, least they tend to reduce interventions to technical endeavors. In Lesotho's case this meant the expansion of state power through technical means. The ensuing chapters will show how some actors, particularly from the financial domain, seek to depoliticize South Africa's transition endeavors.

Secondly, Ferguson's *wariness of technical expertise and packaged solutions*: Ferguson's critique also addresses the development experts and their 'tailored' policy solutions. These oftentimes come as packaged deals lacking history and context and are produced by a small interlocking set of personnel that work within their echo chamber. As I suggested in the introduction, green bonds as a packaged solution seem to not have worked in South Africa yet.

Thirdly, the *function effects* of failed projects: Even formally failed projects carry important political implications. Treating these as not only epiphenomenal but with lasting structural impacts resets the focus on the array of potential effects of transition interventions. While Ferguson focuses this part on state and etatization, bureaucratic state power to emphasize the multiplying, coordinating power relations knotting and congealing through the state apparatus, I focus on the effects of green bond promotion driving a finance-led low-carbon transition.

Lastly, on his *methodology of retrospection and uncovering mechanisms:* Very similar to existing CPE approaches, Ferguson deconstructs the discourse into separate parts, from its construal of a crisis or definition of a problem to the suggested solutions. The retrospective coherence Ferguson outlines through his anti-politics machine ties in nicely with

CPE's approach. We will see to what extent green bond diffusion is laden with similar catch phrases and supposedly straightforward solutions.

In summary, Ferguson's anti-politics machine thus makes for a thematic bridge between CPE and financialization by demonstrating how financial actor depoliticize and simultaneously financialize—as we will see below—development endeavors, whether geared towards economic upliftment or addressing the climate crisis.

The anti-politics machine of rendering technical inherently political processes of development and change has been applied and adapted in the context of climate change research. Li's (2007) research on Indonesian 'betterment schemes" revealed the governmental will to improve (p. 10) as a project many times evaded and contested. In adapting Ferguson, Li helped shift attention to development understood as the 'practice of politics'. In a more recent piece, Müller (2020) uses Li's six elements of assemblage to better understand how climate initiatives such as the REDD+ reach out to subaltern communities, socializes them into roles, but also encourages, categorizes, and functionalizes their agency.

Given the seemingly unsurmountable challenge of climate change and the predominance of technofixes as a result (Markusson et al., 2017; Methmann & Rothe, 2012), the ability of political institutions and politicians to find and maneuver solutions has been questioned (Methmann, 2010; Methmann & Rothe, 2012). Swyngedouw (2017) coined this shift from political to market-oriented processes, wherein state actors concede and devolve (decision-making) power to non-democratic entities and merely perform administrative roles, the 'post-political trap'. This post-political trap hinges on the homogenization and imagining of the people as one unfractured entity, relegating those that disagree to the margins. Seemingly inclusive and participatory stakeholder governance is invoked but not practiced. Rather, politics is reconfigured "to expert management, based on accountancy practices, and to the rituals and choreographies of power" (ibid., p. 58). In other words, this post-politicization does not refer to the disappearance but rather reconfiguration of the modalities of politics (ibid., p. 60). Drawing on the example of the recently established Green Climate Fund as an embodiment of global financial climate governance, Bracking (2015b) synthesizes Swyngedouw's earlier work on climate change (Swyngedouw, 2010) with Ferguson's 'machine' (1994) in diagnosing similar performances of 'anti-politics'. Couched in technocratic expertise and seemingly liberal governance structure, she argues, the fund has produced mainly 'non-outcomes' with civil society's pressure at least resulting in spectacles of non-performativity. In contrast to these attempts of emptying transitions off its political contestation, Mangat et al. (2018) argue that, far from being a public good where all actors share a collective interest in its mitigation, "climate change is intrinsically political in that it expresses fundamental conflicts of interests, power and values: climate change thus has a conflictual, or 'antagonistic', logic" (p. 3).

Climate change discourses may thus be framed through problems and purported solutions that sideline if not exclude certain stakeholder interests, thus depoliticizing transition trajectories. In the opposite vein, however, discursive shifts may also be used to repoliticize climate change pathways. In his recent work, Paterson (2020) aptly shows how the debate around the 'end of fossil fuels' served as a mobilizing imaginary that *repoliticized* climate politics and relied on three key frames. Firstly, by raising the argument of fossil stranded assets, i.e. through the IPCC report; secondly, by academic inquiries consistently flagging the incommensurability of fossil fuel exploitation with the climate targets set under the Paris Agreement; and, lastly, through social movements mobilizing around climate justice demands. All three frames helped shift attention within climate politics to its major pollutants and catalyzed opposition to those corporates in control of fossil fuel exploitation. This repoliticization exposed the conflicting interests between ecological planetary thresholds and the fossil fuel industry's profit imperative and forced climate action to be amended in order to accelerate the end of fossil fuel exploitation not least in South Africa,[4] but across the globe.

In the ensuing chapters, I want to find out what crisis interpretation prevails in the green bond market in South Africa, whether green bonds appear as a packaged solution for climate change and whether similar depoliticizing tendencies surface, rendering the market seemingly non-conflicting but equivocally exclusive. While CPE and the anti-politics machine provide ample footing for these questions, financialization and Transition Studies needs to be introduced to gain a fuller picture of green bond diffusion in South Africa.

---

[4] As part of the climate negotiations, the first calls to 'leave it in the ground' were made by NGOs in Durban, a major port city in South Africa at COP17 in 2011 (Paterson, 2020).

The 'Financial Turn' in Transition Endeavors—Discussing Financialization

Green bonds represent one major cog in the machinery heading to finance low-carbon transitions worldwide (see Introduction). The financialization literature lends itself readily to exploit the growing overlap between financial sector expansion and climate responses. As a literature strand, financialization helps to untangle and reconnect seemingly disparate dynamics in this process and thus adds important insights while building on the previously established theoretical pillars. In the following, I recount relevant features of the financialization literature, drawing especially on Daniela Gabor's 'Wall Street Consensus' to describe prevailing policy recipes and socio-technical understandings of financialization (Eve Chiapello) to theorize financial innovation (Sarah Knuth). These theoretical traits directly relate to my research design. Firstly though, I chart out main pillars in the financialization literature to situate these scholars in these controversial debates.

Sorting Through the Varieties of Financialization

With a focus on capitalist developments in the global North, several scholars, initially from the spheres of heterodox economics and geography, have inaugurated this new strand of thought they call financialization. Originally attributed to Arrighi (1994), financialization has in very broad terms oftentimes been referred to as "the increasing role of financial motives, financial markets, financial actors and financial institutions in the operation of the domestic and international economies" (Epstein, 2005, p. 3).

Quickly gaining popularity across academic disciplines, Christophers (2015) diagnosed financialization to have "fundamentally fragmented. To the degree that it is excessively vague and stretched, it is an increasingly nebulous and even, arguably, unhelpful signifier" (p. 187). Christophers (2015) demanded limits to be set on the concept of financialization to avoid inflationary usage which would potentially diminish its added insight. Various attempts have since been made to heed this advice and organize financialization. Mader, Mertens, and van der Zwan (2020a) provide a comprehensive overview of the different strands within financialization, suggesting various ways to organize it and delineate three core tenets scholars of financialization subscribe to regardless of affiliation.

Firstly, an understanding of finance as not only autonomous of—rather than subservient to—the productive economy but also as increasingly able to influence and even dominate realms of society. Secondly, financialization scholars share a negative assessment of these financializing developments which is then respectively funneled into various forms of critique, be those loss of democratic accountability (Karwowski, 2019a; Pagliari & Young, 2020), social precarity (Lapavitsas & Powell, 2013), or macroeconomic instability (Dafermos et al., 2021). Thirdly and lastly, the stance that finance cannot just be an economic issue (Mader et al., 2020b, p. 5) as evidenced by the array of scholarly disciplines dealing with this phenomenon.

Though initially a Northern theme, the financialization literature focusing on the global South is bourgeoning. Indeed, the void of research on financialization processes in developing and emerging economies that, among others, Bonizzi (2013) had referred to, has increasingly been filled. Popular streams on the global South conceptualize financialization as either dependent (Gabor, 2018, 2020; Rowden, 2019), subordinate (Bonizzi et al., 2020; Kaltenbrunner & Painceira, 2015, 2017; Kvangraven et al., 2020), or variegated (Karwowski, 2020; Karwowski & Stockhammer, 2017), though definitional boundaries are not always clear-cut.

That said, studies on financialization and the green economy on the African continent should be briefly sketched out. Bracking (2016), for example, discusses financialization in the context of Africa's unique dependence on foreign investment, arguing for one that financialized growth carries second-order effects such as draining business of investment capital. Some scholars reiterate the connection between financialization and the green economy, arguing that these green projects propagate 'markets-in-the-making' (Asiyanbi, 2018). Similarly, Elsner et al. (2021), discuss the financializing effects of renewable energy projects in Zambia, arguing among others that these lead to an erosion of local industry demands. This passage illustrated the vast breadth of research pursued under the term financialization. Since my research revolves around one particular financial instrument, namely green bonds, three contributors to the financialization scholarship will offer more concrete advice, namely Daniela Gabor, Eve Chiapello, and Sarah Knuth.

The 'Wall Street Consensus' Meets Socio-Technical Understandings of Financialization

The mantra of the investment gap for climate-aligned infrastructure shifts the debate from public to market actors. For private investors to come in and leverage public funds, the projects to be implemented need to generate a positive return. This profit imperative is the common trait in an otherwise diverse set of green economy discourses in the global South (Death, 2015). In different words, in order to garner private commitment to sustainably restructure the economy, whether in South Africa or in any other emerging market, the respective infrastructural projects need to be 'bankable' (Baker, 2015).

For Daniela Gabor (2020, 2021) this new focus on bankability reframes previously dominant development agendas. The widespread advocacy and use of blended finance bears evidence of an emerging policy paradigm that reframes the 'Washington Consensus' in the language of the Sustainable Development Goals (SDGs). And, indeed, the 17th SDG on global partnerships for sustainable development is testimony to this, as its cross-cutting perspective contributes to institutionalizing the role of private finance at the sustainable energy/development nexus. SDG 7 on universal access to clean energy also includes a provision (Target 7.4), which seeks to "promote investment in energy infrastructure and clean energy technology" (United Nations, n.d.) and thus actively encourages financial and capital market participation.

This shift is particularly visible in the reorganization of financial sectors from a bank-based to a market-based financial system[5] (Gabor, 2019; Rowden, 2019). Initiatives such as the 'billions to trillions' agenda—part of the World Bank's 'Maximizing Finance for Development' framework— or the G20's 'Infrastructure as an asset class' agenda testify to this (G20/OECD/WB, 2018; World Bank Group, 2018; see Mawdsley, 2018 for a critique).

Gabor (2018) describes her own research as belonging to the branch of 'dependent financialization' which she defines as follows:

> Dependent financialization captures the re-engineering of local financial systems towards capital (securities) markets through a partnership between

---

[5] Though differentiating between those circuits of money has become more difficult with big banks operating in the capital markets as well (Knafo, 2022).

transnational financial institutions seeking new asset classes/sources of yield and poor countries seeking financial market-solutions to political problems. (p. 12)

To capture this increasing influence of private finance, Gabor (2020), coined the term "Wall Street Consensus" (WSC) to mean the "effort to reorganize development interventions around questions of 'how to sell development finance to the market'" (p. 3). Beyond the state merely correcting market failures as was the case in the (post)-Washington Consensus years, the state—under this new consensus—is asked "to *compensate* private finance for market failures through derisking bond finance for global institutional investors" (Gabor, 2020, p. 4, my own emphasis). Very broadly, the WSC "allow[s] global institutional investors to become critical actors in international development" (Dafermos et al., 2021, p. 2). What is new, is the increased conflation of de-risking practices and climate- and development finance (see Elsner et al., 2021; Volberding, 2021). Thereby, "green financialization" is ushered in "through which private finance appropriates the climate fight agenda to define the rules of the game and to orchestrate state derisking for greenwashed financial instruments" (Gabor, 2020, p. 4). In other words, development assistance and transition consultancies "become a strategy of green financialization through which private finance manages the environmental crisis" (ibid., p. 15). Contrary to popular perception around the end of the Washington Consensus, the WSC emphasizes the continuity of neoliberal development practices (Babb & Kentikelenis, 2021).

As previously established, the keys to attracting institutional investor attention for low-carbon projects is decent return and manageable risk. The major component of the WSC, according to Gabor (2020, 2021) is the de-risking state, that eases entry for these investors through various instruments, such as partial risk guarantees for project failure or guaranteed returns, i.e. through purchasing power agreements. This state-backing of investment activities is by no means new. Mazzucato (2011) demonstrates along pertinent examples in the US context how the state has strategically funded tech innovations whose profits were subsequently privatized.

As Dafermos et al. (2021) observe, "the WSC has used the growing attention to the climate crisis as an opportunity to promote policy instruments that put finance at the core of climate-aligned development", increasingly heralding a "climate turn" (p. 3). This climate turn in the 'consensus' is pioneered predominantly through four climate-related financial tools: promoting climate infrastructure as an asset class, central banks acting as climate rescuer of last resort, disclosure of climate-related financial risks, and carbon pricing (Dafermos et al., 2021). Apart from carbon pricing, these tools are directly relevant for green bonds, which readily expedite this turn, particularly under the ambit of climate infrastructure as asset classes. In essence, green bonds are market-based solutions of capital. Contrary to traditional loans, they are 'mobile' and can readily be repackaged and sold on secondary markets, thus providing the liquidity so pivotal in financial markets.

After the global financial crisis of 2008, the climate crisis has increasingly challenged the prevailing dominance of global finance. The WSC seeks to integrate this issue in three ways: firstly by creating profitable opportunities for financial institutions in the global North; secondly, by emphasizing—if at least rhetorically—the need to internalize climate issues to restore macro-financial stability, and lastly by claiming that finance-oriented innovations for climate issues are sufficient to fix the failures of capitalism (Dafermos et al., 2021, p. 4). In response to the Coronavirus pandemic, many countries in the global South increased fiscal deficits, which in turn, reinforced the appeal of recoveries driven by infrastructure financed through public-private-partnerships (PPP). Despite weak track records and additional costs, PPPs have recently regained popularity as vehicles for development (Bayliss & Van Waeyenberge, 2018). By not directly contributing to public deficits, PPPs sport a major selling point for public entities. In this vein, public entities backstop private investors while ideologically maintaining fiscal responsibility (Dafermos et al., 2021).

The Covid-19 pandemic induced uncertainty in the global capital markets. In response to the unfolding pandemic globally in 2020 and 2021, many investors shed local currency bonds in emerging markets, resulting in higher yield spreads (Dafermos et al., 2021, p. 5). In response to the crisis, 'green recovery' and 'building back better' are key catch phrases in the private sector-led WSC enamoring World Bank, UN, and governments alike.

Green bonds are the prime example of the WSC's promotion of climate asset classes through taxonomies, i.e. by attaching green labels to financial instruments. Green bonds can, thus, be captured as part of a policy recipe during times of fiscal austerity. Though touching upon multilateral development banks and states as key facilitators of the WSCs, Gabor's

(2020) account of financialization processes lacks an agential and process-oriented understanding beyond the state and its central bank. Who makes up the WSC and through what processes is it enshrined into development prescriptions?

Socio-technical mechanisms underpinning green bond diffusion shed additional light and help to address these shortcomings. By focusing on the practices and techniques with which financialization is implemented, Chiapello (2020) adds this component. Her socio-technical angle looks "into the actual operations performed by the 'workers' of financialization" (Chiapello, 2020, p. 85), and, thus, provides examples of transition endeavors becoming increasingly sucked into financialized circuits. By stressing the role of instruments and actors performing acts of financialization, bridges are established between her take on financialization and, both, the Transition Studies and CPE literature. In her own words: "Financializing an issue, an organization, an activity or a public policy consists of transforming the language and instruments that organize it, and importing practices and ways of thinking that come from the financial world" (Chiapello, 2020, p. 83). She grasps financialization as a "process of 'colonization' by 'financialized' means and practices" (p. 82) which requires a

> wide variety of actors (audit firms, lawyers, rating agencies, fund managers, banks, consultants, but also governments, standard-setters, non-governmental organizations, think tanks and research institutes). It requires [...] systems of visibility creation, metrics, databases, development of theoretical conceptualizations, production of a large number of policy documents and laws, preparation of contracts, and setting up new organizations. (ibid., p. 82)

These enablers of financialization will be at the center of the analysis in the empirical chapter, with new industries emerging to ascribe green credentials, assess climate risk and accredit resilience investments (see also Geels [2019] for a descriptive and Cox [2021], for a more critical application at city level). They are fascinating stakeholders that offer somewhat counter-intuitive insights. By focusing on practices of financialization, avenues also open up to look at means of de-financialization (Karwowski, 2019b). Referring to Karwowski's publication, Hilbrandt and Grubbauer (2020), for example, hint at de-financializing possibilities in green bond standard-setting in Mexico, which arise, i.e. once staff that acquired the network and knowledge to financialize municipal finances were to leave their post (see also Chapter 2).

Chiapello's focus on the workers upholding the market machinery of green bonds corresponds well with Tripathy's assessment of the Climate Bonds Initiative (CBI) as a standard-setting institution that charts out the boundaries of a market-in-the-making (Asiyanbi, 2018). Especially in nascent markets, it will be interesting to find out what novel practices are used to promote green bonds as a product and reduce uncertainties around it. It thus complements CPE literature with its focus on the production of markets.

Lastly, the success of financial innovations such as green bonds depends in large part on its successful promotion, as is highlighted in the CPE section. Yet, one can grasp financial innovation itself as an important facet of financialization. Knuth (2018) does just that and I shall quote her at length here:

> Many scholars of contemporary financialization have defined the process as centrally defined by its proliferation of new financial instruments, novel forms of valuable if intangible property based on practices such as securitization. In this framing, players like investment banks—or new financial startups—are not simply service providers. Rather, they are financial engineers, who use their unique expertise to produce innovative financial products such as asset-backed securities to sell to consumers and (especially) increasingly massive, consolidated institutional investors. This vision argues for ways in which contemporary financialization may function as a permanent secular expansion in capitalism rather than merely a temporary speculative period at the tail end of a genuine productive boom. [...] By extension, it works to legitimize financial specialization as a potentially durable source of global comparative advantage—and thus imagines a long-term future for U.S. financial hegemony, and U.S. financial institutions' ability to extract and (again often only in theory) repatriate rents from a global economy. (p. 8)

Several points of critique are worth noting here: Grasping financialization from an agential point of view through which innovators consolidate market shares; comprehending financialization as legitimizing strategy for global comparative advantage more generally; and understanding green bonds as competitive innovations to secure and bolster the role of the financial sector within green transitions and climate alignment, in particular. The 'secular expansion'[6] of financial products into capital markets and the capital deepening for green transitions is exactly the trend underpinning the expansion of green bonds as advocated by the CBI. Against zero-interest rates prevailing since the global financial crisis, the cofounder of the Climate Bonds Standards, Nick Silver, reportedly, saw inaugurated "the Age of Bonds" (Kidney, 2011, p. n/a). The globally established forums to promote private sector engagement for the fight against climate change outlined in the introduction carries a clear message for Mathews and Kidney (2012), "namely that the financial system is now being enlisted as a player in this most demanding of challenge" (p. 340).

More elusive, yet of particular relevance for my topic are particular 'institutional innovations' (Arent et al., 2017, p. 8f; Sum & Jessop, 2013, p. 399f) that enable new actors to enter the scene and link government entities more readily to capital markets, that, be those renewable energy auction offices (Müller & Claar, 2021) or stock exchanges, themselves (Petry, 2020; Petry et al., 2021). By discussing financialization in light of innovative actors, Knuth (2018) builds bridges with the Transition Studies body of literature.

Furthermore, Knuth's take on financialization nicely ties in with CPE, namely through the role of narratives in driving innovation such as green bonds and turning them into self-fulfilling prophecies. On the abstract political level, narratives carry ideas that are translated into policies. These policies, in turn, shape the organization of the political economy and disclose the inherent set of preferences dominating factions push within the economy. On the more concrete level, green bonds, as debt-instruments, always bet on the materialization of return in the future. Knuth aptly observes in the United States context, that "[a]nnouncements of bold new innovation and investment futures for the region are always part hype—the dream only sometimes fulfilled, that such visions can take off and become self-fulfilling prophesies" (Knuth, 2018, p. 8). Far from conceptualizing financialization in terms of quantifiable metrics, Knuth (2018) offers an interpretist angle towards assessing financialization and the rollout of markets. It is therefore highly commensurable with a CPE approach pursued by the likes of Best and Paterson (2010).

---

[6] Meaning a rise of financial services irrespective of business cycles.

Gabor and colleagues, Chiapello, and Knuth, each provide important arguments for better understanding green bond uptake. The financialization literature, generally, is also very apt in capturing the prevailing and potential drawbacks inherent to a green bond-led transition. These can be broadly categorized in economic, governmental, and redistributive concerns.

Economically, green bonds may introduce several drawbacks that the financialization literature astutely points out. Generally understood, green bonds, as part of financialized transition responses, may advance the emergence of a 'financial monoculture' (Hall et al., 2018), which is not resilient to crises. Low-carbon transitions would thus be exposed to the boom and bust investment cycles and the volatility of international markets (Karwowski, 2019a, p. 1467, see also Dafermos et al., 2021). Gabor (2018), similarly, cautions against globalizing debt provision by opening up domestic capital markets, as transnational credit provision may crowd out credit creation for the development of local productive capacities (see also Elsner et al., 2021).

These economic drawbacks link directly to limitations financialization imposes on the governance of domestic market. For instance, the government's ability to support domestic investment at home is weakened as interest rates must be kept high to attract foreign capital (Karwowski, 2019b) and simultaneously prevent domestic actors from seeking better risk-return profiles abroad (see Ashman et al., 2011a, on the scale of capital flight in South Africa). As discussed in the subordinate strand of financialization in the context of deregulated capital markets, opportunity costs arise for government in need of accumulating hard-currency reserves to cushion potential crises rather than channeling them into other policy priorities (Kaltenbrunner & Painceira, 2017). By advocating for market instruments—like green bonds—as solutions for political problems—like governing a transition—the political space for maneuver shrinks (Elsner et al., 2021). Developing and emerging economies are locked into the dynamics of global financial crises, again limiting domestic financial policy steering (Gabor, 2018). The increasing reliance on bonds in general is inextricably linked to austerity politics that shrink fiscal coffers and enhance their reliance on capital market access (Karwowski, 2019a). And even the clout of central banks to act as "climate rescuers of last resort" (Bolton et al., 2020, pp. 9, 47) is limited; they cannot ultimately curtail or make up for capital outflows (Dafermos et al., 2021). Pagliari and Young (2020) explain that this form of financialization, "reinforce[s] the structural power of the business community and constrained the capacity for states to regulate financial markets and institutions, because the state itself has become dependent on continued financial sector expansion" (pp. 114–115). Especially with economies steeped in fossil path dependence, this development trajectory of the WSC offers no structural alternatives, but rather discloses the barriers to overhauling a system in sustainable ways (Dafermos et al., 2021, p. 10). The governance concern raises questions of accountability and representation that may be eroded through private actors engagement, given both their, at times, opaque ownership structures within corporate organizations (Baker, 2015; G. Epstein, 2020; Kennedy, 2018) and the lack of democratic accountability mechanisms (Karwowski, 2019a, 2019b).

Through the separation of financial and environmental asset (Bracking, 2015a), various issues of inequality in access to services and distribution of benefits and burdens arise. As Dafermos et al. (2021) put it, disclosure does not entail taking responsibility for let alone sanctioning of polluting firms and possibly adversely impact global South actors already at a structural disadvantage. Without substantiating their claim, Dafermos and colleagues (ibid.) lament the WSC's blind spot in not addressing climate justice concerns. As the critical segment in the literature review on green bonds detailed (see previous chapter), the financialization lens sheds light on these issues. Regarding risk distribution, they highlight the potential offloading of risks onto the public (Christophers et al., 2020). With a view to its transformative potential, a study found that green bonds are hardly accessible for issuers with limited creditworthiness (Bigger & Millington, 2019). The instrument's ability to fairly redistribute benefits and transform unequal structures can thus be questioned. Due to financializing access to services—in their case water services in South Africa—Bigger and Millington (2019) conclude that green bonds rather reinscribe and, thus, exacerbate existing inequalities. Investors' fiduciary responsibilities add a structural disadvantage by foreclosing investments in countries with lower credit ratings, oftentimes the case in the global South (Bigger, 2017).

Overall, the financialization literature neatly accommodates attempts at diffusing green bonds as a means to expedite climate resilience and low-carbon transitions. Gabor's 'Wall Street Consensus' (2020) offers a critical inspection of green bonds by foregrounding potential adverse effects of financialized transition endeavors ranging from the macro to the micro level and covering economic, governance, and distributive concerns. Further, green bonds can be well understood as socio-technical practices of financialization (Chiapello, 2020), as much as innovation (Knuth, 2018) to solidify the role of finance as much as the pertinent actors in driving green transitions. The excerpts of Transition Studies will add the finishing touches on this emerging theoretical framework.

TRANSITION STUDIES—A TOOLBOX FOR POLITICAL AND SOCIO-TECHNICAL ASPECTS OF TRANSITIONS ENDEAVORS

Transition Studies is an interdisciplinary approach that possesses two major strengths. It seeks to understand *how* transitions take place and *what* socio-technical and political barriers possibly appear. Due to the pressing need arising from climate change, low-carbon transitions have increasingly gained scholarly attention. Driven by technological *and* socio-political innovation, transitions of energy structures and transport— to name only the biggest carbon dioxide (CO_2) emitting sectors—involve, by necessity, large-scale reconfigurations of institutional arrangements and ownership structures (Swilling & Annecke, 2012). Transitions are generally perceived as lengthy and protracted affairs (Sovacool, 2016). That is why Geels (2002) refers to them as 'socio-technical transitions', encompassing the transformation of production-chains, occupational skills, logistics, and not least consumer habits in order to lower overall CO_2 (Swilling & Annecke, 2012). In contrast to previous large-scale transitions that were predominantly market- and technology-driven and thus considered 'emergent', Geels (2011) terms transitions that address persisting environmental problems 'purposive', drawing on Smith and colleagues (2005). Kern and Markard (2016) aver that these 'purposive' green transitions are highly political due to their normative motivation and high dependence on policy formulation. Therein, both procedural elements—that is governance—as much as redistribute elements—the political economy around the intended effects and unintended externalities—are important. These elements range from technocratic to inclusive for the former and from mere technical fixes to profound socio-technical shifts for the latter. This section spells out the political economic tools a just transition offers for understanding contested transition trajectories and compares them to related environmental and energy justice concepts. It, then, elaborates some of the prisms of analysis that Transition Studies disposes of in order to delve into the particularities of how innovations like green bonds gain momentum.

The 'Just Transition'

The debate around the 'just transition' has gained enormous currency within South Africa and beyond (Newell & Mulvaney, 2013; Swilling & Annecke, 2012). The just transition concept is said to have originated the US labor movement of the 1970s. In the wake of increasing regulation of polluting industries, unions demanded retraining programs for workers and communities, but also more environmentally friendly production processes within the industries (Gordon, 1998). This increasingly led to alliances with environmental movements and local community representatives fighting for environmental *and* social justice. Since then, just transition frameworks have found broader application in political discourses, not only in the US Green New Deal, the Organization for Economic Cooperation and Development (OECD), or the UNFCCC, but also in the European Union.

In South Africa, the term 'transition' is deeply engrained in South Africa's leap for democracy that was accompanied by "fundamental economic problems of inequality and resource exploitation" (Swilling & Annecke, 2012, p. xv, see also Chapter 4). It comes as no surprise that the country's (post)-Apartheid history is full of distinct political struggles around racial equality, energy access, environment protection, and employment generation; some of them heavily draw on the just transition concept (Baker & Phillips, 2019; Barnes, 2022; Swilling & Annecke, 2012; Todd & McCauley, 2021). This literature, however, demonstrates that a just transition is not only an important normative concept for broad-based mobilization but also to monitor and properly implement concrete climate-sensitive projects. The concept has found application in the evaluation of bidding rounds such as the Renewable Energy Independent Power Producers Procurement Program (REI4P) (Baker & Wlokas, 2015; M. Davies et al., 2018; Müller & Claar, 2021), especially also with a focus on participation and development of affected communities (Wlokas et al., 2017). In picking up these diverse political economic threads, the just transition concept navigates social and environmental demands accompanying transition endeavors and helps, I argue, in understanding why certain transition innovations succeed, while others fail.

In light of renewables having reached the point of cost-efficiency across the globe, a powerful 'business case' for environmentally sound investments into renewable energy has been forged.[7] Green bonds aim to consolidate this trend and create additional funding mechanisms to accelerate a green transition. The business case itself does not indicate how, through whom, and to whose benefit these complex transitions evolve. Assessing the role of finance in South Africa's transition, Baker's (2015) emphasis on the incommensurability of bankable and simultaneously equitable locally owned projects delineates clear fault lines between commercial profitability and local accountability. More disparate than most other financial tools, green bonds epitomize the conundrum of geographically spread actors from divergent domains and, hence, prompt questions regarding the modes of governance, issues of local representation in decision-making, but also distribution of benefits and costs associated with projects funded through green bonds. By relying on capital markets steeped in fossil fuels (see Chapter 4), the just transition concept traverses the tight rope of incumbent path-dependent industries and environmentally sustainable and socially inclusive alternatives. The concept thus helps point out political economic bottlenecks inherent to transformative agendas.

The related concepts of environmental and energy justice provide a complementing heuristic to spell out various justice components in purposive transition endeavors. Building on theories of justice that date back to John Rawls (1999), Nancy Fraser and Axel Honneth (2003), and Amartya Sen (1999), they provide three inter-related justice dimensions to use for an analysis of transition processes. They include concerns for *equitable distribution* of costs and benefits of environmental interventions, the *recognition* of stakeholders' interests, values, and perspectives, and the *participation in decision-making processes* (Svarstad & Benjaminsen, 2020). Müller and her colleagues (Müller et al., 2020, 2021), for example, mapped energy transition policies on the African continent along distributive, procedural, and recognitional dimensions of energy justice. A pertinent criticism of this heuristics points to the Eurocentric tendencies evident in the philosophical tradition its couched in and its heavy application in the global North (Lacey-Barnacle et al., 2020). These issues have

---

[7] Still, the relative production of fossil incumbents like BP, Shell, and Total remains more profitable than that of their renewable energy counterparts. What ultimately matters to firms is not just cost, but the bottom line—profit (Christophers, 2021).

recently been increasingly problematized through studies expanding the justice base with non-European thought, i.e. Ubuntu (Sovacool et al., 2017) and dwelling on the overlap between energy (in)justice and racism (Newell, 2021). Still, it is a useful concept to complement and decipher the just transition debate ongoing in South Africa. These political economic informed lenses elaborated above have increasingly informed socio-economic transitions and thus Transition Studies more generally (Geels, 2014; Kern & Markard, 2016).

Beyond these political economic considerations, Transition Studies offers fascinating insights into the emergence and diffusion of socio-technical innovation, whether financial, technological, policy, or otherwise. Through its conceptual frameworks, ranging from 'Strategic Niche Management', 'Multi-Level Perspective', or 'Technological Innovation Systems', Transition Studies offers a powerful toolbox to "provide insights in the agency, processes and dynamics through which newly-created innovations are successfully up-scaled" (Monk & Perkins, 2020, p. 1) into mainstream markets. In the following, I will first dwell on the Multi-Level Perspective as a useful analytical tool to decipher sustainable transition endeavors, before drawing extensively on Monk and Perkins (2020) who deploy these conceptual frameworks to trace the ascent of green bonds as an environmentally conscious asset class. Next to identifying the crucial actors, processes, and landscape developments in driving this innovation, the two authors also chart out important milestones that will similarly be traced in the South African context.

The Multi-Level Perspective (MLP) and Its Application on the Global Green Bond Market

Pioneered by Geels (2002), the Multi-Level Perspective or MLP is an analytical heuristic with which to make sense of transition processes at medium-range. It draws on evolutionary economics, science and technology studies, structuration theory, and neo-institutional theory (Geels, 2011). Transitions are inherently messy endeavors as transitions include alterations in and challenges to the configurations of sectors as diverse as transport, energy, agriculture, but also touch on consumer practices, technology, markets, infrastructure let alone institutional commitments, shared beliefs and discourses, lobbying of incumbents and power relations more generally (Unruh, 2000). Geels (2002, 2011) proposes three analytical levels to cluster these non-linear processes, namely in the *regime*, *niche*, and *landscape* plain. The regime level is "the locus of established practices and associated rules that stabilize the system" (Geels, 2011, p. 26); since transitions entail shifts from one regime to another, it is of crucial importance. Niches refer to protected spaces, where radical innovation can take place. They are oftentimes the main drivers into providing alternative configurations, if alignment of learning processes yields a stable configuration and innovation networks grow to include powerful actors that convey additional legitimacy to niche ideas (ibid.). Still, transitions do not necessarily need to be bottom-up (see bottom-up change bias in Berkhout et al., 2004) and may lead to reconfigurations of regimes rather than total transformation, leaving prevailing ownership structures largely intact (see Geels & Schot, 2007; Köhler et al., 2019 for discussions on different typologies of transitions). The landscape level, which has been criticized as a 'residual' or even 'garbage' category (see Geels, 2011), compiles external contexts the actors at niche and regime levels cannot influence in the short run (ibid.). It includes trends that possibly have destabilizing effects on the regime and thus create a window of opportunity. Climate change effects fall under this category or globally recognized governance practices. This tri-fold clustering will be helpful to assess the diffusion of the green bond concept in South Africa. They also tie in nicely with a CPE understanding that focuses on the production of new markets as well as the ways climate change responses are increasingly financialized.

Monk and Perkins (2020) provide an interesting application of the MLP and related Transition Studies concepts for green bond diffusion on a global scope. Particularly helpful is their division of the green bond market development into five phases: The initial creation and issuance of green bonds (phase 1), can be traced to two multilateral development banks (MDBs). Though not a conventional fixed-income bond, the European Investment Bank issued a climate awareness bond and thus introduced the concept of earmarking debt for environmental investments in 2007. The World Bank then issued the first officially labeled green bond in November 2008. In phase 2 (2009–2013) a slow and incremental uptake of green bonds culminated in a US\$ 1 billion issuance benchmark by the International Finance Corporation (IFC) in 2013, which was significantly oversubscribed and catalyzed stronger growth of green bonds as an asset class by overcoming uncertainty and reaching scale effects. For bankers, not only size, but also peer pressure incentivizes action. As one of Monk and Perkins' (ibid.) interviewees indicated, the wider bond community seems to also be imbued with a certain sense of peer pressure or imitative dynamics: If a big player successfully concludes a green bond, others aspire the same. In the ensuing 3rd phase after this hall mark issuance, average issuance size grew in response to rising demand, which was propelled by a diversification of issuers away from MDBs. In this phase, the state of Massachusetts issued the first municipal bond in July 2013, followed by the city of Gothenburg in October. Corporates followed suit in November, with Electricité de France issuing one of the biggest green bonds to date at US\$ 1.4 billion (Monk & Perkins, 2020). Zurich Insurance became the first institutional investor publicly announcing large commitments of US\$ 1 billion.

In 2014, the International Capital Markets Association (ICMA, 2014) agreed on voluntary process guidelines coined Green Bond Principles (GBPs), which recommend transparency and disclosure, and promote integrity of the market. While the core countries were captured by the "excitement phase" witnessing tremendous market take-off in 2014–2015 (phase 4), phase 5 marked the entrance of periphery actors in the green bond frenzy, as much as the first sovereign issuance by Poland in 2016, with Nigeria following as the first on the African continent in 2017 (Monk & Perkins, 2020).

It is particularly this last phase where my research picks up. Other BRICS (see Cooper, 2016 for a brief introduction) countries like India and China are considered 'fast followers' (Mathews et al., 2011), with China engaging in a "concerted, state-led strategy to promote a domestic innovation system for green bonds" (Monk & Perkins, 2020, p. 11) through the People's Bank of China publishing mandatory green bond guidelines to induce a domestic market to pick up in 2015. In April 2022, South Africa, in turn, launched its green finance taxonomy (Treasury, 2022; more on that in Chapter 6).

In terms of processes, Monk and Perkins (2020) identify learning, standardization, and positive feedback loops as crucial to the early diffusion of green bonds. Given the lack of knowledge on this newly created asset class at the outset, particular when it came to monitoring the use of proceeds for green projects (as the key differentiating factor to conventional bonds), learning was vital to overcome the products' 'liability of newness' (Zhang & White, 2016, cited by Monk & Perkins, 2020, p. 8). Issuers had to garner the expertise required for project selection and evaluation, management of proceeds and reporting, while investors had to comprehend the distinguishing features of and what exactly qualifies as a green asset class. Key here were social networks of investors, issuers, and underwriters forming around the Green Bond Principles (GBPs), later updated in 2018. According to Monk and Perkins (2020), they shared first-hand experience even across traditionally competitive divides. The GPBs, in essence, codified a market-friendly procedural template that "provides definitions of the recognized types of green bonds [and gives] issuers guidance on the key components involved in launching a credible green bond" (ICMA, 2014, p. n/a), thus providing conceptual and educational guidance for newcomers.

At the landscape level, proliferating climate policies, global as much as national and subnational, built pressure on financial and corporate actors to demonstrate legitimacy. Though the financial crisis of 2007–2008 initially slowed green bond market take-off, many of Monk and Perkins's interviewees stressed the financial crisis' dual role in catalyzing green bond market expansion: For one, as the crisis heralded a "sustained critique of financial market actors, calling into question their practices, purpose and legitimacy" (Monk & Perkins, 2020, p. 9). Environmental financial products granted a "'positive' storyline" and, thus, "opportunities for re-legitimation" (Monk & Perkins, 2020, p. 9; see also Paterson, 2010). Beyond that, innovation champions around the CBI, entrepreneurial issuers, underwriters, and investors such as the World Bank, the Swedish investment bank SEB, or the German development bank KFW, have deployed discursive strategies to create a legitimizing narrative of co-benefits around green bonds (primarily improved reputation and internal learning) and sowed expectation for higher levels of market demand and future market growth. The hype around green bonds can also be situated in this light by granting a re-legitimizing narrative for investors to do 'green' (Monk & Perkins, 2020). I will dwell on this later in the South African case.

The growth expectations created a self-reinforcing if not self-fulfilling impetus for the bond market growth in the initial years. As Monk and Perkins (2020) state, "early market formation by the MDBs was essential in creating these self-reinforcing dynamics", creating "a powerful signaling effect [and] demonstrating the existence of genuine demand for the product" (p. 8). They also lend additional creditability to the financial product, but also shielded it from market forces by subsidizing additional costs arising from green issuance. Positive externalities contributed to this hype, whether the proliferation of domestic green bond guidelines or the complementing CBS, GBPs. Also, quality assurance services through external providers such as Cicero and Sustainalytics provided guidance, reduced uncertainties, and facilitated market mechanisms (ibid., p. 9).

Two further take-aways can be drawn from Monk and Perkins (ibid.). Firstly, they underscore the importance of public actors in creating, demonstrating, and commercializing new financial products, whether that are MDBs or committed governments. Similarly, on-state networks, i.e. the CBI providing technical assistance and standards or market participants with first-hand experiences, were crucial in upscaling the green bond niche beyond MDBs on the supply and environmentally oriented investment community on the demand side. We will discuss the driving forces in the South Africa's context, both in terms of innovation regulation and issuing product champions. Secondly, Monk and Perkins (ibid.) identify compatibility with established market convention as key for innovation diffusion. This finding may hint at reasons for the limited expansion of green bonds in South Africa given the economy's heavy reliance on fossil fuels (see Chapter 5).

All these findings are important take-aways to keep in mind when tracing the diffusion of green bonds in South Africa. What Monk and Perkins (2020), however, fail to cover are the competing green finance innovations and the ongoing tussle over the harmonization of national-level taxonomies that dominate global green bond debates. To their credit, especially the latter have gained only recent momentum but should feature in a monography dealing with green bonds in South Africa. The results chapter will shed additional light on these two issues.

This section argued for Transition Studies offering an array of tools that can usefully be deployed to understand the diffusion of green bonds. While Geels' MLP concept helps to order the diverse dynamics, the 'just transition' concept—paired with the justice dimensions I elaborated—will add important elements in tracing the various bottlenecks the green bond diffusion in South Africa has experienced.

FURTHER RESEARCH QUESTIONS

Overall, this chapter sought to provide a theoretical framework to fill the literature gaps identified in the previous chapter. By scrutinizing green bond diffusion in South Africa with an interdisciplinary framework, my research adds to political economic assessments of finance-led transition endeavors. It adds predominantly to the reformist and critical debate on green bonds and explores the promises and shortcomings this green innovation yields in an emerging market context. It also contributes a much-needed qualitative assessment of green bond markets and provides a rich empirical study. By focusing on South Africa, it lastly foregrounds hitherto under-researched emerging markets.

This elaborate theoretical framework yields a few substantiating questions for this research endeavor. As referred to in the introduction, this puzzle revolves around the lack of green bonds being issued in South Africa, despite the apparent benefits the financial practitioners' literature so actively espouses (see Chapter 2). The additional questions are categorized along the three strands of theoretical framework (see Box 3.1), namely CPE (A), financialization (B), and Transition Studies (C). The first set begs for discourse analysis, while the other two foreground financial as well as governmental concerns on the procedural level and material concerns regarding the distributional effects accompanying transitions of that scale.

By combining these three sets of ideas, the South African green bond market can be thoroughly analyzed. Before diving into the empirical findings, a few hypotheses about the distinctive South African context need to be developed. To adequately advance answers to my research questions, I provide an overview of political economic context of my research case.

Box 3.1: Supplementary Research Questions

Cultural Political Economy of green bond diffusion:

A.1: How do green bond advocates portray and narrate green bonds as solutions to driving low carbon transitions?

A.2: How do success stories support green bond market development?

A.3: How do South African financial actors and government representatives justify their (in)actions vis-a-vis climate change?

A.4: How does the green bond market maneuver the contested definitions around what is considered 'green'?

A.5: To what extend do green bond advocates seek to render green bond diffusion a technical and apolitical endeavor?

Financialization through green-bond-led transition endeavors:

B.1: How do green bonds financialize the transition processes in South Africa?

B.2: What weaknesses of green bonds emerge in South Africa as an emerging market?

B.3: What kind of limitations arise from attempting to deploy a market-based innovation like green bonds?

B.4: How do derisking practices intersect with green bond expansion in South Africa?

Policies and politics of finance-led low-carbon transition endeavors:

C.1: How does the predisposition of the domestic capital market affect green bond diffusion in South Africa? What kind of transition do green bonds likely inaugurate?

C.2: How does the regulatory environment incentivize or inhibit green bond diffusion?

C.3: What bottlenecks, barriers and pushbacks has the green bond diffusion experienced in South Africa? How might they be explained?

C.4: How do green bond markets affect concerns for a just transition?

References

Amoore, L., & de Goede, M. (2010). Cultural political economies of the war on terror. In M. Paterson & J. Best (Eds.), *Cultural political economy* (pp. 161–176). Routledge. https://doi.org/10.4324/9780203861394-19

Amsden, A. H. (2008). The wild ones: Industrial policies in the developing world. In N. Serra & J. E. Stiglitz (Eds.), *The Washington consensus reconsidered–Towards a new global governance* (1st ed., pp. 95–118). Oxford University Press. https://doi.org/10.1093/acprof:oso/9780199534081.001.0001

Arent, D., Arndt, C., Miller, M., Tarp, F., & Zinaman, O. (2017). *The political economy of clean energy transitions* (D. Arent, C. Arndt, M. Miller, F. Tarp, & O. Zinaman, Eds., 1st ed.). Oxford University Press.

Arrighi, G. (1994). *The long twentieth century. Money, power, and the origins of our times* (1st ed.). Verso.

Ashman, S., Fine, B., & Newman, S. (2011a). Amnesty international? The nature, scale and impact of capital flight from South Africa. *Journal of Southern African Studies, 37*(1), 7–25. https://doi.org/10.1080/03057070. 2011.555155

Ashman, Samantha, Fine, B., & Newman, S. (2011b). The crisis in South Africa: Neoliberalism, financialization and uneven and combined development. *Socialist Register,* 174–195.https://doi.org/10.1080/00343404.2016.126 2946

Asiyanbi, A. P. (2018). Financialisation in the green economy: Material connections, markets-in-the-making and Foucauldian organising actions. *Environment and Planning A, 50*(3), 531–548. https://doi.org/10.1177/030851 8X17708787

Babb, S., & Kentikelenis, A. (2021). Markets everywhere: The Washington consensus and the sociology of global institutional change. *Annual Review of Sociology, 47,* 521–541. https://doi.org/10.1146/annurev-soc-090220-025543

Baker, L. (2015). The evolving role of finance in South Africa's renewable energy sector. *Geoforum, 64*(July), 146–156. https://doi.org/10.1016/j.geoforum. 2015.06.017

Baker, L., & Phillips, J. (2019). Tensions in the transition: The politics of electricity distribution in South Africa. *Environment and Planning C: Politics and Space, 37*(1), 177–196. https://doi.org/10.1177/2399654418778590

Baker, L., & Wlokas, H. (2015, June). *South Africa's renewable energy procurement: A new frontier?*, 1–34. www.erc.uct.ac.za

Barnes, J. (2022). Divergent desires for the just transition in South Africa: An assemblage analysis. *Political Geography, 97*(April). https://doi.org/10. 1016/j.polgeo.2022.102655

Bayliss, K., & Van Waeyenberge, E. (2018). Unpacking the public private partnership revival. *Journal of Development Studies, 54*(4), 577–593. https://doi. org/10.1080/00220388.2017.1303671

Berkhout, F. G. H., Smith, A., & Stirlingh, A. (2004). Socio-technological regimes and transition contexts. In B. Elzen, F. W. Geels, & K. Green (Eds.), *System innovation and the transition to sustainability* (pp. 48–75). Edward Elgar Publishing Limited.

Best, J., & Paterson, M. (2010). *Cultural political economy* (J. Best & M. Paterson, Eds., 1st ed.). Routledge.

Best, J., & Paterson, M. (2015). Towards a cultural political economy—Not a cultural IPE. *Millennium: Journal of International Studies, 43*(2), 738–740. https://doi.org/10.1177/0305829814557063

Bieling, H.-J. (2011). Theoriefolien: Analyseperspektiven der IPÖ [Theory slides: Analytical perspectives of IPE]. In *Internationale Politische Ökonomie* [International Political Economy] (pp. 27–53). https://doi.org/10.1007/978-3-531-94176-9_2

Bigger, P. (2017). Measurement and the circulation of risk in green bonds. *Journal of Environmental Investing, 8*(1), 273–287.

Bigger, P., & Millington, N. (2019). Getting soaked? Climate crisis, adaptation finance, and racialized austerity. *Environment and Planning E: Nature and Space, 3*(3), 601–623. https://doi.org/10.1177/2514848619876539

Bolton, P., Despres, M., Pereira da Silva, L. A., Svartzman, R., & Samama, F. (2020). *The green swan* (Issue January). https://www.bis.org/publ/othp31. pdf

Bonizzi, B. (2013). Financialization in developing and emerging countries: A survey. *International Journal of Political Economy, 42*(4), 83–107. https:// doi.org/10.2753/IJP0891-1916420405

Bonizzi, B., Kaltenbrunner, A., & Powell, J. (2020). Subordinate financialization in emerging capitalist economies. In P. Mader, D. Mertens, & N. van der Zwan (Eds.), *The Routledge international handbook of financialization* (1st ed., pp. 177–187). Routledge Taylor & Francis. https://doi.org/10.4324/9781315142876-15

Bracking, S. (2015a). Performativity in the green economy: How far does climate finance create a fictive economy? *Third World Quarterly, 36*(12), 2337–2357. https://doi.org/10.1080/01436597.2015.1086263

Bracking, S. (2015b). The anti-politics of climate finance: The creation and performativity of the green climate fund. *Antipode, 47*(2), 281–302. https:// doi.org/10.1111/anti.12123

Bracking, S. (2016). The financialisation of power—How financiers rule Africa. In *The financialisation of power* (1st ed.). Routledge Taylor & Francis. https://doi.org/10.4324/9780415538510

Buckel, S. (2011). Abhandlungen - Staatsprojekt Europa. *Politische Vierteljahresschrift, 52*(4), 636–662. https://www.zar.nomos.de/fileadmin/pvs/doc/Aufsatz_PVS_11_04.pdf

Castree, N. (2010). Neoliberalism and the biophysical environment 2: Theorising the neoliberalisation of nature. *Geography Compass, 4*(12), 1734–1746. https://doi.org/10.1111/j.1749-8198.2010.00407.x

Chang, H.-J. (2003). *Kicking away the ladder—Development strategy in historical perspective* (1st ed., Vol. 2, Issue 2). Anthem Press.

Chiapello, E. (2020). Financialization as a socio-technical process. In P. Mader, D. Mertens, & N. van der Zwan (Eds.), *The Routledge international handbook*

of financialization (1st ed., pp. 81–91). https://doi.org/10.4324/978131
5142876-7

Christophers, B. (2015). The limits to financialization. *Dialogues in Human Geography, 5*(2), 183–200. https://doi.org/10.1177/2043820615588153

Christophers, B. (2021). Fossilised capital: Price and profit in the energy transition. *New Political Economy, 27*(1), 146–159. https://doi.org/10.1080/135 63467.2021.1926957

Christophers, B., Bigger, P., & Johnson, L. (2020). Stretching scales? Risk and sociality in climate finance. *Environment and Planning A, 52*(1), 88–110. https://doi.org/10.1177/0308518X18819004

Claar, S. (2018). *International trade policy and class dynamics in South Africa— The economic partnership agreement.* Palgrave Macmillan.

Cohen, B. (2008). *International political economy—An intellectual history* (B. Cohen, Ed., 1st ed.). Princeton University Press.

Cooper, A. (2016). *BRICS: A very short introduction* (1st ed.). Oxford University Press.

Cox, S. (2021, June). *Inscriptions of resilience: Bond ratings and the government of climate risk in Greater Miami*, 1–16. https://doi.org/10.1177/030851 8X211054162

Dafermos, Y., Gabor, D., & Michell, J. (2021). The Wall Street Consensus in pandemic times: What does it mean for climate-aligned development? *Canadian Journal of Development Studies/Revue Canadienne d'études Du Développement, 42*, 1–14.https://doi.org/10.1080/02255189.2020.186 5137

Davies, M., Swilling, M., & Wlokas, H. L. (2018). Towards new configurations of urban energy governance in South Africa's renewable energy procurement programme. *Energy Research and Social Science, 36*(November), 61–69. https://doi.org/10.1016/j.erss.2017.11.010

Davies, Matt. (2010). Works, products, and the division of labour: Notes for a cultural and political economic critique. In J. Best & M. Paterson (Eds.), *Cultural political economy* (1st ed., pp. 48–63). RIPE Series in Global Political Economy, Routledge. https://doi.org/10.4324/9780203861394-11

Death, C. (2015). Four discourses of the green economy in the global South. *Third World Quarterly, 36*(12), 2207–2224. https://doi.org/10.1080/014 36597.2015.1068110

Deitelhoff, N. (2022). Zurück auf Null - Putins Krieg und die deutsche Sicherheitsordnung [Back to Zero - Putin's war and German security]. *Die Blätter Für Deutsche Und Internationale Politik* [Pamphlets for German and International Politics], 6(June), 69–76. https://www.blaetter.de/ausgabe/2022/ juni/zurueck-auf-null#_ftnref12

Elsner, C., Neumann, M., Müller, F., & Claar, S. (2021). Room for money or manoeuvre? How green financialization and de-risking shape Zambia's renewable energy transition. *Canadian Journal of Development Studies, 43*(2), 276–295. https://doi.org/10.1080/02255189.2021.1973971

Epstein, G. (2020). The bankers' club and the power of finance. In P. Mader, D. Mertens, & N. van der Zwan (Eds.), *The Routledge international handbook of financialization* (1st ed., pp. 437–447). Routledge Taylor & Francis. https:// doi.org/10.4324/9781315142876-39

Epstein, G. A. (2005). *Financialization and the world economy*. Edward Elgar Publishing Limited. http://search.lib.cam.ac.uk/?itemid=%7Cdepfacf mdb%7C434152

Ferguson, J. (1994). *The anti-politics machine. Development, depoliticization, and bureaucratic power in Lesotho*. University of Minnesota Press.

Fine, B., & Rustomjee, Z. (2018). The political economy of South Africa. In B. Fine & Z. Rustomjee (Eds.), *The political economy of South Africa* (1st ed.). Routledge. https://doi.org/10.4324/9780429496004

Fraser, N., & Honneth, A. (2003). *Redistribution or recognition? A political-philosophical exchange* (1st ed.). Verso.

G20/OECD/WB. (2018). *G20/OECD/WB Stocktake of Tools and Instruments Related to Infrastructure as an Asset Class—Background report* (Issue July). https://www.oecd.org/g20/G20-OECD-WB-Stocktake-of-Tools-and-Instruments-Related-to-Infrastructure-as-asset-class.pdf

Gabor, D. (2018). *Understanding the financialisation of international development through 11 FAQs*. https://us.boell.org/sites/default/files/financialisatio nfaqs.pdf

Gabor, D. (2019). *Securitization for sustainability – Does it help achieve the sustainable development goals*. https://us.boell.org/sites/default/files/gabor_ finalized.pdf

Gabor, D. (2020, April). *The Wall Street Consensus* (Working Paper, 1–23). https://doi.org/10.31235/osf.io/wab8m

Gabor, D. (2021). The Wall Street Consensus. *Development and Change, 52*(3), 429–459. https://doi.org/10.1111/dech.12645

Geels, F. W. (2002). Technological transitions as evolutionary reconfiguration processes: A multi-level perspective and a case-study. *Research Policy, 31*(8–9), 1257–1274. https://doi.org/10.1016/S0048-7333(02)00062-8

Geels, F. W. (2011). The multi-level perspective on sustainability transitions: Responses to seven criticisms. *Environmental Innovation and Societal Transitions, 1*(1), 24–40. https://doi.org/10.1016/j.eist.2011.02.002

Geels, F. W. (2014). Regime resistance against low-carbon transitions: Introducing politics and power into the multi-level perspective. *Theory, Culture & Society, 31*(5), 21–40. https://doi.org/10.1177/0263276414531627

Geels, F. W. (2019). Socio-technical transitions to sustainability: A review of criticisms and elaborations of the multi-level perspective. *Current Opinion in*

Environmental Sustainability, 39, 187–201. https://doi.org/10.1016/j.cos
ust.2019.06.009

Geels, F. W., & Schot, J. (2007). Typology of sociotechnical transition pathways. *Research Policy, 36*(3), 399–417. https://doi.org/10.1016/j.respol.
2007.01.003

Gordon, R. (1998). "Shell no!": OCAW and the labor-environmental alliance.
Environmental History, 3(4), 460–487. https://doi.org/10.2307/3985207

Hall, S., Roelich, K. E., Davis, M. E., & Holstenkamp, L. (2018). Finance and justice in low-carbon energy transitions. *Applied Energy, 222*, 772–780.
https://doi.org/10.1016/j.apenergy.2018.04.007

Helleiner, E. (2010). The culture of money doctoring: American financial advising in Latin America during the 1940s1. In M. Paterson & J. Best (Eds.), *Cultural political economy* (pp. 91–109). Routledge. https://doi.org/
10.4324/9780203861394-14

Hilbrandt, H., & Grubbauer, M. (2020). Standards and SSOs in the contested widening and deepening of financial markets: The arrival of Green Municipal Bonds in Mexico City. *Environment and Planning A, 52*(7), 1415–1433.
https://doi.org/10.1177/0308518X20909391

Huysmans, J. (2006). The politics of insecurity: Fear, migration and asylum in the EU? In B. Buzan & R. Little (Eds.), *The new international relations* (1st ed., Vol. 45, Issue 1, pp. 219–219). Routledge. https://doi.org/10.1111/j.
1468-5965.2007.00709_9.x

ICMA. (2014, June). *The green bond principles 2014*. The Green Bond Principles—Brochure, 6.

Jessop, B. (2010). Cultural political economy and critical policy studies. *Critical Policy Studies, 3*(3–4), 336–356. https://doi.org/10.1080/194601710036
19741

Jessop, B., & Oosterlynck, S. (2008). Cultural political economy: On making the cultural turn without falling into soft economic sociology. *Geoforum, 39*(3),
1155–1169. https://doi.org/10.1016/j.geoforum.2006.12.008

Kaltenbrunner, A., & Painceira, J. P. (2015). Developing countries' changing nature of financial integration and new forms of external vulnerability: The Brazilian experience. *Cambridge Journal of Economics, 39*(5), 1281–1306.
https://doi.org/10.1093/cje/beu038

Kaltenbrunner, A., & Painceira, J. P. (2017). The impossible trinity: Inflation targeting, exchange rate management and open capital accounts in emerging economies. *Development and Change, 48*(3), 452–480. https://doi.org/10.
1111/dech.12304

Karwowski, E. (2019a). How financialization undermines democracy. *Development and Change, 50*(5), 1466–1481. https://doi.org/10.1111/dech.
12537

Karwowski, E. (2019b). Towards (de-)financialisation: The role of the state. *Cambridge Journal of Economics, 43*(4), 1001–1027. https://doi.org/10. 1093/cje/bez023

Karwowski, E. (2020). Economic development and variegated financialization in emerging economies. In P. Mader, D. Mertens, & N. van der Zwan (Eds.), *The Routledge international handbook of financialization* (1st ed., pp. 162– 176). Routledge Taylor & Francis. https://doi.org/10.4324/978131514287 6-14

Karwowski, E., Fine, B., & Ashman, S. (2018). Introduction to the special section 'Financialization in South Africa.' *Competition and Change, 22*(4), 383–387. https://doi.org/10.1177/1024529418791762

Karwowski, E., & Stockhammer, E. (2017). Financialisation in emerging economies: A systematic overview and comparison with Anglo-Saxon economies. *Economic and Political Studies, 5*(1), 60–86. https://doi.org/10. 1080/20954816.2016.1274520

Katz-Rosene, R. M., Kelly-Bisson, C., & Paterson, M. (2021). Teaching students to think ecologically about the global political economy, and vice versa. *Review of International Political Economy, 28*(4), 1083–1098. https://doi.org/10. 1080/09692290.2020.1748092

Kennedy, S. F. (2018). Indonesia's energy transition and its contradictions: Emerging geographies of energy and finance. *Energy Research and Social Science, 41*(June 2017), 230–237. https://doi.org/10.1016/j.erss.2018. 04.023

Keohane, R. O., & Nye, J. S. (1977). Power and interdependence—World politics in transition. In R. O. Keohane & J. S. Nye (Eds.), *Power* (1st ed.). HarperCollins.

Keohane, R. O., & Nye, J. S. (1998). Power and interdependence in the information age. *Foreign Affairs, 77*(5), 81. https://doi.org/10.2307/200 49052

Kern, F., & Markard, J. (2016). Analysing energy transitions: Combining insights from transition studies and international political economy. In T. Van de Graaf, B. K. Sovacool, A. Ghosh, F. Kern, & M. T. Klare (Eds.), *The Palgrave handbook of the international political economy of energy* (1st ed., pp. 291–318). Palgrave Macmillan. https://doi.org/10.1057/978-1-137- 55631-8

Kidney, S. (2011). *3 simple reasons why Climate Bond Standards are important.* Climate Bonds Initiative, 1–4. https://www.climatebonds.net/2014/05/3- simple-reasons-why-climate-bond-standards-are-important

Knafo, S. (2022). The power of finance in the age of market based banking. *New Political Economy, 27*(1), 33–46. https://doi.org/10.1080/13563467.2021. 1910646

Knuth, S. (2018). "Breakthroughs" for a green economy? Financialization and clean energy transition. *Energy Research and Social Science, 41*(April), 220–229. https://doi.org/10.1016/j.erss.2018.04.024

Köhler, J., Geels, F. W., Kern, F., Markard, J., Onsongo, E., Wieczorek, A., Alkemade, F., Avelino, F., Bergek, A., Boons, F., Fünfschilling, L., Hess, D., Holtz, G., Hyysalo, S., Jenkins, K., Kivimaa, P., Martiskainen, M., McMeekin, A., Mühlemeier, M. S., … Wells, P. (2019). An agenda for sustainability transitions research: State of the art and future directions. *Environmental Innovation and Societal Transitions, 31*, 1–32.https://doi.org/10.1016/j.eist.2019.01.004

Kranke, M. (2014). Which "C" are you talking about? Critical meets cultural IPE. *Millennium: Journal of International Studies, 42*(3), 897–907. https://doi.org/10.1177/0305829814529472

Krasner, S. D. (1994). International political economy: Abiding discord. *Review of International Political Economy, 1*(1), 13–19. https://doi.org/10.1080/09692299408434265

Kvangraven, I. H., Koddenbrock, K., & Sylla, N. S. (2020). Financial subordination and uneven financialization in 21st century Africa. *Community Development Journal*, 1–22. https://doi.org/10.1093/cdj/bsaa047

Lacey-Barnacle, M., Robison, R., & Foulds, C. (2020). Energy justice in the developing world: A review of theoretical frameworks, key research themes and policy implications. *Energy for Sustainable Development, 55*, 122–138. https://doi.org/10.1016/j.esd.2020.01.010

Lapavitsas, C., & Powell, J. (2013). Financialisation varied: A comparative analysis of advanced economies. *Cambridge Journal of Regions, Economy and Society, 6*(3), 359–379. https://doi.org/10.1093/cjres/rst019

LeBaron, G., Mügge, D., Best, J., & Hay, C. (2020). Blind spots in IPE: Marginalized perspectives and neglected trends in contemporary capitalism. *Review of International Political Economy, 28*(2), 283–294. https://doi.org/10.1080/09692290.2020.1830835

Lehmann, I. (2019). When cultural political economy meets 'charismatic carbon' marketing: A gender-sensitive view on the limitations of Gold Standard cookstove offset projects. *Energy Research and Social Science, 55*(May), 146–154. https://doi.org/10.1016/j.erss.2019.05.001

Levy, D. L., & Spicer, A. (2013). Contested imaginaries and the cultural political economy of climate change. *Organization, 20*(5), 659–678. https://doi.org/10.1177/1350508413489816

Li, T. M. (2007). *The will to improve* (1st ed.). Duke University Press.

Lisle, D. (2010). Joyless cosmopolitans: The moral economy of ethical tourism. In J. Best & M. Paterson (Eds.), *Cultural political economy* (1st ed., pp. 139–157). Routledge. https://doi.org/10.4324/9780203861394

MacKenzie, D. (2006). An engine, not a camera—How financial models shape markets. In *Massachusetts Institute of Technology* (1st ed., Vol. 1). MIT Press. https://doi.org/10.1080/15265160902874361

MacKenzie, D. (2009). Making things the same: Gases, emission rights and the politics of carbon markets. *Accounting, Organizations and Society, 34*(3–4), 440–455. https://doi.org/10.1016/j.aos.2008.02.004

Mader, P., Mertens, D., & van der Zwan, N. (Eds.). (2020a). *The Routledge international handbook of financialization* (1st ed., Vol. 1, Issue 1). Routledge Taylor & Francis.

Mader, P., Mertens, D., & van der Zwan, N. (2020b). Financialization—An introduction. In P. Mader, D. Mertens, & N. van der Zwan (Eds.), *The Routledge international handbook of financialization* (1st ed.). Routledge Taylor & Francis.

Mangat, R., Dalby, S., & Paterson, M. (2018). Divestment discourse: War, justice, morality and money. *Environmental Politics, 27*(2), 187–208. https://doi.org/10.1080/09644016.2017.1413725

Markusson, N., Dahl Gjefsen, M., Stephens, J. C., & Tyfield, D. (2017). The political economy of technical fixes: A case from the climate domain. *Energy Research and Social Science, 23*, 1–10. https://doi.org/10.1016/j.erss.2016.11.004

Mathews, J. A., Hu, M. C., & Wu, C. Y. (2011). Fast-follower industrial dynamics: The case of Taiwan's emergent solar photovoltaic industry. *Industry and Innovation, 18*(2), 177–202. https://doi.org/10.1080/13662716.2011.541104

Mathews, J. A., & Kidney, S. (2012). Financing climate-friendly energy development through bonds. *Development Southern Africa, 29*(2), 337–349. https://doi.org/10.1080/0376835X.2012.675702

Mawdsley, E. (2018). From billions to trillions': Financing the SDGs in a world 'beyond aid. *Dialogues in Human Geography, 8*(2), 191–195. https://doi.org/10.1177/2043820618780789

Mazzucato, M. (2011). The entrepreneurial state. In *Soundings* (Vol. 49, Issue 49). Demos. https://doi.org/10.3898/136266211798411183

McNamara, K. R. (1999). The currency of ideas—Monetary politics in the European Union. In *The currency of ideas* (1st ed., Vol. 1). Cornell University Press. https://doi.org/10.7591/9781501711930

Methmann, C. (2010). "Climate protection" as empty signifier: A discourse theoretical perspective on climate mainstreaming in world politics. *Millennium: Journal of International Studies, 39*(2), 345–372. https://doi.org/10.1177/0305829810383606

Methmann, C., & Rothe, D. (2012). Politics for the day after tomorrow: The logic of apocalypse in global climate politics. *Security Dialogue, 43*(4), 323–344. https://doi.org/10.1177/0967010612450746

Monk, A., & Perkins, R. (2020). What explains the emergence and diffusion of green bonds? *Energy Policy, 145*, 111641. https://doi.org/10.1016/j.enpol.2020.111641

Müller, F. (2020). Can the subaltern protect forests? REDD+ compliance, depoliticization and Indigenous subjectivities. *Journal of Political Ecology, 27*(1), 419–435. https://doi.org/10.2458/V27I1.23198

Müller, F., & Claar, S. (2021). Auctioning a 'just energy transition'? South Africa's renewable energy procurement programme and its implications for transition strategies. *Review of African Political Economy, 48*(169), 333–351. https://doi.org/10.1080/03056244.2021.1932790

Müller, F., Claar, S., Neumann, M., & Elsner, C. (2020). Is green a Pan-African colour? Mapping African renewable energy policies and transitions in 34 countries. *Energy Research and Social Science, 68*. https://doi.org/10.1016/j.erss.2020.101551

Müller, F., Neumann, M., Elsner, C., & Claar, S. (2021). Assessing African energy transitions: Renewable energy policies, energy justice, and SDG 7. *Politics and Governance, 9*(1), 119–130. https://doi.org/10.17645/pag.v9i1.3615

National Treasury. (2022, April 1). *Media statement: South Africa's first national green finance taxonomy launched to assist the financial sector response to climate change and support sustainable development.* http://www.treasury.gov.za/comm_media/press/2022/2022040101 Media statement - Green Finance Taxonomy.pdf

Newell, P. (2021). Race and the politics of energy transitions. *Energy Research and Social Science, 71*(October 2020), 101839. https://doi.org/10.1016/j.erss.2020.101839

Newell, P., & Mulvaney, D. (2013). The political economy of the "just transition." *Geographical Journal, 179*(2), 132–140. https://doi.org/10.1111/geoj.12008

Ogman, R. F. (2018, October). *Crisis, hegemony, and the social investment market The cultural political economy of an emerging governance strategy*, 1–319.

Pagliari, S., & Young, K. L. (2020). How financialization is reproduced politically. In P. Mader, D. Mertens, & N. van der Zwan (Eds.), *The Routledge international handbook of financialization* (1st ed., pp. 113–124). https://doi.org/10.4324/9781315142876-10

Palan, R. (2009). The proof of the pudding is in the eating: IPE in light of the crisis of 2007/8. *New Political Economy, 14*(3), 385–394. https://doi.org/10.1080/13563460903087540

Paterson, M. (2010). Legitimation and accumulation in climate change governance. *New Political Economy, 15*(3), 345–368. https://doi.org/10.1080/13563460903288247

Paterson, M. (2020). SS-03 'The End of the Fossil Fuel Age'? Discourse Politics and Climate Change Political Economy. *New Political Economy, 26*(6), 923–936.https://doi.org/10.1080/13563467.2020.1810218

Paterson, M., & Stripple, J. (2010). My space: Governing individuals' carbon emissions. *Environment and Planning D: Society and Space, 28*(2), 341–362. https://doi.org/10.1068/d4109

Peterson, V. S. (2006). Getting real: The necessity of critical postrstructuralism in global political economy. In M. De Goede (Ed.), *International political economy and poststructural politics* (1st ed., pp. 119–139). Palgrave Macmillan.

Petry, J. (2020). From national marketplaces to global providers of financial infrastructures: Exchanges, infrastructures and structural power in global finance. *New Political Economy, 26*(4), 574–597. https://doi.org/10.1080/13563467.2020.1782368

Petry, J., Koddenbrock, K., & Nölke, A. (2021). State capitalism and capital markets: Comparing securities exchanges in emerging markets. *Environment and Planning A: Economy and Space*, 1–22. https://doi.org/10.1177/0308518x211047599

Polanyi, K. (n.d.). The great transformation—The political and economic origins of our time. In *Politics, health, and health care: Selected essays* (Second Pap). Beacon Press. https://doi.org/10.7208/chicago/9780226278130.003.0005

Rawls, J. (1999). A theory of justice. In *Theory and decision* (2nd ed., Vol. 4, Issues 3–4). The Belknap Press of Harvard University Press. https://doi.org/10.1007/BF00136652

Rowden, R. (2019). *From the Washington Consensus to the Wall Street Consensus. The financialization initiative of the World Bank and multilateral development banks.*

Sau, A. (2021). On cultural political economy: A defence and constructive critique. *New Political Economy, 26*(6), 1015–1029. https://doi.org/10.1080/13563467.2021.1879758

Scherrer, C., & Kunze, C. (2011). *Globalisierung* (1st ed.). Vandenhoeck & Ruprecht.

Sen, A. (1999). *Development as freedom* (1st ed.). Oxford University Press.

Smith, A., Stirling, A., & Berkhout, F. (2005). The governance of sustainable socio-technical transitions. *Research Policy, 34*(10), 1491–1510. https://doi.org/10.1016/j.respol.2005.07.005

Sovacool, B. K. (2016). How long will it take? Conceptualizing the temporal dynamics of energy transitions. *Energy Research and Social Science, 13*, 202–215. https://doi.org/10.1016/j.erss.2015.12.020

Sovacool, B. K., Burke, M., Baker, L., Kotikalapudi, C. K., & Wlokas, H. (2017). New frontiers and conceptual frameworks for energy justice. *Energy Policy, 105*, 677–691. https://doi.org/10.1016/j.enpol.2017.03.005

Stockhammer, E. (2012). Financialization, income distribution and the crisis. *Investigación Económica, 71*(279), 39–70.

Strange, S. (1970). International economics and international relations: A case of mutual neglect. *International Affairs, 46*(2), 304–315. https://www.bu.edu/pardeeschool/files/2018/02/Susan-Strange's-"International-Economics-and-International-Relations-A-Case-of-Mutual-Neglect.pdf

Sum, N.-L. (2009). The production of hegemonic policy discourses: 'competitiveness' as a knowledge brand and its (re-)contextualizations. *Critical Policy Studies, 3*(2), 184–203. https://doi.org/10.1080/19460170903385668

Sum, N.-L., & Jessop, B. (2013). *Towards a cultural political economy—Putting culture in its place in political economy* (N.-L. Sum & B. Jessop, Eds., 1st ed.). Edward Elgar Publishing Limited.

Svarstad, H., & Benjaminsen, T. A. (2020). Reading radical environmental justice through a political ecology lens. *Geoforum, 108*(March), 1–11. https://doi.org/10.1016/j.geoforum.2019.11.007

Swilling, M., & Annecke, E. (2012). *Just transitions—Explorations of sustainability in an unfair world* (1st ed., Vol. 1, Issue 4). United Nations University Press. https://doi.org/10.1080/02652038509373556

Swyngedouw, E. (2010). Apocalypse forever?: Post-political populism and the spectre of climate change. *Theory, Culture and Society, 27*(2), 213–232. https://doi.org/10.1177/0263276409358728

Swyngedouw, E. (2017). Unlocking the mind-trap: Politicising urban theory and practice. *Urban Studies, 54*(1), 55–61. https://doi.org/10.1177/0042098016671475

Todd, I., & McCauley, D. (2021). Assessing policy barriers to the energy transition in South Africa. *Energy Policy, 158*(February), 112529. https://doi.org/10.1016/j.enpol.2021.112529

United Nations. (n.d.). *SDG 7: Affordable and clean energy—Ensure access to affordable, reliable, sustainable and modern energy.* SDGs. https://www.un.org/sustainabledevelopment/energy/

Unruh, G. C. (2000). Understanding carbon lock-in. *Energy Policy, 28*(12), 817–830. https://doi.org/10.1016/S0301-4215(00)00070-7

van der Merwe, J. (2016). An historical geographical analysis of South Africa's system of accumulation: 1652–1994. *Review of African Political Economy, 43*(147), 58–72. https://doi.org/10.1080/03056244.2015.1049521

van Heur, B. (2010a). Beyond regulation: Towards a cultural political economy of complexity and emergence. *New Political Economy, 15*(3), 421–444. https://doi.org/10.1080/13563460903290938

van Heur, B. (2010b). Research and relevance: Response to Jessop and Sum. *New Political Economy, 15*(3), 453–456. https://doi.org/10.1080/135634 61003789811

Volberding, P. (2021). Leveraging financial markets for development. In *Leveraging financial markets for development*. https://doi.org/10.1007/978-3-030-55008-0

Walters, W. (2010). Anti-political economy: Cartographies of "illegal immigration" and the displacement of the economy. In M. Paterson & J. Best (Eds.), *Cultural political economy* (pp. 113–138). Routledge. https://doi.org/10.4324/9780203861394

Warren, L., & Seal, W. (2018). Using investment appraisal models in strategic negotiation: The cultural political economy of electricity generation. *Accounting, Organizations and Society, 70*, 16–32. https://doi.org/10.1016/j.aos.2018.04.001

Watts, N., & Scales, I. R. (2020). Social impact investing, agriculture, and the financialisation of development: Insights from sub-Saharan Africa. *World Development, 130*, 1–11. https://doi.org/10.1016/j.worlddev.2020.104918

Williams, R. (1960). Culture and society, 1780–1950. In *Anchor books*. Kansas City Public Library.

Wlokas, H. L., Westoby, P., & Soal, S. (2017). Learning from the literature on community development for the implementation of community renewables in South Africa. *Journal of Energy in Southern Africa, 28*(1), 35–44. https://doi.org/10.17159/2413-3051/2017/v28i1a1592

World Bank. (2018). *Financing for development: New approach, new commitment*. https://olc.worldbank.org/system/files/Financing_for_Development_at_the_WBG_Brochure.pdf

Wullweber, J., & Scherrer, C. (2010). Post-modern and post-structural international political economy. In A. Robert (Ed.), *The international studies encyclopedia* (pp. 1–25).

Zhang, W., & White, S. (2016). Overcoming the liability of newness: Entrepreneurial action and the emergence of China's private solar photovoltaic firms. *Research Policy, 45*(3), 604–617. https://doi.org/10.1016/j.respol.2015.11.005

CHAPTER 4

The Political Economy of Greening South Africa's Capital Markets

Green bonds are undoubtedly a recent phenomenon in South Africa's capital markets, and so are the wider efforts of greening this sector. In very broad strokes, this chapter traces the historical factors that contributed to South Africa's current political economic capital market setup. The very establishment of the Johannesburg Stock exchange as a major turnstile for natural resources for the world market in 1887 was marked by mining and, thus, also colonial pursuits. While fossil path dependency will certainly emerge as a red thread running through its history, this chapter will also touch upon the peculiar side effects of the first global divestment campaign against the Apartheid regime on the country's capital market setup. In the second part, this chapter will recount some of the major challenges the successive presidents of post-Apartheid South Africa faced and how this led to a crisis of the governing liberation party as well as democracy more generally. In its last part, this chapter dwells on the interrelated crises of inequality, energy, and climate, especially between the global financial crisis in 2008 and the Covid-19 pandemic of 2020–2022. This selective approach does not seek to provide a full genealogy in a historical sense but will rather help to understand some major facets of the current disposition of South Africa's political economy. This chapter argues for four overarching political economic themes on which

© The Author(s), under exclusive license to Springer Nature Switzerland AG 2023
M. Neumann, *The Political Economy of Green Bonds in Emerging Markets*, International Political Economy Series, https://doi.org/10.1007/978-3-031-30502-3_4

the green bond discourse latches on: the persistence of the Minerals-Energy-Complex (MEC) slowing green alternatives; a governing party facing a legitimacy and capacity crisis, which inhibits their ability to drive the transition; the uneven and unequal aftermath of the financial crisis, which bolstered and emboldens South Africa's financial markets; and lastly climate change governance facing significant competition from other crisis moments.

EARLY EXTRACTIVISM AND LASTING PATH DEPENDENCE—THE EMERGENCE AND PERSISTENCE OF THE MINERALS-ENERGY COMPLEX

The root to South Africa's establishment of its capital markets lies in its colonizers' resource pursuits. The discoveries of diamonds near Kimberley in 1867 and gold near Witwatersrand in 1886 inaugurated the British-led scramble for resource exploitation (van der Merwe, 2016). Railways were built to connect the mines with the ports, heavy machinery brought in from Europe and excavation and evacuation of the mined minerals ensued. As van der Merwe notes, the burgeoning minerals trade drove the infrastructural advancements for the regional economy and soon turned the city of Johannesburg into "a regional focus of mining, finance and banking" (ibid., p. 62). A good year into the gold discoveries, the Johannesburg Stock Exchange (JSE) was founded by the British businessman Benjamin Minors Woollan in November 1887 as a trans-shipment center for these resources, thus kick-starting the globalization of South African primary markets (Jones, 2003, p. 240). By the late nineteenth century, the country had shifted from a primarily Agrarian to a minerals-exporting economy (Southall, 2012, p. 8). Mining became synonymous with the rise of the British mining elites, who were often referred to as the 'Rand-lords', among them politically highly influential figures like Cecil Rhodes (van der Merwe, 2016). Due to the colonial settlements between the British and the Afrikaners (the British focusing on mining, the Afrikaners on large-scale agriculture Fine & Rustomjee, 1996; Nölke et al., 2020)), economic growth hinged on mining extraction and energy-heavy production setting the ground early for deepening the dependence of the South African economy on what later became known as the Minerals-Energy Complex, or MEC (Fine & Rustomjee, 1996). The MEC signifies a system of accumulation based on abundant coal, cheap black labor, and export of mining and mineral products. Due to it providing vital inputs, the MEC exuded significant influence on many other sub-sectors of manufacturing. Its tight ownership structures comprise state, corporate capital and financial system actors (Karwowski et al., 2018). During the Apartheid years, mining conglomerates were still predominantly in British ownership and diversified across the economy, particularly absorbing financial services (Karwowski et al., 2018). Moving beyond their base in gold, diamonds, and coal, the conglomerates spanned finance, industry, minerals by the 1960s (Southall, 2012, p. 8). Cheap black labor and abundant mineral resources made for a dual extractive industry with the national energy utility Eskom as the combustion engine that drove the economy under Apartheid (Davies et al., 2018).

With the loss of internal political stability in the 1970s which culminated in the Soweto uprisings in 1976, the systemic racial segregation administered and overseen by the Apartheid regime drew increasingly heavy criticism from around the world. These took the forms of divestment campaigns and yielded corporate accounting guidelines for multinational companies operating in South Africa such as the Sullivan Principles[1] in the USA (Arnold & Hammond, 1994; Padayachee, 2013). With the Apartheid government declaring a military state of emergency in 1985, companies and investors ultimately conceded their limited leverage for political reform and started withdrawing from South Africa.

By ostracizing South Africa from global capital markets and world trade, the globally enacted sanctions on the Apartheid regime yielded a few unintended side effects. Karwowski and her colleagues (2018) observe, that these sanctions led to "the containment of capital within the domestic economy, giving rise both to increasing development of financial markets and concentration of ownership of productive capital and finance within the conglomerate mining houses" (pp. 383–384). Six conglomerates, also known as the six capital axes and core pillars of the MEC (Fine & Rustomjee, 1996, pp. 103, 108; van der Merwe, 2016) commanded 83% of market capitalization in 1988. Among them were Sanlam, SA Old Mutual and Liberty/Standard, three financial services and insurance companies, Anglo-American Corporation, the biggest mining company, Rembrandt/Volkswas, an Afrikaner monopoly capital turned ABSA bank,

---

[1] Similar principles in other regions were struck in other regions as well, such as the Code of Conduct of the European Economic Community (EEC) in 1977 (ibid.).

and Anglovaal, a conglomerate with huge holdings in mining, finance, and industry. Van der Merwe (2016) points out, that

> Other than the highly concentrated ownership, [it] is the 'mutually reinforcing' role played between the areas of finance, mining, and manufacturing, and how collusion between these spheres was a deliberate strategy employed by the ruling oligarchy to gain control of the South and southern African economy. Once their control of the economy was secure, they were able to play a decisive role in southern African politics. (p. 63)

This control of political affairs the large capital interest group wielded also extended to factions in the increasingly emboldened liberation movement in the last years of Apartheid. This held particularly true for the African National Congress (ANC). Just as capitalist factions safeguarded their wealth under Apartheid, so did the ANC protect their interest in the long term with approaching independence. The ANC regenerated its political clout through its connections to big business (van der Merwe, 2016). Due to these diverse yet compounding factors, the MEC thus emerged from the Apartheid period as a largely consolidated and politically immensely powerful force with the largest state-owned enterprise Eskom firmly at the helm.

South Africa's liberation from colonial rule was a highly anticipated, auspicious, and much fought for achievement. The election of Nelson Mandela as the first president of a democratic South Africa in 1994 raised expectations for broad-based political and economic transformation. Karwowski et al. (2018) identify several features that propelled the promise and expectations around socio-economic and political transformation. For one, there was the "dream ticket" (ibid., p. 384) coalition between the ANC, the South African Communist Party, the militant domestic Mass Democratic Movement and the leading trade union federation, the Congress of South African Trade Unions. This alliance enjoyed international solidarity especially in light of the universal animosity to Apartheid rule, also conceived as internalized colonialism and credibly represented a turn for progressive change. Nelson Mandela further conjured up hopes as a charismatic leader with internationally renowned standing. And so did the election manifesto that the ANC put to the table: With the Reconstruction and Development Plan (RDP), labor, more generally, hoped to gear the state towards "beginning to meet the basic needs of people: Jobs, land, housing, water, electricity, telecommunications, transport, a clean and healthy environment, nutrition, health care, and social welfare" (Visser, 2005, p. 6). With geopolitics clearly titled towards liberal capitalism at the end of the 'cold war', South Africa's progressive agenda represented "the last throw of the twentieth century revolutionary dice" for a socialist project (Karwowski et al., 2018, p. 384). The political stakes were thus incredibly high at the advent of democracy in South Africa.

The democratic settlement with the colonizers, however, was tied to a few compromises. Thus, three broad factors contributed to this transformative agenda increasingly diluting over time. Firstly, Ashman and her colleagues (2011) argue, that the negotiation to end the Apartheid rule ultimately yielded political liberation taking precedence over the question of economic redistribution. In exchange for political equality through constitutional amendments, ownership structures in and the functioning of the economy were largely held intact—though the state could appropriate private assets if in the public interest (Southall, 2016). The ANC itself soon left by the wayside its own Freedom Charter—which foresaw the nationalization of mines, banks, and monopoly industries (Freund & Padayachee, 1998)—and other interventionist policy measures to upend Apartheid legacies. The political settlement also included the corporate sector striking a deal with incoming ANC elites by way of employment opportunities, board membership, and investment opportunities that would later be institutionalized in the Black Economic Empowerment (BEE) program (Bowman, 2019; Southall, 2016). Bond (2000) fittingly called South Africa's shift into democracy an 'elite transition'.

Secondly, the National Party had bled dry the fiscal coffers to stave off its replacement, resulting in rising public sector debt levels and inflation into the early 1990s (Freund & Padayachee, 1998). As a result, South Africa's first independent democratic government essentially accepted Apartheid-era debt (Southall, 2016). Upon interacting with local and international actors after his release from prison, Mandela and the ANC downgraded their populist economic pronouncement for fear of hurting its favorable image with international financial markets and business media (Mohamed, 2012).

Thirdly, the ANC's agenda focused on political liberation, leaving a void in economic know-how. Indeed, the ANC's freedom charter only prescribed vague economic policy prescriptions in the areas spelled out earlier (Freund & Padayachee, 1998). Though a Macro-Economic

Research Group with South African researchers was set up at the University of the Witwatersrand in Johannesburg and tasked with charting out economic policy between 1991 and 1993, the ANC increasingly abandoned its progressive policies gearing up to the election (Sam Ashman et al., 2012; Segatti & Pons-Vignon, 2013). Rather, "[white] capital, the National Party and the ANC leadership increasingly came together around the pursuit of economic growth through 'competitiveness', faith in private sector investments, liberalization, privatization, Central Bank independence, etc." (Samantha Ashman et al., 2011, p. 182), which culminated in the replacement of the Reconstruction and Development Plan with the Growth, Employment and Redistribution Program (GEAR) in 1996. While GEAR's neoliberal footing sought to encourage foreign direct investments into the country, the policy package effected quite the opposite: By lifting exchange controls, the outflow of domestic capital towards safer capital havens increased while investment inflows failed to meet expected levels (Ashman et al., 2011).

Capital flight dominated the post-Apartheid years after 1994 with many large conglomerates—most notably Billiton, South African Breweries, Anglo-American, Old Mutual, and Liberty Life—moving their primary listings from JSE to the London Stock Exchange (Mohamed, 2012). Whereas the three conglomerates Anglo-American, Sanlam, and Old Mutual controlled 75% (R425bn) of the total capitalization (R567bn) of the JSE in 1990, they only accounted for 24.4% by December 2008, despite an increase in overall market capitalization to R1.1 trillion (Southall, 2012). By 2006, tellingly, 66% of outward foreign investment from South Africa went to Europe, followed by 24% to the Americas and only 6.4% being absorbed by other African countries (Southall, 2012, p. 7, citing Daniel & Bhengu, 2009, p. 142). Beyond moving business overseas, this is due to major conglomerates opting to realize shareholder value by unbundling and selling non-core assets which they had acquired because of their inability to invest abroad under Apartheid. Domestic institutional investors like the Public Investment Corporation, private pension funds, and emerging BEE players gobbled up these non-core assets. But foreign investors, also, moved in to purchase South African assets. By late 2007, 45% of JSE's issued shares were held by foreign entities, up from 18.9% a year earlier (Southall, 2012). This magnified the exposure of the economy to global market sentiments, be those currency fluctuations, high interest rates, or capital outflow. All of this occurred ensuing the dotcom crisis in the early 2000s (Mohamed, 2012), serving as a precursor for what was to come later in the decade. Almost three decades into an independent South Africa, the MEC, for its part, still controlled large swaths of the economy, whether primary sectors, manufacturing, or finance. The demand for mining was actively supported through industrial and energy policies that entrenched and locked in a seemingly impenetrable system of subsidies that upheld and undergirded continued demand in fossil fuel based energy (Burton et al., 2018). While mining's direct contribution to GPD fell from 12.1% in 1951 to about 9% 70 years later (Naidoo & Njini, 2021; Southall, 2012, p. 8), the heightened demand for rare earth across the globe has rendered South African mining more profitable. Combined with the price inflation in fossil fuels in the wake of Russia's invasion of the Ukraine, South Africa is well positioned to supply the world with rare earth and excess coal. Already the fasted growing sector at 11.8% in 2021 (Stats SA, 2022), South African mining currently supplies half the world's palladium, 75% of the world's platinum and 90% of the world's rhodium (Stark, 2022). Western sanctions on Russia have additionally forced investors to look for markets elsewhere. In South Africa, the price per ton of exported coal is up 300% from before Russia's invasion of Ukraine (ibid.). And despite falling into the bottom ten (75 out of 84) of the Fraser Institute's Investment Attractiveness Index (an index specializing in mining) in April (Yunis & Aliakbari, 2022), investments worth ZAR 46.5 billion (US$ 2.91 billion) were pledged towards mining and mineral beneficiation at the fourth South Africa Investment Conference in March 2022 (Ramaphosa, 2022). At the mining conference in Cape Town in May 2022, President Cyril Ramaphosa set the target to reclaim 5% of global exploration expenditure it last had in 2003 within the next three to five years (Department of Mineral Resources & Energy, 2022). Against this background, one can readily ascertain that MEC still holds massive sway over the direction of South Africa's economy and, thus, its transition trajectory.

I have traced the emergence of the MEC and emphasized its persistence not only at the JSE's capital markets but also the wider economy. In the next section on the governing crisis in South Africa, we will revisit the MEC's influence on political decision-making and on shaping and exacerbating the effects of the financial crisis, particularly on energy provision. We will also return to the MEC in the last section of this chapter to understand how exactly the fossil path dependence and technological lock-ins I described above interfere with the promotion of green bonds in the country.

THE CRISIS OF GOVERNANCE EXEMPLIFIED ALONG MANDELA'S SUCCESSORS

Whether Thabo Mbeki, Jacob Zuma, or Cyril Ramaphosa—each of these presidents[2] succeeding Nelson Mandela wrestled with different sets of challenges that sharpened the crisis topography. I draw especially on the ANC and the country's post-Apartheid presidents to exemplify the exacerbating crisis of governance crisis around the ANC.

Thabo Mbeki had made a name for himself not only as a movement activist in exile, but also when negotiating with and dissociating militant Afrikaner and Zulu factions from opposing elections in 1994. Upon prolonged discussion with the extended ANC leadership, Mandela was swayed to opt for Mbeki as his running mate over his own preferred choice, Cyril Ramaphosa (Gevisser, 2009, pp. 234–245).

During Mbeki's time as President, the expansion of the electricity sector was largely driven by mining (see previous section) and its energy-intense processes; the mining and industry sectors have historically been the primary beneficiaries of state electricity expenditure (McDonald, 2011). Eskom almost exclusively accounted for the country's electricity generation at the time, sourcing most of that (roughly 80–85%) from five coal contractors, formerly known as the six axes (Baker, 2015a; Eberhard, 2011). Starting under Mbeki's administration, these mutual ties were enshrined through long-term coal contracts. Among the nine of Eskom's coal power stations with long-term contracts, six have fixed price and three cost-plus contracts (Eberhard, 2011). With little incentive for cost reduction and quality upgrading, Eskom's generation performance has dwindled to the point of the electricity crisis in 2008, right at the end of Mbeki's presidency. With the help of the multinational consultancy PricewaterhouseCoopers, the government had floated the idea of 'unbundling' Eskom into separate entities (generation, transmission, and distribution) and introducing a competitive electricity market through independent power producers already in 1999 (McDonald, 2011), the

---

[2] Kgalema Motlanthe briefly served as president after Mbeki's resignation. Given his limited time in office and his shallow imprint on South Africa's political economy, I skip his contributions and focus on the other successors to Mandela instead.

idea was also deliberated in a White Paper in 1998 (Baker et al., 2021). As late as 2004, however, the government had backtracked from these reforms for lack of private investment and political buy-in, particularly from trade unions (Eberhard, 2011). By this time, the country had lost years of investing in the country's energy infrastructure. Between 1998 and 2003, no new generation capacity was built (Baker et al., 2021). Growing demand soon outstripped supply, resulting in the first blackouts in 2006. Poor operative management on Eskom's part and diminishing coal stockpiles, unseasonal rain, and financial constraints added to the crisis, which forced Eskom to roll out loadshedding in early 2008 (ibid.). Under Mbeki's administration the overhaul of the energy sector, nowadays the most important destination of green investment globally, was attempted and failed.

Mbeki tarnished his legacy beyond repair by failing to adequately respond to the AIDS crisis that rocked the country (Gevisser, 2009, p. 277; Marais, 2012) during his administration. When he hastily seized the opportunity to sideline his deputy Jacob Zuma after a botched arms deal, the party sentiment had irreversibly swung in Zuma's favor. The court would later rule Mbeki politically interfered in the court proceedings and, thus, treated Zuma unfairly through his "political meddling" (ibid., p. 334), resulting in Mbeki leaving office in September 2008, six months before the end of his term.

Backed by the Communist Party and COSATU, as well as elements in emergent black business elite, Jacob Zuma, emerged as the new President of the ANC at their party Summit in Polokwane in 2007, preventing Mbeki from pursuing a third term at the party's helm. The election results at Polokwane, however, are likely less to do with Zuma's own strength but rather with the negative legacy Mbeki left behind (Butler, 2012). Zuma inherited the internal party rifts, that were initially cut open over the country's economic policy trajectory, and exploited and deepened them further after taking office as President of the state a good year later.

Zuma's administration continued Mbeki's neoliberal economic trajectory (Butler, 2012). He also built onto Mbeki's efforts for more centralization of authority, but with more adverse effects. The administration gradually stifled cabinet deliberation, parliamentary autonomy, and the security and criminal justice systems, i.e. by appointing Zuma associates.

Zuma also took advantage of the internal party divisions, replacing Xhosas by Zulus in key locations such as intelligence services and fanning factional struggles also within parastatals and the public service provision at provincial and municipal level (Southall, 2012). An increasingly refined state patronage system ensued broadening avenues for graft and corruption that Zuma himself was embroiled in.

Zuma rattled the energy sector with his attempt to procure nuclear energy to meet the country's energy needs. After installing his ally Tina Joemat-Pettersson to head the Department of Energy, Zuma's administration announced an intergovernmental agreement with the Russian company Rosatom for nuclear power plants with installed capacity of up to 9.6 gigawatts (GW) in October 2014 (Southall, 2016). Zuma had bypassed most of his ministers by negotiating directly with Russian president Putin in July and September 2014, fomenting suspicion around personal illicit enrichment (ibid.). Though ultimately an unsuccessful endeavor during his terms, his attempt to remove nuclear policy from public scrutiny stands evidence to a wider pattern of declining government transparency (ibid., p. 83).

The most jarring reflection of Zuma's lack of integrity, which also compromises the ANC's credibility and ability to deliver, is the so-called state capture, that an academic inquiry convened by Mark Swilling characterized as "Betrayal of the Promise: How South Africa is being stolen" in their report with the same title (Bhorat et al., 2017). Godinho and Hermanus (2018) define state capture as

> a political-economic project whereby public and private actors collude in establishing clandestine networks that cluster around state institutions in order to accumulate unchecked power, subverting the constitutional state and social contract by operating outside of the realm of public accountability. (p. 1)

Central to state capture in South Africa are the Gupta brothers, an Indian-born South African family with a vast business conglomerate that used its strong personal and professional ties with President Zuma to siphon state funds. Former Public Protector Thuli Madonsela released the State of Capture report in November 2016. Therein, it is alleged that the Zuma and Gupta families, as well as their associates, influenced appointment and removal of state ministers and board members at state-owned enterprises, especially Eskom, Transnet, and Denel. They allegedly faced conflicts of interest and information sharing to their benefit, received special treatment, and are implicated in incidents of fraud, corruption, and bribery

(Godinho & Hermanus, 2018). The Judicial Commission of Inquiry into State capture (colloquially known as the Zondo Commission after its Deputy Chief Justice) that Zuma established in one of his last moves before leaving office, had 278 witnesses take the stand and collected 51,669 pages of recorded transcripts by December 2020 (Businesslive, 2000). After holding more than 400 hearings featuring Zuma as well as Ramaphosa and other party leaders on the stand, the inquiry is closed at the end of September 2021. The first report of the Zondo Commission was made public in January 2022 with the fifth and last report handed over on June 22, 2022 (Daily Maverick, 2022; South African Government, 2022). In them, the embroilment of state entities such as Eskom, South African Airways, and Transnet with corrupt practices are traced.

The ever-increasing record of maleficence on Zuma's part swept Ramaphosa to seize the ANC Presidency in Johannesburg in December 2017. In the immediate aftermath, the ANC pressed Zuma to resign by recalling him as President of South Africa less than a year before the end of his second term. Faced with a vote of no confidence in the National Assembly, Zuma grudgingly stepped down in February 2018, thus making way for Ramaphosa to take the reins as the country's president.

Cyril Ramaphosa made a name for himself long before he became president. He founded the National Union of Mineworkers (NUM) in the 1980s and led the negotiations of the country's post-Apartheid constitution as the Secretary General of the ANC in 1991. When Mbeki became President, Ramaphosa turned businessmen and became one of the richest men in Africa by breeding exotic cattle, thereby benefiting from the Black Economic Empowerment program he had helped to create (Hartley, 2017).

Against the backdrop of accusations of graft and corruption piling up in front of the then President Zuma and the lasting damage it inflicted not only on the ANC but also on the democratic institutions more generally, Ramaphosa became vocal about fighting corruption, when he perceived public as well as party opinion decisively shifting towards desire for more accountability (Hartley, 2017). In his bid for the ANC presidency in 2017, his campaign encapsulated "the promise of a new dawn, a return to moral stature, and a need to regain the trust of ordinary South Africans following Zuma's nine wasted years" (Kotze & Bohler-Muller, 2019, p. 365).

After securing the ANC leadership, Ramaphosa had five months before South Africa went to national elections in 2019. As the face of the campaign, Ramaphosa's conquest to rekindle voters' trust in the ANC did materialize in the general electoral results: Though dipping below 60% for the first time, the ANC seized a comfortable majority of 58%, ahead of the Democratic Alliance at close to 21% and the Economic Freedom fighters at almost 11% (Keane, 2019). Still, voter apathy, especially among the youth has steadily increased over the past 25 years; only 49% of the eligible population cast their ballot (Roberts et al., 2019). This trend is attributed among others to poor public service delivery and lack of trust in political parties (Kotze & Bohler-Muller, 2019; but see also Roberts et al., 2019, for an in-depth analysis of voter behavior; and Bornman et al., 2021, for an analysis of voter sentiments among the post-Apartheid youth).

Though Ramaphosa has increasingly gained the upper hand in the factional head-to-head by sidelining Ace Magashule, his main sparring partner from Zuma's faction (Cele, 2021), fighting corruption remains a hard nut to crack. And though deeply implicated in corrupt practices, Zuma still enjoys support by a broad platform. Upon his incarceration, violent protests coupled with vandalism rocked havoc in KwaZulu-Natal and Gauteng bear testament to this erosion of trust and the heightened disillusion and disenfranchisement felt by pockets of South African society (McKenzie et al., 2021). News emerged in June 2022, that Ramaphosa, himself, covered up an alleged robbery on his game farm in February 2020 where thieves are said to have seized US$ 4 million worth of foreign-denominated currency stuffed in his couch (Vecchiatto & Goko, 2022). Not only his credibility to tackle, but corruption head-on has taken a hit. Also, the broad-based support for re-election as ANC president in December 2022 has diminished.

The post-Apartheid governance legacy of the ANC has, thus far, not met the high expectations of 1994. Rather, the successive leaders, chief among them Zuma, widened the gulf of disillusion with the government's capability to address people's needs. Rather than pursuing people-centered development, the ANC seems to have squandered lots of the broad-based voter support it enjoyed when seizing power in 1994.

Let me, at this point, briefly return to the introductory claim of the crisis of legitimacy and governance that has engulfed the ANC after independence. I have selectively outlined some events that contributed to the crisis of governance. Indeed, all presidents are implicated—though in varying degrees—in practices that have contributed to the erosion of trust in public representation. Given the political nature of transition endeavors (Kern & Markard, 2016), governments, in general, need to credibly represent and drive voters' interests and their demands, i.e. for a just transition. The growing disenchantment of South Africans increasingly viewing politicians not as servants of the people but with their own parochial vested interests is an important contextual factor in understanding the government's and public institutions' limited capacity to steer green transition endeavors and, thus, also the regulatory framework within which green bonds are conceived.

The financial sector and the energy sector hold the most prominent position in driving innovations like green bonds, with the former sourcing the investments and the latter presenting the green investment opportunities. The next section will take a closer look at these sectors in the aftermath of the financial crisis in 2008. This is necessary to better understand South Africa's economic predicament and impetus for transitioning to a greener economy. In the end, some preliminary effects of the Covid-19 crisis are discussed.

The Financial Sector Lessons from the Global Financial Crisis

The impact from the global financial crisis on South Africa's economy varied significantly. While many sectors in the economy took significant hits, the financial sector survived the financial crisis relatively unscathed, as no banks had to be bailed out. We briefly look at the lessons drawn from the global financial crisis in the South African context.

Thanks to a global commodity boom, South Africa's economy experienced consistent growth after independence. The increased internationalization and financialization of the economy had until this point reinforced the economy's dependence on the fossil commodity exports. The reliance on MEC-based resource exports, however, backfired when the global financial crisis of 2008 made demand for these goods plummet (Swilling, 2012). The growth spirt ground to a hold, though it had already shown downward trends before the global financial crisis hit (Mohamed, 2012). Official unemployment was consistently well over 20 percent with opportunities declining in manufacturing and services grew mostly on the backdrop debt-driven consumption, leading Mohamed to assert that the GDP growth, despite it being around 5% per year between

2004 and 2007, was the "'wrong kind of economic growth for South Africa" (ibid., p. 39). In the wake of the global financial crisis, growth declined to 3.1 percent in 2008 and that went into reverse in 2009 (ibid.). Employment decreased by 770,000 in 2008–2009 and the number of 'not economically active' people increased by almost 1.1 million (ibid.).

Not all sectors were equally affected by the crisis, however. And though they transmitted the crisis into South Africa's economy, the banking and financial sectors emerged fortified and untarnished out of the financial crisis. Southall (2012) attributes this to "[a] fortuitous combination of the Apartheid legacy of control and post-Apartheid macroeconomic stringency [which] had ensured that the financial sector had remained quite tightly regulated" (p. 8), thus avoiding the extreme over-lending practices in Europe and North America. And unlike other countries with very sophisticated and mature financial markets, South Africa's financial sector did not require public money to stay afloat and no banks collapsed (BASA, 2020; Southall, 2012). Despite the increased capital flight and growing global interconnection, which has heightened the risk of external economic shocks and spillovers materializing in currency fluctuation and inflation, the financial sector came out emboldened rather than humbled from the global financial crisis.

Since the financial crisis, the financial sector witnessed only some 'cosmetic' reforms. Regulation was upped with the aim to stabilize the sector and avoid undue clashes of interest. The Financial Sector Regulation act took effect in 2018 and with the Prudential Authority as well as the Financial Sector Conduct authority, the so-called Twin Peak framework was established, separating regulatory responsibilities (BASA, 2020). In line with global best practice, reporting requirements for corporate investments were upped through successive reporting guidelines, the so-called King Principles (Padayachee, 2013). The second iteration introduced the triple bottom line in investment decision-making, expecting companies to report on environmental and social aspect beyond financial metrics. King III expanded on this, recommending the integration of environmental, social and governance criteria according to the Global Reporting Initiative's Sustainability Reporting Guidelines instead of producing separate sustainability reports (Makiwane & Padia, 2013).

In the banking sector, the country's 'big four' banks—Standard Bank, Nedbank, ABSA, and FirstRand—have also repositioned themselves at least nominally to account for their actions taken in response to climate change (see Neumann & Elsner, forthcoming for an assessment of

Nedbank and Standard Bank). The 'big four' essentially still operate in a system with relatively little global competition and provide financial services such as credit provision at their terms. According to Simatele (2015), South Africa has a very concentrated banking industry. Increasing the competition by promoting capital market integration has, thus far, not yielded significant regulatory changes.

Against an economy steeped in fossil resource extraction and a financial sector seemingly validated by its crisis-proven business models, it will be interesting to see how green bonds are conceived and taken up by South Africa's financial markets. We will look at the regulation and regulatory actors for green bonds more closely in the empirical chapter.

The Energy Sector—Incremental Reforms Amid Loadshedding

Investment cuts for new power stations and the failed reform under the Mbeki administration had laid early ground for an energy crisis to coincide with the global financial crisis in early 2008. Electricity demand first overshot supply in 2007.

In response to the energy crisis, two huge coal-fired power plants named Kusile and Medupi, at 4.8GW each (the third and fourth largest in the world) were hastily commissioned in 2007 and 2008 to avert future energy shortages. Rather than projectably coming online in 2012 and 2014, respectively, these megaprojects added to Eskom's crisis (Gregory, 2020). As things stand, both plants have yet to be fully completed, face significant cost overruns (Medupi's price tag went up from an initial R79 billion to an estimated R234 billion, whereas Kusile's price tag increased from R69.1 billion to R460 billion) and still perform well below capacity (Tshidavhu & Khatleli, 2020). The long-term investment climate in the energy sector generally, but particularly Eskom has been severely inhibited by compounding factors such as Eskom's demands for price increases to mirror their costs (especially high due to long-term contract with coal mines (Eberhard, 2011), political infighting and board reshuffles, less affluent municipalities unable to pay their energy bills to Eskom, general mismanagement, disproportionately high staff salaries, failed structural reforms, mounting stranded assets and above all its embroiling in state capture (Southall, 2016, Butler, 2012, Bischof-Niemz and Creamer, 2019). All of this resulted in Moody's, one of the credit rating agencies, downgrading the utility's long-term debt to junk status (Hill, 2018). This left Eskom struggling to attract investments and debt piling up to ZAR 484 billion in 2020, ZAR 83 billion of which could be resolved through repayments on matured bonds, refinancing, and a favorable exchange rate (Vecchiatto, 2021). Whereas Eskom boasted one of the cheapest energy sources worldwide in 1994, coal-based energy prices had escalated to a degree, where renewables were half as expensive in 2016 (Davies et al., 2018). Eskom's unbundling—floated under the Mbeki administration as a policy idea—is still on the table today and currently envisioned to be implemented incrementally in late 2021 and by the end 2022 (Vecchiatto, 2021). In the meantime, loadshedding persists. In April 2022, an unprecedented 1054 gigawatt hours were shed; the country is on track to exceed annual records in controlled blackouts (Burkhardt, 2022).

Despite the currently bleak outlook, a few reforms were implemented that will prove interesting for the remainder of this work. For one, the Zuma government introduced the Integrated Resource Plan (IRP) as the country's new energy planning tool in 2011 (Baker et al., 2021). Against the backdrop of the NDCs the government passed in accordance with the Paris Agreement of 2015, the IRP set a renewable energy target of 17.8 GW until 2030 of renewable energy. This contributes to government's greater ambition to decommission 35 GW of the country's coal fleet by 2050, a tremendous task given Eskom's total installed capacity at 48GW (M. Mkhize & Radmore, 2021).

The key tool to shift the energy sector into renewable futures is the Renewable Energy Independent Power Producer Procurement Program (REI4P). The tender program resulted from the setup of the Independent Power Producers (IPP) Office in 2010, which lent the initial impetus for a market-oriented restructuring, targeting independent power producers, mostly, but not exclusively, from renewable sources such as wind and solar. In this vein, the IPP Office introduced the REI4P bidding scheme to attract private investments into renewable energy generation, supplanting a Feed-in Tariff (Baker et al., 2021; Baker, 2015b). Since its establishment, the tender program procured 6.4 GW of electricity from renewables of which a little over 4 GW has been connected to the grid as of March 2021 (M. Mkhize & Radmore, 2021). In policy terms, South Africa's REI4P program garnered global attention for its success in attracting transnational investment for renewables and forcing prices down below their fossil counterparts and thus highly competitive levels (Baker, 2015a; Baker et al., 2021; M. Mkhize & Radmore, 2021; Müller & Claar, 2021). It is hailed across the continent as a policy blueprint for its innovative bidding criteria (Müller et al., 2020, 2021) but also garnered criticism for increasingly privileging large transnational developers able to muster the legal and financial costs associated with the bidding process (L. Baker et al., 2021; see also Claar, 2020, for the role of transnational classes). In 2021, the 5th bidding window opened, foreseeing a doubling the currently installed 6.4GW in renewable generation by 2024. The fifth bidding window, however, had long been held back by regulatory and political gridlocks, involving Eskom's unwillingness to connect these IPPs to the grid, thus fueling uncertainty among investors and acting as a spoiler for renewable alternatives (Baker et al., 2021; Lawrence, 2020).

The energy sector is marred with conflicting interests, whether that is the delay in promulgating the new IRP or the various means to sustain technologies at its attached job opportunities increasingly under pressure from renewables. The main results chapter will help assess to what extent green bonds bought into the REI4P program, and whether the program helped alleviate climate as much as wider development concerns.

As the section on the MEC already indicated, South Africa is heavily reliant on its coal exploitation, which Kusile and Medupi, will, upon their eventual completion, at least sustain. According to ClimateScope (2022), non-renewables like fossil fuel, oil, and nuclear comprise 85.08% as of 2021. Given the looming climate crisis, South Africa faces urgent calls to green its energy sector in particular, and the economy more broadly. According to a recent study (Blended Finance Taskforce & Centre for Sustainability Transitions, 2022), at least US$ 250 in climate finance will be needed over the next three decades just to transition South Africa's energy systems.

These examples demonstrate how deep the MEC has driven the country into fossil path dependence is. With increasing global concern for climate change, Baker (2015b) observes how the MEC has reinvented itself as a leading destination for renewable energy investments by merging with foreign capital. Even Eskom, the national utility and key behemoth in the MEC, considers a diversification into renewable energy. They signed a deal with the World Bank for battery storage to bolster an ailing energy infrastructure (World Bank, 2021) and floated plans to invest in wind and solar (Businesstech, 2021). Eskom, as the energy monopolist and central embodiment of the MEC, faces competing interests to power the transition to greener futures (Müller & Claar, 2021), it might as well act as a spoiler. The distribution of revenues and burdens from natural resource extraction (see Okpanachi & Chowdhari Tremblay,

2021, for insights specifically on Sovereign Wealth funds premised on natural resource extraction) is highly dependent on domestic politics.

Covid-19 Exacerbating Socio-Economic Challenges

Despite evidence of Southern Africa warming at alarmingly higher rates than the global average (Engelbrecht et al., 2015) and South Africa persistently breaking maximum temperature records (Mcbride et al., 2022), other challenges require similarly urgent addressal. When the Covid-19 pandemic engulfed South Africa in 2020, climate mitigation and adaptation—as in many other countries—once again took the political backseat.

On March 5, 2020, the National Institute for Communicable Diseases (Z. Mkhize, 2020) confirmed the first case of Covid-19 in the country. The national treasury responded with several measures to curtail social hardship. For workers facing redundancy, an unemployment insurance fund of ZAR 30 billion was set up (Akrofi & Antwi, 2020, p. 5). Treasury granted subsidies for small businesses were granted and the Reserve Bank reduced its base rate by 100 basis points (ibid.). The pandemic also reinvigorated debates about a basic income grant to cushion the worst-off in society (Businesstech, 2022). The social relief grant for those severely affected which will be extended until April 2023 (SA News, 2022).

The pandemic has disrupted trade and travel in and beyond the country. In 2020, the economy contracted by 6.4% only to bounce back by 4.9% in GDP the following year (AfDB, 2022, p. 171). To avert additional hardship caused by the pandemic, public spending, meanwhile, reached a new record at 10% of GDP (ibid.). The country still witnessed its already high unemployment levels rise further, leaving only 14 million with work in the formal and informal sector, out of a population of 60 million (Naidoo, 2021). The pandemic also magnified inequality in a society, that has been among the most unequal in the world, persistently leading the global GINI coefficient chart (World Bank, 2022). According to the latest World Inequality report of 2022, the richest 10% command 67% of national income (Chancel et al., 2022, p. 32), while the poorest 50% hold just 5%, of national income (ibid., p. 33). Especially black communities—disenfranchised before and after Apartheid—suffer this employment precarity and limited access to energy (Koomson & Awaworyi Churchill, 2022). Against the backdrop of persistent (racial) inequality, it, is thus, no surprise that those bearing the brunt of the prevailing injustices engrained in society back the call for a just transition. In hardly any other place in the world, the need to address the climate crisis in a social manner is so urgent. It is in this vein that (Qobo et al., 2022) identify improving government capacities as a key bottleneck towards seizing the pandemic as an opportunity for inclusive structural reforms, among others in the areas of public health and community interventions.

As this chapter demonstrated, however, the government may be ill-equipped to adequately prioritize and address these concerns. With a public purse strained over the years of independence and all but emptied in the Covid-19 pandemic, limited capacity at state, provincial, and municipal level, and mounting social hardship, tackling climate change has powerful competition for policy priority. It comes as no surprise, that President Ramaphosa envisions institutional investors to take the lead in driving the infrastructural overhaul for the country, ideally providing decent jobs and increasing economic competitiveness while advancing climate adaptation and mitigation.

This chapter set the stage for the main body of this work: the stalling diffusion of green bonds in South Africa. By drawing on historical trends and events, I sought to cobble the political economic ground, on which green bonds are issued. In this chapter, I made four propositions that I backed through in-depth discussion. Firstly, I traced the persistence of the Minerals-Energy-complex and the brakes it puts on the socio-technical as much as political transformation needed to avoid a climate disaster. I further argued that the governing party faces a legitimacy and capacity crisis by tracing the corrupt practices culminating in 'state capture'. Thirdly, I demonstrated how the financial sector persevered through the global financial crisis and remained largely intact, with regulation only marginally shifting. Lastly, I showed how climate responses, despite all their urgency and importance, do face competition for attention from other developmental concerns, like the prevailing energy crisis. The Covid-19 pandemic amplified these concerns. The empirical chapter will shed light on these issues and contribute a few answers to the question, whether green bonds can provide a combined answer to not only tackle climate change concerns, but also alleviate some of the socio-economic plights many South Africans suffer.

References

AfDB. (2022). *African Economic Outlook 2022*. https://www.afdb.org/filead min/uploads/afdb/Documents/Publications/African_Economic_Outlook_ 2018_-_EN.pdf

Akrofi, M. M. C., & Antwi, S. H. (2020). COVID-19 energy sector responses in Africa: A review of preliminary government interventions. *Energy Research and Social Science, 68*(June), 1–10. https://doi.org/10.1016/j.erss.2020. 101681

Arnold, P., & Hammond, T. (1994). The role of accounting in ideological conflict: Lessons from the South African divestment movement. *Accounting, Organizations and Society, 19*(2), 111–126. https://doi.org/10.1016/0361-3682(94)90014-0

Ashman, S., Fine, B., & Newman, S. (2012). *Chapter*. In B. Fine, J. Saraswati & D. Tavasci (Eds.), *Beyond the Developmental State: Industrial Policy into the 21*, 1–20.

Ashman, S., Fine, B., & Newman, S. (2011). The crisis in South Africa: Neoliberalism, financialization and uneven and combined development. *Socialist Register, 174–195*. https://doi.org/10.1080/00343404.2016.1262946

Baker, L. (2015a). Renewable energy in South Africa's minerals-energy complex: A 'low carbon' transition? *Review of African Political Economy, 42*(144), 245–261. https://doi.org/10.1080/03056244.2014.953471

Baker, L. (2015b). The evolving role of finance in South Africa's renewable energy sector. *Geoforum, 64*(July), 146–156. https://doi.org/10.1016/j.geo forum.2015.06.017

Baker, L., Hook, A., & Sovacool, B. K. (2021). Power struggles: Governing renewable electricity in a time of technological disruption. *Geoforum, 118*(July), 93–105. https://doi.org/10.1016/j.geoforum.2020.12.006

BASA. (2020). *Banking matters - 2019 and beyond*. https://www.banking.org. za/wp-content/uploads/2019/04/Banking-Matters-Publication.pdf

Bhorat, H., Buthelezi, M., Chipkin, I., Duma, S., Mondi, L., Peter, C., Mzukisi, Q., Swilling, M., & Friedenstein, H. (2017). Betrayal of the promise: How South Africa is being stolen state capacity research project convenor: Mark swilling. In *State Capacity Research Project* (Issue May). http://cdn.24.co. za/files/Cms/General/d/4666/3f63a8b78d2b495d88f10ed060997f76.pdf

Blended Finance Taskforce, & Centre for Sustainability Transitions. (2022). *Making climate capital work: Unlocking $ 8.5 billion for South Africa's just energy transition*. https://static1.squarespace.com/static/5acdc066c258b4b d2d15050b/t/628e373f28dafe216b114042/1653487452874/Making+Cli mate+Capital+Work+-+FINAL+REPORT.pdf

Bond, P. (2000). *Elite transition: From apartheid to neoliberalism in South Africa*. Pluto Press/University of Natal Press.

Bornman, E., Harvey, J., Janse van Vuuren, H., Kekana, B., Matuludi, M. F., Mdakane, B., & Ramphele, L. (2021). Political engagement and opinions of youth in post-apartheid South Africa: A qualitative study. *Politikon, 48*(3), 372–390. https://doi.org/10.1080/02589346.2021.1913554

Bowman, A. (2019). Black economic empowerment policy and state–business relations in South Africa: The case of mining. *Review of African Political Economy, 46*(160), 223–245. https://doi.org/10.1080/03056244.2019.160 5587

Burkhardt, P. (2022, May 10). South Africa set for worst year of power cuts as plants fail. *Bloomberg*. https://www.bloomberg.com/news/articles/2022- 05-10/south-africa-set-for-worst-year-of-power-cuts-as-plants-fail

Burton, J., Lott, T., & Rennkamp, B. (2018). Sustaining carbon lock-in: Fossil fuel subsidies in South Africa. In J. Skovgaard & H. van Asselt (Eds.), *The politics of fossil fuel subsidies and their reform* (1st ed., pp. 229–245). Cambridge University Press. https://www.cambridge.org/core/books/pol itics-of-fossil-fuel-subsidies-and-their-reform/sustaining-carbon-lockin/9AC 7F2DA4AB31EB649EE84EA58C3708B

Businesslive. (2000, December 21). More cabinet ministers should have testified, Raymond Zondo says. *Businesslive*, 1–2. https://www.businesslive.co.za/bd/ national/2020-12-21-more-cabinet-ministers-should-have-testified-raymond-zondo-says/

Businesstech. (2021, August 31). Eskom's R106 billion wind and solar investment plan. *Businesstech*. https://businesstech.co.za/news/energy/517014/ eskoms-r106-billion-wind-and-solar-investment-plan/

Businesstech. (2022, June 13). Warning over higher taxes to fund basic income grant in South Africa. *Businesstech*. https://businesstech.co.za/news/bus iness-opinion/596260/warning-over-higher-taxes-to-fund-basic-income-grant-in-south-africa/

Butler, J. (2012). The African National Congress under Jacob Zuma. Chapter 6. In J. Daniel, P. Naidoo, D. Pillay & R. Southall (Eds.), *New South African review − 2010: Development or decline?* (pp. 164–183).

Cele, S. (2021, July 9). South African court upholds Ramaphosa Foe Magashule's suspension. *Bloomberg*. https://www.bloomberg.com/news/articles/ 2021-07-09/south-african-court-upholds-ramaphosa-foe-magashule-s-suspen sion#xj4y7vzkg

Chancel, L., Piketty, T., Saez, E., & Zucman, G. (2022). *World inquality report*. https://wir2022.wid.world/www-site/uploads/2021/12/WorldIneq ualityReport2022_Full_Report.pdf

Claar, S. (2020). Green finance and transnational capitalist classes − Tracing vested capital interests in renewable energy investments in South Africa. *Journal Für Entwicklungspolitik [Journal for Development Politics]*,

XXXVI(4–2020),   110–128.   https://www.mattersburgerkreis.at/dl/lLk
qJMJKONMJqx4KooJK/JEP_2020_4_6_Claar_Green_Finance_and_Transa
tional_Capitalist_Classes.pdf
ClimateScope. (2022). *South Africa - Energy market*. BloombergNEF. https://
global-climatescope.org/markets/za/
Daily Maverick. (2022, June 22). Here you go: The final State Capture report
recommendations - at last. *Daily Maverick*. https://www.dailymaverick.co.
za/article/2022-06-22-here-you-go-the-final-state-capture-report-recomm
endations-at-last/
Davies, M., Swilling, M., & Wlokas, H. L. (2018). Towards new configurations
of urban energy governance in South Africa's Renewable Energy Procurement Programme. *Energy Research and Social Science, 36*(November), 61–69.
https://doi.org/10.1016/j.erss.2017.11.010
Department of Mineral Resources and Energy. (2022). *South Africa's exploration
implementation plan* (Issue 46246). https://www.gov.za/sites/default/files/
gcis_document/202204/46246gon2027.pdf
Eberhard, A. (2011, January). Market, investment, and policy challenges for
South African coal. *The global coal market supplying the major fuel for emerging
economies*, 164–203. https://doi.org/10.1017/CBO9781316136058.005
Engelbrecht, F., Adegoke, J., Bopape, M. J., Naidoo, M., Garland, R., Thatcher,
M., McGregor, J., Katzfey, J., Werner, M., Ichoku, C., & Gatebe, C. (2015).
Projections of rapidly rising surface temperatures over Africa under low miti-
gation. *Environmental Research Letters, 10*(8). https://doi.org/10.1088/
1748-9326/10/8/085004
Fine, B., & Rustomjee, Z. (1996). The political economy of South Africa: Intro-
duction. In *Poverty and governance in South Asia* (pp. viii–16). https://doi.
org/10.4324/9781315741932-8
Freund, B., & Padayachee, V. (1998). Post-apartheid South Africa: The key
patterns emerge. *Economic and Political Weekly, 33*(20), 1173–1180.
Gevisser, M. (2009). *Thabo Mbeki – The dream deferred: Vol.* Jonathan Ball
Publishers. https://doi.org/10.1038/132817a0
Godinho, C., & Hermanus, L. (2018). *Reconceptualising state capture - With a
case study of South African Power Company Eskom 1*, 22–24. http://www.gsb.
uct.ac.za/files/ReconceptualisingStateCapture.pdf
Gregory, J. (2020). Governance, scale, scope: A review of six South African
electricity generation infrastructure megaprojects. *Utilities Policy, 66*(August),
101103. https://doi.org/10.1016/j.jup.2020.101103
Hartley, R. (2017). *Ramaphosa – The man who would be king*. Jonathan Ball
Publishers.
Hill, L. (2018, March 28). Moody's downgrades South Africa's Eskom citing
lack of clear plan. *Bloomberg*. https://www.bloomberg.com/news/articles/
2018-03-28/moody-s-downgrades-s-africa-s-eskom-citing-lack-of-clear-plan

Jones, S. (2003). The banking sector in the 1990s. *South African Journal of Economic History, 18*(1–2), 238–274. https://doi.org/10.1080/101134303 09511161

Karwowski, E., Fine, B., & Ashman, S. (2018). Introduction to the special section 'Financialization in South Africa.' *Competition and Change, 22*(4), 383–387. https://doi.org/10.1177/1024529418791762

Keane, F. (2019, May 11). *South Africa election: ANC wins with reduced majority.* BBC, 1–11. https://www.bbc.com/news/world-africa-48211598

Kern, F., & Markard, J. (2016). Analysing energy transitions: Combining insights from transition studies and international political economy. In T. Van de Graaf, B. K. Sovacool, A. Ghosh, F. Kern, & M. T. Klare (Eds.), *The Palgrave handbook of the international political economy of energy* (1st ed., pp. 291–318). Palgrave Macmillan UK. https://doi.org/10.1057/978-1-137-55631-8

Koomson, I., & Awaworyi Churchill, S. (2022). Employment precarity and energy poverty in post-apartheid South Africa: Exploring the racial and ethnic dimensions. *Energy Economics, 110*(June), 1–3. https://doi.org/10.1016/j.eneco.2022.106026

Kotze, J. S., & Bohler-Muller, N. (2019). Editorial: Quo Vadis? Reflections on the 2019 South African General Elections. *Politikon, 46*(4), 365–370. https://doi.org/10.1080/02589346.2019.1692520

Lawrence, A. (2020). Energy decentralization in South Africa: Why past failure points to future success. *Renewable and Sustainable Energy Reviews, 120*, 109659. https://doi.org/10.1016/j.rser.2019.109659

Makiwane, T., & Padia, N. (2013). Evaluation of corporate integrated reportin in South AFrica post King III release South Africa - An exploratory enquiry. *Journal of Economic and Financial Sciences, 6*(2), 421–438. http://phys.org/news/2012-03-lung-doctors-respiratory-diseases-worsen.html

Marais, H. (2012). The polarising impact of South Africa's AIDS epidemic. In J. Daniel, P. Naidoo, D. Pillay, & R. Southall (Eds.), *New South African Review 1* (pp. 305–325). https://doi.org/10.18772/22010115164.20

McBride, C. M., Kruger, A. C., & Dyson, L. (2022). Trends in probabilities of temperature records in the non-stationary climate of South Africa. *International Journal of Climatology, 42*(3), 1692–1705. https://doi.org/10.1002/joc.7329

McDonald, D. A. (2011). Electricity and the minerals-energy complex south africa. *Africa Review, 3*(1), 65–87. https://doi.org/10.1080/09744053.2011.10597305

McKenzie, D., Bairin, P., & Beech, S. (2021, July 14). *South Africa Protests: More than 70 Killed in Violence after Former President Jacob Zuma is Jailed.* CNN Website, 1–7. https://edition.cnn.com/2021/07/13/africa/south-afr ica-violence-protests-intl/index.html

Mkhize, M., & Radmore, J. (2021). *Utility-scale renewable energy market intelligence report.* https://www.greencape.co.za/assets/Renewable_Energy_MIR_2021_31_3_21.pdf

Mkhize, Z. (2020, March 5). First Case of Covid-19 Coronavirus Reported in SA. *National Institutite for Communicable Diseases.* https://www.nicd.ac.za/first-case-of-covid-19-coronavirus-reported-in-sa/

Mohamed, S. (2012). The state of the South African economy. In J. Daniel, P. Naidoo, D. Pillay, & R. Southall (Eds.), *New South African Review 1* (1st ed., pp. 39–64). Wits University Press. https://doi.org/10.18772/22010115164.6

Müller, F., & Claar, S. (2021). Auctioning a 'just energy transition'? South Africa's renewable energy procurement programme and its implications for transition strategies. *Review of African Political Economy,* 1–19. https://doi.org/10.1080/03056244.2021.1932790

Müller, F., Claar, S., Neumann, M., & Elsner, C. (2020). Is green a Pan-African colour? Mapping African renewable energy policies and transitions in 34 countries. *Energy Research and Social Science, 68*(July 2019), 101551. https://doi.org/10.1016/j.erss.2020.101551

Müller, F., Neumann, M., Elsner, C., & Claar, S. (2021). Assessing african energy transitions: Renewable energy policies, energy justice, and SDG 7. *Politics and Governance, 9*(1), 119–130. https://doi.org/10.17645/pag.v9i1.3615

Naidoo, P. (2021, August 24). South Africa unemployment rate rises to highest in the world. *Bloomberg.* https://www.bloomberg.com/news/articles/2021-08-24/south-african-unemployment-rate-rises-to-highest-in-the-world

Naidoo, P., & Njini, F. (2021, July 6). Iconic South African Mines Ravaged Economy's Unlikely Savior - Bloomberg. *Bloomberg.* https://www.bloomberg.com/news/articles/2021-07-06/iconic-south-african-mines-are-ravaged-economy-s-unlikely-savior

Nölke, A., ten Brink, T., May, C., & Claar, S. (2020). *State-Permeated Capitalism in large emerging economies* (A. Nölke, T. ten Brink, C. May, & S. Claar (Eds.); RIPE Series). Routledge.

Okpanachi, E., & Chowdhari Tremblay, R. (2021). *The political economy of natural resource funds* (E. Okpanachi & R. Chowdhari Tremblay (Eds.); 1st ed.). Palgrave Macmillan.

Padayachee, V. (2013). Corporate governance in South Africa: from "Old Boys Club" to "Ubuntu"? *Transformation: Critical Perspectives on Southern Africa, 81*(1), 260–290. https://doi.org/10.1353/trn.2013.0006

Qobo, E. M., Soko, M., & Ngwenya, N. X. (2022). *The Future of the South African Political Economy Post-COVID 19* (1st ed.). Palgrave Macmillan.

Ramaphosa, C. (2022). *Key Note address: Investing in African Mining Indaba.* https://www.gov.za/speeches/president-cyril-ramaphosa-2022-investing-african-mining-indaba-10-may-2022-0000

Roberts, B. J., Struwig, J., Gordon, S. L., & Davids, Y. D. (2019). The unconvinced vote: The nature and determinants of voting intentions and the changing character of South African electoral politics. *Politikon, 46*(4), 481–498. https://doi.org/10.1080/02589346.2019.1687120

SA News. (2022, February 23). Government extends R350 COVID-19 grant by 12 months. *SA News (Government)*, 1–4. https://www.sanews.gov.za/south-africa/government-extends-r350-covid-19-grant-12-months

Segatti, A., & Pons-Vignon, N. (2013). La stabilisation à tout prix? La politique macro-économique de l'Afrique du Sud postapartheid entre conversion idéologique et capture technocratique. *Review of African Political Economy, 40*(138), 537–555. https://doi.org/10.1080/03056244.2013.858430

Simatele, M. (2015). Market structure and competition in the South African banking sector. *Procedia Economics and Finance, 30*(15), 825–835. https://doi.org/10.1016/s2212-5671(15)01332-5

South African Government. (2022). *Presidency on final report of Zondo Commission*. The Presidency. https://www.gov.za/speeches/interference-judiciary-20-jun-2022-0000

Southall, R. (2012). Introduction: South Africa 2010: From short-term success to long-term decline. In J. Daniel, P. Naidoo, D. Pillay, & R. Southall (Eds.), *New South African Review 1: Development or decline?* (1st ed., Vol. 1, pp. 1–21). Wits University Press.

Southall, R. (2016). The coming crisis of Zuma's ANC: The party state confronts fiscal crisis. *Review of African Political Economy, 43*(147), 73–88. https://doi.org/10.1080/03056244.2015.1083970

Stark, V. (2022, May 10). South Africa poised to exploit growing demand for platinum group metals. *Voa News*, 1–3. https://www.voanews.com/a/south-africa-poised-to-exploit-growing-demand-for-platinum-group-metals-/6565894.html

Stats SA. (2022). *The South African economy records a positive fourth quarter*. Statistics South Africa. http://www.statssa.gov.za/?m=2019

Swilling, M. (2012). Growth, resource use and decoupling: Towards a "Green new deal" for South Africa? In J. Daniel, P. Naidoo, D. Pillay, & R. Southall (Eds.), *New South African Review 1* (pp. 104–135). Wits University Press.

Tshidavhu, F., & Khatleli, N. (2020). An assessment of the causes of schedule and cost overruns in South African megaprojects: A case of the critical energy sector projects of Medupi and Kusile. *Acta Structilia, 27*(1), 119–143. https://doi.org/10.18820/24150487/as27i1.5

van der Merwe, J. (2016). An historical geographical analysis of South Africa's system of accumulation: 1652–1994. *Review of African Political Economy, 43*(147), 58–72. https://doi.org/10.1080/03056244.2015.1049521

Vecchiatto, P. (2021, May 25). South Africa's Eskom Slashes Debt by a Fifth; Bonds Rally. *Bloomberg.* https://www.bloomberg.com/news/articles/2021-05-25/south-african-power-utility-eskom-makes-headway-in-cutting-debt

Vecchiatto, P., & Goko, C. (2022, June 6). Mysterious Wildlife Farm Robbery Puts Ramaphosa on Back Foot. *Bloomberg.* https://www.bloomberg.com/news/articles/2022-06-06/ramaphosa-pleads-innocence-as-south-african-police-probe-robbery

Visser, W. (2005). Shifting RDP into gear: The ANC government's dilemma in providing an equitable system for social security for the'New'South Africa. *ITH-Tagungsberichte 39, "Mercy or Right": Development of Social Security Systems,* 105–124.

World Bank. (2021). South Africa - Eskom Renewables Support Project (P122329). *World Bank Disclosure Report.* https://doi.org/10.1136/bmj.318.7187.822

World Bank. (2022). *World Population Review - Gini Coefficient by Country 2022.* https://worldpopulationreview.com/country-rankings/gini-coefficient-by-country

Yunis, J., & Aliakbari, E. (2022). *Annual Survey of Mining Companies 2021.* https://www.fraserinstitute.org/studies/annual-survey-of-mining-companies-2021?utm_source=Facebook-and-Twitter&utm_campaign=Annual-Survey-of-Mining-Companies-2021&utm_medium=Social&utm_content=Learn_More&utm_term=415

CHAPTER 5

A Stalling Green Bond Take-Off

To approach the overarching research question and decipher reasons for the lack of green bond market expansion in South Africa, this chapter elaborates on the findings of my empirical research and touches on different compounding factors that inhibit the uptake of green bonds in the country. I structured findings into seven complementary pillars that mirror the order of my theoretical approaches. Each provides insights into answering my research question.

In a first step, the general opportunities promoted by green bond advocates will be delineated and assessed against South Africa's background as an *emerging* green bond market. Second, Cape Town's green bond, widely perceived as the most successful green bond issuance in South Africa to date, will be scrutinized more closely and the importance of success stories emphasized to grow so-called markets-in-the-making. In a third step, the requirement for green bonds to be 'simple' will be substantiated and the conceptual limitations as well as inherent trade-offs discussed. In the subsequent section, controversial bond issuances, fanning debates around greenwashing at a global stage, will be juxtaposed with the ongoing deliberations around a national taxonomy for green bonds in South Africa. In an important fifth step, I dwell on the peculiarities of the South African capital markets and discuss pertinent actors, inherent bottlenecks to capital market greening as well as attempts

© The Author(s), under exclusive license to Springer Nature Switzerland AG 2023
M. Neumann, *The Political Economy of Green Bonds in Emerging Markets*, International Political Economy Series, https://doi.org/10.1007/978-3-031-30502-3_5

to overcome said bottlenecks. Then, I revisit my interviewees' perception of competing policy trajectories, dwelling specifically on concerns for a just transition. Lastly, I illustrate the attempts at depoliticizing low-carbon transition governance more generally and of green bond diffusion in particular and compare these with the contested and repoliticized arenas green bonds have (unintentionally) created. Each section will reference and relate to aspects of the theoretical framework in Chapter 3 and zoom in from remote to concrete levels of abstraction. To add analytical depth, some findings will also be linked with the hypotheses raised in Chapter 4.

The Purported Opportunities of Green Bonds Hardly Transpire in Emerging Markets

As evident in the exponential growth rates at global scale, green bonds carry characteristics that induce investors to opt for these capital debt instruments with environmental benefits. Financial practitioners, indeed, put forth a sequence of arguments in favor of green bonds that will briefly be recapitulated before assessing some of them in an emerging market context. I first touch on a popular crisis interpretation and green bonds as the proposed solution for the climate crisis.

The Climate Bonds Initiative and Its Crisis Interpretation

There are key global actors pushing green bonds as instruments to fund the decarbonization of economies. The Climate Bonds Initiative (CBI), described by Tripathy (2017) as a "collateral institution, interpreting green bond market data" (p. 248), is one such key advocate, producing and advocating standards for this nascent market. The initiative is based in London and funded by a range of non-profit and public organizations (see Climate Bonds Initiative, 2022b). Its so-called 10-point case for green bonds, their webinar on green bonds in South Africa, and their country report on South Africa provide valuable insights into their crisis interpretation and proposed solution. To set the bar, the CBI credits climate change as "an extraordinary challenge facing the world community [… threatening] uncontrollable change" (CBI 10-point case, p. 1: 195). This challenge, according to the London-based organization, has a temporal, an economic, and a geographical component: Given the time "constraint", there is "urgency" (CBI 10-point case, p. 1: 1209) to act swiftly on climate change in order to stay within the 2 °C warming boundary. And given the nascency of many path-compliant technologies, there are little economies of scale and thus huge up-front costs initially. And lastly, given the arising opportunity costs for poorer countries to focus on other policy priorities like poverty eradication, the developing world is targeted as the arena where the battle against climate change is won or lost. Notedly, CBI's CEO Sean Kidney, the 'go-to person' for parties interested in rolling out green bonds (Hilbrandt & Grubbauer, 2020; Monk & Perkins, 2020), walks a fine line when framing climate change in the beginning of the green bond webinar in South Africa in August 2021. He describes climate change as a "challenge" (CBI webinar, 2021, p. 2: 1854) rather than a crisis on the one hand and cites wildfires in the USA and floods in China as vivid global examples of the disruptive effects—were climate change not to be reined in—on the other. This three-pronged approach to climate change forms the premise on which a key institution like the CBI premises its case for green bonds. Accordingly, this climate crisis consists of three oftentimes intertwined arguments: There is a sense of *urgency*, in that action is required swiftly to retain the stability of the system. That action requires institutional and technical *innovation*. And if done right, climate change offers plenty of great *opportunities* for profit and reputation.

Interestingly, however, rather than presenting a purely techno-optimist stance on innovation doing the trick, the CBI's 10-point case for green bonds avers that "the solution paths [towards low-emission futures] are largely understood" (p. 1: 139), suggesting that it is not purely techno-optimism that will suffice to address climate change ramifications. Instead, the key obstacle is for these technologies to gain economies of scale and become cost competitive. This statement, thus, shifts attention to questions of funding and distribution and introduces the funding gap as a key obstacle to be closed.

The 'Other' Side of the Investment Gap

Scholars, policy-makers and activists in the field of global climate governance and its political economy have heard this refrain: To align our economies with the 1.5 °C target of the Paris Agreement will require huge amounts of capital investments (see Chapter 1). The African economic outlook estimates funding needs for the updated NDCs to range from US\$55 billion to 59 billion between 2020 and 2030 (AfDB, 2022, p. 171). According to another slightly earlier report (Cassim et al., 2021,

p. 4), total climate-related finance, whether public, private or blended, totaled ZAR62.2 billion (US$4.28 billion) for 2017 and 2018. That converts to ZAR31 billion (US$2.14 billion) per annum and will (if assumed to remain stable throughout 2030) cover only 36–39% of the required funding. Unless efforts are significantly upscaled, the country's funding gap, thus, remains enormous.

Arthur Wood, the moderator of the green bonds webinar targeting South African municipalities organized by the Green Growth Knowledge Partnership (GGKP),[1] identifies the closing of the funding gap as the overarching challenge in this "decade of action" (GGKP webinar, 2021, pos. 13). The peculiarity of the green bond debate is, however, that it takes a slightly different starting point: Rather than starting from the premise of an *unprecedented demand* for capital, the green bond discourse starts from the premise of an *untapped supply* of capital. CBI's CEO Sean Kidney, again, paints this illustrative arc when discussing funding issues for South Africa's transition:

> Above all, we need a lot of capital to shift their economies, to shift our industrial infrastructure to shift our land use our mining industries. We're going to need to invest in what the transition is. The good news this is /where we get the good news, we have a world awash in capital. In Europe, some 21% of all institutional investment capital is invested in near zero or negative interest rate bonds – I mean that is crazy. There is no way to pay my pension when I finally retire putting it in negative interest rate bonds so, if you like, we have capital in search of yields as a dominant factor in the world now. (CBI webinar, 2021, p. 3: 2267)

Capital, he argues, is *not* the scarce resource. Rather, it is the return-oriented investment opportunities that are missing—with possibly adverse effects on his and every hard-working person's pensions. The challenge is, thus, reframed not as a lack of capital available, but as a lack of funding opportunities for capital markets. We will turn to what constitutes 'funding opportunities' below when discussing the financialization of Transition Studies more generally and the bankability of projects specifically.

---

[1] GGKP comprises various South Africa's Ministry of the Environment, Forestry & Fisheries and development institutions including the United Nations Environment Program (UNEP) and the German Development Agency (GIZ).

Kidney is by no means and outlier with his statement. Arthur Wood, the aforementioned moderator of the GGKP webinar, similarly summarizes

> the exciting opportunity of mobilizing local capital markets to get to the SDGs, something that's often ignored in the developed world and the fact that there is two trillion that sits in local pension funds in local currencies and up to up to five million in various other local currencies [...] is that exciting opportunity. (GGKP webinar, 2021, pos. 965–970)

And even within South Africa, this argumentation has tremendous currency as a former investment banker turned advisor to the South African government and solar industry representative argued:

> We certainly need to attract other capital markets into this space. And there is a huge amount of money out there. There is probably R3-4trillion worth of money that sits in these kinds of capital markets, sit in bonds and other tradeable instruments that so far have not tapped into this sector. (RE Industry representative, pos. 34)

The first important takeaway in framing green bonds as an economic imaginary is its repositioning capital markets as ready dispensers for the green transition. The coin is discursively upended from an 'unprecedented demand' for capital to 'untapped supply' of funds for green investment projects.

From Opportunities to 'Bankability' as the Binding Constraint for Capital Markets

To untap this capital supply for climate-related action requires creating not so much environmental but rather economic opportunities. The 9th of the 10 points in case that the CBI (CBI 10-point case) lists, therefore, is: "The transition to a low-carbon economy presents capital with what is likely to become the largest *commercial opportunity* of our time: investing in clean energy and low-carbon infrastructure" (p. 2: 2755, *own italics*). 'Commercial opportunities' are invariably at the center of the argument to enlist actors in the greening of financial sectors specifically and the wider economy more generally. This focus on commercial opportunities through green bonds already insinuates the predominant motivation underpinning the shift to 'green' financial innovations like green bonds: The promise of profits. The discursive frames for green bonds, thus, draw up climate change as an urgent challenge and presents commercial opportunities for capital markets keenly scanning markets for return.

Investment opportunities are readily identified in the South African context. The CBI report envisions "transition opportunities" (CBI & Agora Energiewende, 2021, p. 10) for Eskom and Sasol, the biggest CO_2 emitters in South Africa, or the short-term decarbonization of the energy sector more generally as the best bet (citing, ironically, the NDC's lack of clarity as a reason for identifying this opportunity in the first place (ibid., p. 10]). This would turn South Africa into "the first global South coal-based economy to make a successful transition to a low carbon economy" (ibid., p. 2). A chief analyst of South Africa's capital market's unit at one of the big five banks in South Africa further argued that the pricing in of climate change issues may yield tremendous returns, pointing at water treatment as a key area the state could administer to simultaneously fulfill its role as charting out just transition projects (Banker 1, pos. 33, 41; see also RE industry Representative, pos. 26, 29). This stance is largely seconded by a senior representative of the Independent Power Producers (IPP) office, who refers to the "huge opportunities when you think of water, food, energy nexus from renewables [...and] the costs coming down" (IPP office representative, pos. 48). Lastly, even local NGOs "see[s] the green economy as one of the sort of biggest opportunities for that economic development. [...] So, all of the sectors that we work in, we believe have an economic business case behind them", according to a representative (Civil Society actor 1, pos. 13–15).

Commercial returns, however, do not merely form the key incentive for capital markets to shift money into climate-aligned products, but are also their sine qua non. As one institutional investor puts it, "green bonds in terms of the African context are in their infancy. And certainly, I think the market is ready for more. Again, it needs to [...] operate on the same commercial principles as would any other bond" (Asset Management Consultant 1, pos. 52). When reaching out to investors, an employee at one of the municipal treasuries (Municipal representative 1, pos. 152) summarized his experience with interested investors as such: "I mean, everybody likes the idea of investing in green, but they are not [ready] to sacrifice return". A representative of the International Capital Market Association (ICMA) and senior employee at Old Mutual, one of the biggest insurance companies on the African continent and avid investor in South Africa's renewable energy tender program, substantiates this position:

> I don't think anyone is going to say, 'Listen, you know, you have a mandate to pursue the green attributes and we prepare to accept a 30 or 20 percent lower yield', I don't think that's going to be the case. But you know you might find a willingness to sort of be more flexible on the margin to get the green attribute. (Old Mutual Representative, pos. 159)

On the challenges on making green bonds attractive for investors, the former JSE senior sustainability manager, involved in setting up the green segment, takes the same line of argument:

> The challenge with anything that has a green label is always, whether equity or bond, is whether it delivers on what it promises. And the question is: What does it promise? With the Green Label you are creating the expectation that it will deliver not only a financial return but a green return as well. And the challenge is – I don't know whether that is a weakness – is how to balance the two, because investors have not yet gotten to the point where they are willing to compromise on a financial return, but some of them are happy to settle for a neutral return; they just don't want to be losing any money. (JSE Representative 1, p. 8: 1633)

The CEO of an NGO advocating the greening of banking in South Africa echoes this unwillingness to compromise returns by connecting it to the short-terminism that dominates markets: "So I don't think that you are going to find a lot of investors in South Africa who will say okay we will take a short term hit on our returns for the sake of doing this good for the long term you know. I don't think so" (Civil Society actor 2, p. 6: 769). The recurring message across the spectrum of interviewees is: Green investments require similar returns as business-as-usual ones.

Yet how much return on investment, i.e. interest rates, are we talking about? These differ tremendously not least depending on the length of tenure, the repayment type and schedule, the technology in question, market outlook, and of course the perception of risk. Driven by development bank support and increased competition, profit margins in the renewable energy space, for example, tightened. The Chamber of Commerce representative (pos. 44) estimates smaller RE projects like biogas or rooftop PVs to garner market interest rates of 10–14% with DFIs offering various types of concessions, either through first-loss tranches (Kreditanstalt für Wiederaufbau, KfW) or below market lending rates (Agence Française de Développement). A fund manager and investor in the country's renewable energy tender said with view to bidding rounds 3 and 4:

> And the reality is that now they are trading in twelve fourteen percent return is the kind of space that wind farms and solar farms trade at. Which is half of what the initial ones were in round one before any had been constructed. (Fund Manager 1, pos. 46)

In defense of bankability, this investment banker of the big five banks retorts upon prompting: "Why would you take on more credit risk for a lesser return? Everything that we have been taught since most of us went to school, is on risk-return-reward" (Banker 2, pos. 51). His reasoning for defending the notion of bankability is equally straightforward, boiling down to the economic trade-offs of investing scarce capital need to add up to the risks that investment entails:

> The problem that you have is, that if you are unbankable, and your project is unbankable, the bank is not going to put scarce resources just to prove that you were unbankable. [...] Every project requires a certain level of economic stability or economic feasibility. And the level of risk in that project needs to be offset either through collateral or equity or track record or something. You can't just say this thing is feasible, irrelevant of risk. As soon as you start making that risk-return trade-off, now it starts becoming a real sustainable project. Otherwise, what happens is you start spending a lot of money on lots of roads that go nowhere. And then when you have a monstrously big deficit you say: 'Man, capital was a scarce resource – I am now in trouble.' As we can see in the left or the right of the globe. So that is the trade-off. (Banker 2, pos. 38)

This overriding concern for bankability also dominates policy-making, for example when charting out the country's renewable energy tender program. "Engagement with the market was a key thing", according to a senior representative of the Independent Power Producers office, "sitting down with potential lenders and understanding what would make [the projects] bankable. What would make [the lenders] walk away?" (pos. 10).

Pension funds significantly complicate the picture as they oversee the pensions of masses of working people. In line with CBI's Sean Kidney's first concern for his own pension money needing return to finance retirement, a South African institutional investor argues:

> but it all needs to come at a point where you know you can build a project which still ... meets return hurdles so the widows and orphans that we have money that will get a decent return (Fund Manager 1, pos. 44).

These examples carry three takeaways. For one, bankability, i.e. a project structure yielding calculable returns on (up-front) investments, imposes a binding constraint on attaining funding. Beyond the bankable structure, however, the quantity of return also matters. My interviewees hint at the fact that investors are currently largely unwilling to compromise there, though many climate advocates—whether in finance or in politics—hope for this return hurdle to diminish over time. Thirdly, institutional investors justify their uncompromising stance—in the case of pension funds—with their 'stewardship' of people's retirement money.

The compromises on returns are also epitomized in global debates around the so-called *greenium* or the premium investors at times pay (in the form of reduced coupon rates) for a climate-aligned as opposed to a regular project. These debates around the *greenium* have escalated to a point where investors attack the lower return for climate-aligned projects as distorting the market which should return to its pricing fundamentals, namely risk perception and outlook (see environmental finance debates Hurley, 2021; Michaelsen, 2018).

This binding constraint of ensuring the bankability (Baker, 2015; Gabor, 2021; Maltais & Nykvist, 2020; Müller et al., 2020; Sovacool et al., 2017) of climate-aligned projects discloses the first rift between opportunities green bonds offer on the one hand and the lack of investable projects on the other.

The Dearth of Bankable Projects in South Africa
Regardless of more or less concrete opportunities for green alternatives, whether "transition opportunities" (CBI & Agora Energiewende, 2021, p. 10) to shift the coal economy or pricing in climate change at the water, food, and energy nexus (IPP office representative, pos. 48–51; Banker 1, pos. 33, 41), many interviewees bemoan the lack of bankable projects as the key constraint to roll out green bonds. Across the interviewed spectrum, whether the South African investment community, NGOs, or developers, they affirm a the lack of bankable projects

as the key concern already raised among financial practitioners in the literature review (McInerney & Bunn, 2019). By engaging with the institutional investor landscape, the NGO representative gathered that "the biggest roadblocks are lack of investable opportunities or investable alternatives" (Civil Society actor 2, p. 5: 185). To put this into perspective, an interviewed development banker argues:

> I mean you know that depth of the South African capital markets. They can find the infrastructure we have for the next 30 years. I mean it's deep, it's sophisticated, it's developed. But you know other than the REI4P [the renewable energy tender program], what else has there been to invest in? Nothing. (Development Bank Representative 1, pos. 114)

At another point in the interview, he put it even more bluntly, "there are no projects, so there are no project bonds" (Development Bank Representative 1, pos. 23). And that is not due to a lack of investor demand for green projects. An institutional investor with a track record of investing in green bonds says:

> I don't think there's a lack of appetite. I think local investors are looking for new opportunities. But the opportunities need to be something really attractive from an underlying project perspective, and a written perspective. […] [T]here's a lack of product but that purely because I think it's a very new concept in South African market. (Futuregrowth employee, pos. 46, 48)

Indeed, the ICMA representative I talked to indicated that they have been quite vocal in the media and with issuers, speaking in particular to banks as to why they are not bringing more of these products to the market (Old Mutual Representative, pos. 14). Developers affirm this tremendous demand for green investable products like green bonds. Explaining how a development bank supported the process of issuing their maiden green bond, one developer recounts:

> They gave us some funding to do the research into green bond. So, we modelled various scenarios and we did a couple of road shows. We met all of the asset managers and discussed what rates we could get and how it could be structured. And we got a very, very positive response. (Developer 1, pos. 8)

When offering sound business plans that are adequately asset-backed and meet the risk criteria of investors, projects seem to be quickly gobbled up. This is evident in the vast oversubscription of most the green bonds at the JSE, regardless of the 'shade' of climate alignment (CICERO, 2021b) they attained. We'll return to this finding below.

Public Sector Struggles Around Meeting Bankability Requirements
Where there are no private issuers, public issuers could come in and offer projects to investors willing to drive climate alignment. Quite in contrast to the investment community's charge of missing projects, public actors, specifically municipalities but also the Industrial Development Corporation (IDC) insist that they have plenty of climate-aligned projects that lack funding to get implemented. An IDC representative, for example, observed that "lately, there are all these people trying to develop projects but there's no big offtake" (IDC employee, pos. 32). Quite in line with this observation, the treasury representative of one of the few municipalities that successfully issued a green bond argued:

> We had more projects to fund, but the CBI standards were limited. And they were still in the process of developing standards for the other infrastructure projects. It is all green oriented. So, it was very limited projects for the CBI to give accreditation. They could not give accreditation to all our projects because they never had a standard in place. (Municipal representative 2, pos. 26)

These seemingly incommensurable positions of (public) projects lacking funding and funders lacking (investment) projects can be reconciled when zooming into green bond requirements. The mismatch sketched out above boils down to issues of bankability, which essentially explains the gulf between private and public sector perceptions of the projects in question. Three reasons explain this imbalance between lack of projects bemoaned by investors on the one hand and the projects lacking private funding that public actors point to on the other: Missing know-how on how to attain bankability, the lack of solvent and credit-worthy municipalities, and the missing overlap between private sector needs for profitability and public sector projects geared for social outcomes.

The development banker cited earlier points to the capacity shortfall inhibiting municipalities, specifically, from tapping institutional funds:

The problem you got in South Africa is that the municipalities – they don't like to admit this – they don't have the ability to take projects from feasibility to bankability. So, when we went to see the asset managers in the banks, I said, we would support a structure of this type. We're looking for those types of assets, they suit our portfolio but everything we've seen so far is not in a bankable form. (Development Bank Representative 1, pos. 95–97)

Even the municipality I interviewed concedes that the projects need to also meet the city's investment policy and oftentimes "these investments are not liquid" (Municipal representative 1, pos. 149). Despite several de-risking tools and funding opportunities for climate-aligned projects that will elaborated later, a chamber of commerce representative soberly concludes that the conditions ensuring bankability are very hard to fulfill: "Once you familiarize yourself with these conditions, you soon realize, how difficult it is to get the money. It is buried under so many imponderables, even though it is right there" (Chamber of Commerce Representative, pos. 40).

And this issue has already been identified by various domestic and international development banks:

The problem is you need to develop the municipalities' ability to take projects from feasibility or from drawing board to bankability. So, that's the challenge. So, to me it's not a case of funding. There's more than enough money out there. To me, the real challenge is to give or support or provide resources to the municipalities to be able to put together bankable projects" (Development Bank Representative 1, pos. 110).

For the senior employee at Futuregrowth, the key missing ingredient that would make more projects bankable—next to clear cost structures, proper collateralization, and a reliable rate of return—is the missing track record of the implementing engineers that public entities like municipalities solicit:

So, we're always on the outlook for this type of climate friendly environmental-friendly projects to fund. And they fall in-between at the moment. They all fall in-between. Lots of great ideas of people having started companies and it's in early stage, it's in pilot phase, it's in – they've launched it, no track record, it's not investible for us at the moment. (Futuregrowth employee, pos. 78–79)

And beyond hardly attainable conditionalities, solvency issues loom large, particularly at municipal level. These preclude many second and third tier municipalities from even attempting to issue a green bond. The interviewees refer to the low number of creditworthy municipalities (JSE Representative 2, p. 7: 3074), variously speaking of only fourteen bankable municipalities (eight in the Western Cape and six in the rest of the country, Development Bank Representative 1, pos. 73–75), that could chart out investment projects with technical and financial support or four municipalities that can by themselves raise debt in the capital markets (Old Mutual Representative, pos. 42). Given the structural public sector management crisis that led to widespread financial insolvency and capacity shortfalls (Butler, 2012; Southall, 2016), the struggle of municipalities to meet bankability thresholds is unsurprising.

At the same time, it is important to note that these solvency capacity issues have not afflicted every municipality. As the same development banker argues:

> Now, when Joburg does it or Cape Town, they don't even, they can list any project they want there, these guys [institutional investors] turn a blind eye because they're really banking Cape Town's balance sheet. Cynical but it's true. (Development Bank Representative 1, pos. 109)

In summary, requirements of bankable projects inhibit the uptake of green bonds in both the private and public spheres. This stark difference in the public sphere between the few municipalities that can access capital market funding and those that cannot exemplifies (Bigger, 2017; Bigger & Millington, 2019) findings that green bonds deepen existing structural inequalities (Caprotti et al., 2020). By favoring those municipalities with functioning balance sheets over those not endowed with similar capital stock, green bonds contribute to magnifying these structural inequalities. This problem, similarly, surfaces in the private sector, where incumbents with solid track records outcompete new arrivals over low-carbon funding opportunities (effectively leaving the market to a few multinational firms, as will be discussed further below). These examples demonstrate some shortcomings of interventions premised on bankability. As a tool for upliftment of structurally disadvantaged actors, they hardly offer a suitable avenue. There are several more compounding factors that contribute to the lack of green bond take-off particularly in emerging markets.

Investor's Reluctance to Shoulder Construction Risks

To understand the second major hurdle that prevents the advantages of green bonds to transpire in an emerging market context like South Africa, we turn to green bond's unique selling point—their use-of-proceeds setup—and recap basic project finance rationales.

The use-of-proceeds setup requires the issuer to identify projects that will be funded through the green bond. Though exceptions exist (we will discuss Nedbank's earliest attempt later), green bonds encourage a project finance setup. Usually, issuers create a separate special-purpose-vehicle (SPV) to segregate risks accrued in this project in order to avoid a potential bankruptcy of the project to afflict the issuer's wider balance sheet (Fund Manager 2, pos. 174). Through the SPV, in short, the risk is backed by the project asset to be constructed.

The major concern that particularly risk-averse institutional investors raise is the mismatch between very high up-front costs of a green project like a solar park coinciding with high risks underpinning the projects in their early phases particular before construction is completed. Given the even higher risk perception in emerging markets (Haag & Müller, 2019; Volberding, 2021; Waissbein et al., 2013), large institutional investors are very hesitant to engage in project finance in emerging markets. Global regulations, such as Basel III, have heightened capital requirements for banks five years into lending, thus creating markets for institutional investors to participate in the less risky phases of these project investment cycle (Developer 1, pos. 101). Upon asked whether her employer would consider shouldering construction risk, a senior employee at Futuregrowth responds:

> So, I don't see that–we wouldn't – but obviously construction risk has a bigger risk element to it. We don't, you know, we prefer not to participate with this construction risk. We are, not to say that we haven't in the past. [...] So, I think of some of non-REI4P [the country's renewable energy tender program] projects that we have funded with some DFIs [Development Finance Institutions]. They would come in and do the subsidized finance and do the construction finance. And then we would take over, step in once construction has actually been completed. (Futuregrowth employee, pos. 17–19, 29)

When asked the same question about considering funding projects with construction risks, a senior employee of Old Mutual, similarly, remarked:

So, and obviously when there's new capital issuances from large listed corporates then we're in conversation but sort of more on the project finance sort of side of things. We buy that debt only once they're fully derisked and up and running. (Old Mutual Representative, pos. 28)

The Futuregrowth employee links this hesitancy to engage in construction risk with the risk mandate the respective institutional investor is endowed with:

So, each investment manager has parameters around the type of risks that they can take and the product that they offer on that resource spectrum. You get your private equity firms, they can take a lot more risk on [...] Some private equity firms could do funding of pilot projects, some won't, but some will do early-stage VC [venture capital] type of investments, you know [...]They have that specific mandate. So, to your earlier question around, would pension funds participate? It also depends on the pension funds risk appetite and the risk parameters that they've set out for their fund. And some pension funds will invest a portion in private equity and then they would specify that perhaps they would not do venture capital, but they would do more private equity in the early growth stage. You know what I'm saying? But I think that funds still have a fiduciary duty to invest in any investment they make has got to be, offer suitable risk returns for the underlying beneficiaries. (Futuregrowth employee, pos. 79–82)

In the South African context, few institutional investors are willing to take on construction risk as their mandate or fiduciary duty precludes them from investing funds into projects perceived as riskier. The "four or five" that would take on construction risks such as during the heavily state-backed renewable energy tender program "have staffed up their project finance capabilities" (Development Bank Representative 1, pos. 132).

Developers have gotten a similar sense, though being optimistic that that might change with a developer' successful track record:

But again, the current fund managers will not look at constructions. They are absolutely allergic to it. So, you need to take from here and five years from now I think you can go to a fund manager and say okay well, they take some construction risk. You know once you set five years of track record, he's got a return. He's comfortable, he will probably look at [it], but right now they will definitely not look at it. Every one of them says 'Don't come to us with construction risk. We'll only look at projects that are in, that are grid code compliant and they're in operations'. [...] And if you're a good developer, I think they're, you know there's a, I think you've got a track record, you perform well, they've already got a bond with you, they'll look at it but certainly not now. (Developer 1, pos. 105, 107)

To the senior capital market analyst of one of the big five banks in South Africa, major hurdles for green bond take-off still need to be bridged in the realm of perceived risks:

Project bonds in this country haven't had a glorious start or support, because we are missing one or two participants in the risk management framework. The risk appetite is such that you have got banks that are prepared to get onboard with a project, banks will fund projects based on club deals and bilateral arrangements. So, we are talking project bonds, we talk about listed notes to offer opportunities for that broader investment universe I spoke about: Investment asset managers, pension funds, life [insurance] companies. They have got big money; they also want to invest in a new investment class. So, we sit in a conundrum in this country, where there is lots and lots of liquidity and very few assets that are available, too. Project bonds would be an ideal investment alternative for them. (Banker 1, pos. 12–13)

He goes on to point out the mismatch in skills and risk appetite that prohibit green bond take-up:

However, having said that, project bond skills reside within banks and not within institutional asset managers. So, they would only want to participate once it has become kind of 'brown fields', when it is up and running and established. Basically, they were not happy to participate in the construction risk element of a project which then leads you to think, well they will only start participating once it has been de-risked to a certain extend. They don't have the risk etc. or haven't had in the past, or the mandate, since it is very much a conservative investment environment, driven to say: I am going to invest in construction risk of a project. (Ibid., pos. 13)

He, also, identifies development banks as key actors able to bridge the risk divide and refers to the key advantage of green bonds over regular loans:

So, what we are missing is, we have got the banks that can bridge fund in the beginning, maybe up to 3-4 years, you have the asset managers who are happy to take the 'brown fields' once it is running. There is no one to bridge in-between. That is where we have got to bring in the DFIs. We have seen the IFC, the World Bank host a conference to get a project bond market up and going. The Canadians have a fantastically vibrant project bond market. That is because you have got the Canadian government and DFIs happy to stand in to plug that gap to take some of the construction risk in the interim before passing it on. That is the missing link in our chain. And I think our government and the DFIs domestically have enough on their plates. So, what it has done is forcing banks to take longer-term positions, but it kept it all in the loan market hasn't kept it in the bond market. It is important to make a distinction between the loan world, and the bond world, because they are two very different channels or mechanisms of financing. Loan world, very bespoke bilateral between banks. No one is really focused on green loans. But everyone is getting very excited about green bonds. Why is that? Bonds are obviously a lot more tradeable, they are out there, they are more public, the profiling behind bonds is a lot more appropriate. It lends itself a lot more towards profiling, whereby bilateral loans are quite bespoke, and you want to keep the terms and conditions inhouse because they are propriety. (Ibid., pos. 13)

In the South African financial markets, green bonds sit in a risk vacuum that neither banks nor institutional investors with their respective risk tranches are willing to fund and fill. There are a few intermediaries, like the Industrial Development Corporation, who have taken on investment risk for pension funds in the renewable energy tender (IDC employee, pos. 184–90). We will also cover the renewable energy tender and a few of the DFI's de-risking measures in later subsections. But that most institutional investors do not take on construction risk—for reasons of risk aversion, missing skills, and lack of mandate—strip green bonds of some of their leverage to fund a transition up-front.

Patchy 'Greenium' for Issuers in Emerging Markets

Yet not only investors, but also issuers struggle to cash in on green bond benefits in emerging markets. As the third bullet for benefits of green bonds indicates, in the CBI's green bond report on South Africa (CBI & Agora Energiewende, 2021) "[g]reen bonds can attract a lower cost of capital" (p. 3). According to the report, this purported benefit is derived from an earlier CBI study (Harrison, 2021) and focused on US$ and EUR-denominated bonds. The report goes on to argue that green bonds,

> tended to attract larger book cover and spread compression during the book-building process, which can allow issuers to squeeze the pricing, potentially to the point of achieving a '*greenium*' (a *greenium* occurs when the green bond prices inside the yield curve and results in cheaper cost of capital for the issuer). While the analysis is based on the most liquid part of the market, there are multiple anecdotal examples of local currency bonds achieving tighter pricing than expected. (CBI 2021, p. 3)

The question whether a *greenium*, and thus a monetary benefit for issuers, actually materializes in South Africa is somewhat contested. As the report itself acknowledges, anecdotal evidence exists. An employee of the JSE's secondary trading unit provides said examples upon reviewing the latest bond issuances on his screen:

> I think the pricing is always better. Just using the Growthpoint as an example. Their five-year note was five basis points better than their last vanilla issue. And their seven-year note was one basis point better than their last issue. And even when you look at the subscription, just the overall subscription, the management of that company came out to say that they believe that the oversubscription to the issue is a result of it being green. (JSE Representative 3, p. 10: 467)

His colleague, the head of the sustainability segment, seconds with another example:

> What I understood from the Cape Town example, it provided a unique opportunity for comparison: because the time the City of Cape Town did their issuance, the [unclear, another company] did at the same time: similar credit rating, all else being equal, Cape Town was oversubscripted on the green bond. So firstly, the quality of the debt, as the first pass, was the same between the two. The issuance happened at the same time which gave an absolutely unique opportunity to compare. The only differentiator was the one was green and the other one wasn't. And Cape Town got the oversubscription, I think it was between 4 or 5 times. And they also saw attacking of the spread, i.e. they came in under what the guidance was on the pricing. (JSE Representative 2, p. 10: 467, 1504)

As pointed out earlier, these examples do not extend beyond anecdotal relevance. Even this second comparison of issuances extends across
two *different* entities (which affects the investors' risk perception) and
thus, does not reach the required scientific scrutiny as other studies (see
i.e. Harrison et al., 2020; MacAskill et al., 2021). Germany's so-called
Twin Bond issuance garnered lots of attention exactly for providing the
"dream case study" (Lester, 2021a), by simultaneously issuing a green
and a vanilla bond with otherwise matching market characteristics in all
but its size.

And as is often the case with anecdotal evidence, anecdotal counterevidence is also found, though a lot more muted. An interviewed economist
working with the African Centre for Cities in Cape Town recounts this
experience from the municipality of Ethekwini:

> The municipality was looking to garner a water bond in response to
> the drought in 2015. Due to previous bond issuance, the balance sheets
> and the know-how was there. Guaranteed offtake through various sub-
> municipal arms were also given. But when Old Mutual and Sanlam were
> approached as potential investors, their response was: 'Yes, we do want
> this novel financial tool.' But their wanted 13% interest. At the time, the
> municipality paid 11% for regular infrastructure bond. No financial gain.
> Only the schedule for payment as such is advantageous. (Civil Society actor
> 3, pos. 13)

Overall, the examples cited by my sources in South Africa neither validate
the *greenium* as an incentive for issuers to safe costs in the South African
context nor do they delve into the underlying reasons for particular price
mechanisms to take shape.

Zooming into Pricing Factors in South Africa's (Green) Bond Market
The pricing of (green) bonds results from supply and demand of said
bonds and their respective assessment through investors. The pricing
benefit for the issuer directly translates into a loss of revenue for
the investor. In the previous subsection, I alluded to the institutional
investors' lack of willingness to take a cut on returns to fund green
projects. Indeed, the important question around the *greenium* is whether
the green characteristics are actually a defining element driving down the
costs of capital for the issuer. To the former ICMA spokesperson and Old
Mutual investor, the answer is 'no'. That the city of Cape Town's green

bond was four times oversubscripted definitely signaled that "the pricing benefit sits on their end...because of the high demand in our markets" (Old Mutual Representative, pos. 167). This fact turns issuers if not into "price makers" that at least "price benefiters" (ibid., pos. 167). But he argues that the demand for the green bond does not stem from the green characteristics:

> And there, the yield wasn't reduced as a consequence of the greenness, the yield was reduced as a consequence of the fact that there's such a small amount of good quality, long issued paper in South Africa that when anything comes to market, that's long and it just gets/ everyone wants to buy it. [...]
>
> So, there's a general sort of low level of issuance in the market. So, anything that's coming to the market has got a lot of buyers, which you know I don't know whether the greenness had anything to do with the oversubscribed nature of it. I don't think it did. I just think it was just generally a desire for that kind of [tenured] paper, you know? (Old Mutual Representative, pos. 167, 174)

The domestic development bank representative agrees with this opinion and provides another argument as to what inhibits the effectiveness of green bonds in South Africa:

> So, in my opinion, green bonds are not effective in South Africa yet. Okay? And I say so for two reasons. [...] One is to attract or increase the investor base, in other words you're tapping into normal funds plus alternative investment plans. That is number one. And number two, it should also result in a more competitive pricing for the bond. Because of the nature of the being a green bond and having to be fitting into portfolios. Okay? So, those are the two reasons 'why a green bond', the advantages of green bonds. I mean besides, of course, the use for proceeds. [...] Now, in South Africa, those two characteristics do not exist. So, when Cape Town issue their green bond or when Joburg issued their green bond, they didn't attract any new investors. And I guarantee if they called it a black bond, a pink bond, or yellow bond, blue bond, they would have got exactly the same pricing, okay. So, what they were doing is they weren't actually banking the bond, they were banking Cape Town's balance sheet. (Development Bank Representative 1, pos. 5–13)

These two interconnected arguments achieve two things. First, they question whether the oft-cited examples of a successful *greenium* in the South

African context materialized due to its green credentials rather than the issuer's overall commercial credentials as a credit-worthy institution. They argue that a regular bond would have likely achieved a similar pricing. Indeed, Cape Town's praised green bond actually incurred a slightly higher pricing than their current cost of capital—approximately 10.17% versus 9.95% (Sullivan, 2020).

I was unable to verify whether Cape Town or Johannesburg did, indeed, diversify their investor base. The City of Cape Town report merely alludes to non-financial benefits including "conversations with [a] new mix of asset managers (26 bidders)" (ibid., p. 6). The diversification of the investors' mix, which is purported as a key motivation to issue green debt (CBI & Agora Energiewende, 2021; Maltais & Nykvist, 2020; Nanayakkara & Colombage, 2019; Ng & Tao, 2016), however, ultimately serves to bring down capital costs for the issuer. That the Cape Town green bond was "in fact more expensive" and that "[t]he funds, which you can get in the market is *(sic!)* much cheaper than what you will get from a green bond" (Municipal representative 2, pos. 7–8) underscores—at least in this case—that the *greenium* has not delivered.

As the senior capital market analyst at Nedbank concludes on a general note, "there is no obvious pricing benefit as yet for green" (Banker 1, pos. 33) in South Africa. And also Bridget Boulle from the CBI acknowledges in the webinar presenting South Africa's green bond report that "there's a lot of talk about pricing [...] but we are seeing much greater evidence of better pricing in liquid currencies so particularly US$ and Euros" (CBI webinar, 2021, p. 5: 930). The CBI's green bond report (CBI & Agora Energiewende, 2021) flags this issue:

> The incredibly low cost of debt capital seen across the developed world has led many commentators, including Climate Bonds Initiative, to note that now is the perfect moment in history to finance a green economy.
> Such conditions, however, do not exist across much of the developing world, including in South Africa. The yield curve comparison with the US demonstrates this with the yield for 5-year bonds for the South African sovereign at 6.8% compared to 0.361% for the USA. (p. 4)

Indeed, the yield spread of emerging market bonds is more pronounced than developed country bonds in global comparison. Currently, the 20 best vanilla bonds at the JSE, routinely captured in the index with the misnomer 'All-Bonds Index', trade at 8.8% (FTSE Russel, 2022) for tenures 7–12 years, whereas the bonds at S&P 500 Bond Index[2] (to pick a global index) produce an annualized return of 4.07% on a 10-year note, less than half that. The added risk premium does, in part, rest on the domestic capital market being denominated in Rands. Particularly foreign institutional investors are unlikely to shoulder the currency risk of investing in a rand-denominated market (Gabor, 2021; Volberding, 2021). Thus, green bonds have limited effect in subordinate capital markets (Kaltenbrunner & Painceira, 2015; Kvangraven et al., 2020).

The Old Mutual representative's statement on the issuer-friendly pricing stemming from the lack of investable options points to another more fundamental weakness of green bonds that deter it from gaining traction in South Africa and even beyond. As that same representative put it:

> There is nothing to preclude institution investors buying the green bond, but they wouldn't buy it on the basis of its greenness. They're going to buy it on the basis of the commerciality of the yield. So, it must compete, you know. (Old Mutual Representative, pos. 149)

This quote powerfully demonstrates not only the unconditionality of commercial viability of any project, but also speaks to Bracking's concern over separating environmental from economic return (Bracking, 2015; Jones et al., 2020). As things stand, market fundamentals seem to drive pricing on these bonds, whether vanilla or green. The 'performance' of the green attribute is separated from the economic performance and the latter prioritized over the former. Thus, irrespective of a largely anec-dotal discussion in South Africa, we may summarize that the *greenium* largely elides South African issuers, with the few ambiguous outliers dully noted. Thus, another key selling point of the green bond narra-tive has not materialized in this emerging market context, offering a CPE-informed explanation for the green bond market's stagnant growth. The next section delves deeper into pertinent narratives that accompany innovations, potentially helping them thrive.

---

[2] https://www.spglobal.com/spdji/en/indices/fixed-income/sp-500-bond-index/#ove rview.

THE STORY MATTERS—WHETHER IN THE ABSENCE OF SUCCESS STORIES OR THROUGH STORIES OF FAILURE ELSEWHERE

Innovative products benefit from success stories that serve as market benchmarks and kindle the interest of a market-in-the-making (Asiyanbi, 2018; Hajer, 1995; Lehmann, 2019). This subchapter focuses on the channels of information provision on the green bond market to then zoom in the stories in the (South) African context. Sometimes, failed attempts set as much an example as successful ones. We will cover both in this section.

To promote the expansion of a nascent market like green bonds, stakeholders and financial practices stretch far beyond the narrow set of immediate stakeholders to a green bond issuance, such as the issuers, underwriters, certifying agencies, a bond exchange, and investors. These market promoting practices range from information provision on market metrics to best practice handbooks (CICERO, 2021a; KfW, 2022), from webinars showcasing successful municipal green bond issuances (GGKP webinar, 2021) or the state-of-play in South Africa's green bond market (CBI webinar, 2021), and ideas to overcome bottlenecks to trainings on green finance tools, either free of charge (SEB & GIZ, 2021) or accessible via subscriptions (World Bank, 2016). Environmental finance, a leading magazine for financial practitioners in the green bond realm (Monk & Perkins, 2020), features annual award ceremonies with an ever-expanding list of prizes and winners (up from 11 in 2015 [Cripps, 2015] to 49 in 2020 [Lester et al., 2020]) for various innovations and drivers in the labeled bond market—subscribers are even encouraged to submit their nomination (Environmental Finance Awards Committee, 2021) for these awards. The discourse celebrates breakthroughs in size of market, with successive barriers successfully overcome and the next already being in plain side: US$5 trillion a year by 2025 (see Climate Bond Initiative's Twitter channel as of June 21, 2022).

On media outlets such as Environmental Finance and Responsible Investor, similarly, large single issuances are celebrated, new actors welcomed, and incumbents fed with market details in recurring market round-ups (Lester et al., 2021), database reports (Environmental Finance, 2021b), or newsletters (Kidney, 2021). Decisions to exclude issuers from indices are communicated and reasons provided to safeguard integrity

(Cripps, 2017). The discourse is, thus, not only about delineating *arguments* in favor of green bonds. More so, it is about the *channels* to transmit the core messaging of green bonds as funding the transition across as big an interested audience as possible. The different channels through which information and updates regarding market issuances and regulation are provided speak to the financial practices deployed to further the market and, thus, yield important examples for Chiapello's work (2020). Beyond the examples outlined above, these channels are also used to spread success stories around green bonds.

In a podcast, organized by the International Capital Market Association (ICMA), Christa Clapp, the CEO of the Center for International Climate Research (CICERO) a leading second-opinion provider on green bond certification (see last subsection in Sect. 3), recalls the most interesting bond issuances she witnessed the previous year. Her recollection serves as a good example of a success story aiming to shine a trajectory for the market. In this podcast, she refers to CICERO's annual best practice report as a "resource for market actors" featuring outstanding examples that will hopefully find "some replication" (C. Clapp podcast, 2020, pos. 8). After paying dues to the most promising sector (electric transportation) benefiting from green bond issuances recently (C. Clapp podcast, 2020, pos. 9), she recaps Grieg Seafood's green bond listing, a first move into aquaculture. Through the second-opinion process, the Norwegian company pressured its suppliers to prove they avoided deforestation, thus helping to reduce the company's scope 3 carbon footprint deep down its supply chain. As a result, they were awarded a medium-green rating (see CICERO, 2021b for its different 'shades of green' framework) and even made it into a Financial Times article (C. Clapp podcast, 2020, pos. 10; see Terazono, 2020). This example underscores the ingenuity to drive change deep down into a company's supply chain and advances into hitherto unchartered forays, in terms of both sector and scope 3 emission reduction. It serves as a perfect reference or success story to be emulated by the market in the future. Globally, noteworthy success stories are a key ingredient to channel the hype around a growing market into new outlets (Knuth, 2018). In South Africa, it is predominantly the municipal green bond issued in Cape Town that garnered international praise.

The Cape Town Bond—A Success Story

The global popularity of Cape Town's first green offering is linked to the contextual setting it addresses and ingenious marketing efforts. The green bond was issued in 2017 in the wake of water crisis afflicting Southern Africa more generally but also Cape Town in particular. The city barely avoided 'Day Zero'—when water supplies would empty out completely—in 2018 and only at great personal and societal costs (Water specialist at PDG Development Consultants in Cape Town). That the green bond specifically aimed at improving the dire water situation was praised across the globe. As Bridget Boulle observed in the CBI webinar:

> Particularly, the City of Cape Town [bond issuance] was picked up around the world. Obviously, the timing was quite good. It was in the middle of the water crisis. Everybody was talking about that not just in South Africa but all around the world. And then, the bond attracted a lot of attention with its resilience component so that was kind of something quite interesting. That was really before many resilience bonds had come out yet. (CBI webinar, 2021, p. 7: 560)

That the use of proceeds addressed such an imminent crisis upgraded the bond's standing. Combined with the auspicious timing, it showcased exactly what green bonds can be capable of: Providing the finance to avert climate-related crises. It was, thus, the timing and the urgency of the crisis that benefited the bond's reputation. One investor also referred to the palpably lower rainfalls, which have been "sporadic" and "unpredictable" in the country off late, and its effects on agriculture and food output, which the bond helped to address (Futuregrowth employee, pos. 66–70). She concludes:

> So, I think at a provincial level, the governments residing over the province recognize that there are big environmental risks that they need to start factoring in, into medium and long-term in terms of how cities are run. And I think the City of Cape Town is a very good example of a city that is thinking and planning in that way. It's a new way of thinking and a new way of planning. (Futuregrowth employee, pos. 71)

The City of Cape Town made the most out of its issuance. Mayor Patricia De Lille was cited for a roadshow of the bond (De Lille, 2017). The municipal media office published an article captioned with "Green Pays"

(City of Cape Town Media Office, 2017) and also the municipal treasury said, proper (double) accreditation and promotion were key to attaining good market rates for the bond (Municipal representative 1 and 2, pos. 25).

Yet, not only did that improve the bond's coupon structure for the city. It also enhanced its global reputation as a sought-after destination for capital (confer with Kong [2007] on the competition for capital between cities and Sassen [2005] on what makes a global city), especially among the C40 imitative, a network of big city mayors seeking to address climate issues (Civil Society actor 3, pos. 9–10). In the municipal treasury's own words, the bond demonstrated:

> That the city would like to support, not only in words, but indeed that it will fund climate orientated projects with the city's rates payers to fund. So, it is more to make a statement that they are serious in supporting the C40s objectives. And we then decided maybe we must look to make also the city's name, put it on the radar that we are all in support of that. So that was the sole driver of going through the green bond. (Municipal representative 2, pos. 7)

Crafting the right message is an important component of the green bond market. That also extends to the debate around the country's just transition, where success stories are tremendously needed to garner trade union (Fund Manager 1, pos. 73) and investor support (Civil Society actor 2, p. 8: 275). However, beyond the City of Cape Town bond, there aren't any noteworthy domestic green bond success stories to emulate. While Nedbank tested the waters with a retail green bond that banked the bank's balance sheets and was used to refinance existing portfolios (Banker 1, pos. 29), Johannesburg's earliest attempt at a green bond did not even steer global investor attention enough to raise eyebrows at Cape Town marketing its green bond "as the first African city bond" (Civil Society actor 3, pos. 10). In fact, Johannesburg issued their green bond beforehand, but only self-declared it as green without going through third-party accreditation (Development Bank Representative 2, pos. 10).

The Cape Town bond was neither remarkable in its size at ZAR1 billion (US$76 million) nor particularly innovative in the projects it was funding (water resilience and low-carbon transport). The Cape Town bond made headlines in financial circles around the world for the urgent crisis it addressed. It thus provided an important success story to refer to in order to justify the instrument and bolster the growth of the market. That green bond issuances can also garner criticism was made clear in the previous subsection. Here, I want to also juxtapose the need for success stories with the threat that accompany failed issuances and missed opportunities.

The Threat of a Failed Story: Reception of Nigeria's First Sovereign Bond

Nigeria wanted to become the first (!) sovereign to issue a green bond worldwide. Due to internal political conflicts that caused significant delays (Mullin, 2018), Poland snubbed away this informal but prestigious title in December 2016 (Cripps, 2016), being celebrated as the unexpected number one (Monk & Perkins, 2020) and even featuring as a case study in the CBI's sovereign green bond issuance handbook (Climate Bonds Initiative, 2017). It was, thus, Poland and not Nigeria that garnered the targeted visibility needed to diversify the country's investor base down the line. Nigeria, in turn, finally issued its inaugural green bond in December 2017,[3] valued at 10.8 billion naira (US$30 million) and becoming the first *African* sovereign to issue a green bond. Still the market reception was lukewarm at best.

The Environmental Finance commentator plauded the government's perseverance to operationalize its green bond framework and push through a green offering despite significant headwinds (Mullin, 2018). Amina Mohammed, the key driver in the Ministry of Environment, left the ministry to become the UN's Deputy Secretary General in February 2017. Persistent conflicts between ministries and lacking data capabilities, particularly on project risk assessment, further complicated and delayed the issuance process (Mullin, 2018). The Nigerian government had even gone the 'extra mile' by establishing a green bond Private–Public Sector Advisory Group, comprising government ministries, regulators, capital market agencies and the World Bank, IFC, AfDB, UNEP, and CBI. The bond ultimately obtained an excellent GB1 rating by Moody's. Despite

---

[3] Both France and the Fiji had issued sovereign green bonds in the meantime (Roumpis, 2018). By comparison and as per the Sustainable Bond Insight report (Environmental Finance, 2021a, p. 3), Germany was the largest sovereign green bond issuer with two issuances for a combined US$13,616 million.

these extra efforts, however, all these hurdles, the commentator argued, resulted in:

> a rather wonky and illiquid bond that from the outside looks short on green ambition, when Africa's largest economy could have tapped into rampant international demand for green product and funded its entire NGN150 billion program in one visit, was arguably a missed opportunity to create a capital markets splash. (Mullin, 2018, p. 2)

The mediocre size of the offering was perceived as "underwhelming" with investor response being "subdued" (ibid., p. 3). Given the fossil path dependency in the country, this offering "won't move the needle" on the country's NDCs (ibid., p. 4). The only consolation is that it may serve as a "catalyst" (ibid., p. 4) for further green bond issuances now that the framework has been tried and tested. The Nigerian sovereign has only issued one green bond since and of similarly small size (CBI, 2019, pp. 9, 16).

This example powerfully demonstrates the potential reputational risks that come along with expanding into unchartered territory, like green bond issuances. In Nigeria's sovereign issuance case, the country's reputation as a possible destination for foreign investment suffered rather than improved, even if the offering turned out slightly over-subscribed in the end. This exemplifies the importance of the reception of each bond. Some actors stand to gain significantly and even provide a success story that is repeated across the globe. But it can also result in a damning reception with little to gain apart from the loaned capital. This reputational risk attached to green bond issuances gains relevance in light of the high degree of risk aversion characterizing the South African investor landscape (see section "The Peculiarities of South Africa's Capital Markets Inhibit Green Bond Uptake"). It also explains why Nedbank tested the waters first by issuing a retail bond to set up the monitoring for the proceeds (see also the last subsection in section "The Peculiarities of South Africa's Capital Markets Inhibit Green Bond Uptake").

This section underscores the importance of success stories (Lehmann, 2019) as much as the unpredictability or risk of the green bond 'hype' (Knuth, 2018) unexpectedly turning favors (Fund Manager 3, pos. 66). It also demonstrates the relevance of cultural political economic approaches (Best & Paterson, 2010) that highlight exactly these undergirding pillars of yet to be established markets. Successful and innovative green bond issuances, like the Cape Town or Cargill's green bond, are celebrated in financial magazines and annual reports. They serve as reference points in the market. The market information provision upholds and powers the rising market trajectory adding interesting insights into how markets are created and bolstered (Chiapello, 2020; Tripathy, 2017). Beyond the attention industry, the conceptual setup of the financial innovation in question is also quite relevant for its success. We turn to these traits in the next section.

GREEN BONDS' NEED FOR SIMPLICITY CARRIES TRADE-OFFS

As section "The Purported Opportunities of Green Bonds Hardly Transpire in Emerging Markets" established, market fundamentals seem to drive pricing. That does not come as a surprise, given the great lengths standardizing institutions like the Climate Bonds Initiative go through to turn climate concerns into palatable metrics for the investor community and offering guidance for these markets in the making, as the previous section demonstrated. What's more, green bonds epitomize an attempt to cater to institutional investors with an instrument that is *recognizable* and offers traits they are comfortable with. This section deals with some conceptual components of green bonds and its resulting weaknesses.

The simplicity of the green bond with its ingenuity essentially boiling down to the earmarking of its use of proceeds for climate-aligned investments caters to investors' needs for metrics that can be pressed into risk-return matrices. This is particularly relevant in new climate-linked investment arenas like renewables where knowledge gaps deter investments. One developer puts it very bluntly:

And I think what we found for most of the fund managers is that they don't understand REI4P [the renewable energy auction program], they don't understand renewables, they don't, they're very risk averse. So, what they're looking at is a structure they can invest in where they've got the protections of JSE and everything else. (Developer 1, pos. 23)

He goes on to explain the investors' requirements in more detail:

So, they want it listed, rated, and [that it] also covers many mandates if you do that. So, we'd already budgeted to get a reduced rating for our green bond to be listed on the JSE. And then we would have an asset management function as well which would manage the assets like a typical bank would have managed their lending in the same way as an independent party. So that the fund managers are comfortable that we just have one point of entry to talk to. So, they could understand that. So, that's, we're busy with that structure, we know how to do it. But it's all about making it easier for a fund manager because traditionally, they're very risk averse and they're very lazy. So, they want one document a month, they want to know what their returns are, they don't want to hear from you again. (Ibid., pos. 23)

Although a tongue-in-cheek statement, other green bond stakeholders do support this assertion, albeit from the opposing investor perspective. Whether praised as pursuing a "known pathway" by CBI's Bridget Boulle (CBI webinar, 2021, p. 9: 1927) or arguing that "this simplicity [of the green bond concept] has been key to its success" (CBI & Agora Energiewende, 2021, p. 3), green bonds are simple *by design* in order to be the marketable product investors are willing to take up. In that sense, one can add 'simple' to 'boring' (Bigger & Millington, 2019) as key credentials that—though negatively connoted in a general sense—drive home the message of green bonds advantages over riskier and more complex alternatives. Simplicity thus morphs into a key selling point used by green bond proponents.

The JSE conjoins this simplicity of the green bond structure with the constraint for bankability. Upon prompted with a story of an institutional investor who had canvassed institutional investors on green bonds yielding in not one being willing to compromise on return, the leader of the green segment retorted:

> JSE Rep 2: Yes, that is true. But that is what we said up-front. It has got to meet our vanilla bond criteria firstly.
> [author]: So is it in a sense an add-on that investors would not compromise in terms of...
> JSE Rep 2: Return, yes. The point to make there is of course that you have a very broad set of investors, right. Investors vary in terms of what their returns profile is, what each one's requirements are. [...] So, I think we would first map out the characteristics of the return profiles of the investors to instill whether this is suitable or not. Our market certainly, remember this is a listed instrument,

which would still meet our market criteria of a vanilla bond first.
(JSE Representative 2, p. 8: 604)

A green bond, thus, must meet requirements of a vanilla bond to be
eligible for funding. However, this very simplicity that seeks to lure
in institutional investors carries drawbacks that are visible in the South
African context and beyond. I will touch on six conceptual limitations,
namely the lack of actual innovation, the questionable resilience of market
actors amid crises, technical shortcomings, the missing ability to sanction
against green default, the lack of impact and charges of greenwashing. As
will become clear at the end of this section, these shortcomings substantiate the concerns raised in the literature around financialization but also
explain its limited progress.

The Lack of Actual Innovation

Pursuing a trodden path with green bonds has its downsides. As a fund
manager cheekily comments, green bonds remind him of an

> Ostrich feather commodity [chuckles], maybe slightly exotic now...but
> there is nothing in the [green bond] market that is fundamentally new.
> It is the same old-fashioned techniques to address these challenges. (Fund
> Manager 3, pos. 67)

Referring to blended economics as a sideshow that never get treated on
a like-for-like basis, he comments on carbon tax with these words:

> It is unlikely, similar to green bonds, to fundamentally drive behavior. What
> is driving behavior is worries about quality of supply, uncertainty around
> costs of electricity from Eskom [the national energy utility], for example.
> These tools may influence decisions but won't be the starting point. They
> serve as incentives and nudges to make decisions. But carbon tax in a 20
> year horizon of a developer will not be relevant. Especially in developing
> countries there isn't a political will to get the price on carbon big enough
> to fundamentally change behavior due to the risk of losing competitiveness.
> (Fund Manager 3, pos. 70)

Though his comments are very insightful also with regard to the political
will preventing a loss of competitiveness in favor of more environmentally stringent guidelines (which we will touch on below when discussing

South Africa's green bond taxonomy and its 'right to develop'), he also argues that green bonds just like the carbon tax lack the punch to drive investment decisions. He, thus, seconds the institutional investor's earlier refrain that market fundamentals dominate investment decisions over green performance. The merit of green bonds ultimately lay in its exotic guise that appeal to buyers with particular ESG commitments (Fund manager 3, pos. 56). The hype around these instruments is volatile and may as quickly dissipate as it appeared (Fund manager 3, pos. 66).

An equally important drawback of the simple design of and lack of innovation around the green bond concept is well-captured by this truism: Green bonds are still bonds. Or as one interviewee puts it, "[i]t is still just debt by another name" (Civil Society actor 3, pos. 12). That means, if you don't have the balance sheet to entice investors, it is not going to work. It is still tied to the market fundamentals that enable those to benefit from the instrument that are already better positioned (Bigger & Millington, 2019) and, thus, does not bring anything fundamentally new to the table, apart, of course, from creating a green capital market outlet.

The Questionable Resilience of Market Actors Amid Crises

The CBI avers that "green bonds offer a competitive advantage at a time of instability" (CBI & Agora Energiewende, 2021, p. 4). They base this claim on research demonstrating the crisis proneness and resilience green bonds enjoy in capital markets, at least in comparison with vanilla bond. In a webinar, CBI's Brigdet Boulle recounts the "emerging evidence of better liquidity" during the Covid-19 pandemic; when the market ground to a halt in March and April 2020, investors feedbacked that "they were still able to transact green bonds when they weren't able to transact very much else" (CBI webinar, 2021, p. 5: 1151). Sean Kidney concurs later in the webinar:

> The green transformation is effectively providing a damper to volatility we have an increased volatility in bond markets right now globally but we see very clearly the green bond mark green bonds are less volatile which is very useful for investors as well as treasuries because of the belief in these things are going to be lower risk going forward and I think that's a clue in the last 10 years we've seen a switch from green transformation investments as being seen as high risk and scary to actually being precursors of change

coming through and, therefore, lower risk because they're less likely to be impacted negatively by policy changes. (CBI webinar, 2021, p. 22: 2406)

The CBI's own issuance data, however, add an important caveat to these observations. Since Covid-19 became a global pandemic, growth came largely through public sector issuers while private sector volumes either remained static or shrunk (CBI & Agora Energiewende, 2021, p. 7), supporting the notion that the confidence of private issuers plummets in times of crisis. The supply of bonds can, thus, skew towards the public sector during crises. In 2020 alone, South Africa witnessed a net outflow of portfolio investments of US$2.2 billion largely attributable to the Covid-19 pandemic (AfDB, 2022, p. 27). In addition, green bond funding is currently biased towards mitigation rather than adaptation as these projects lend themselves more readily for business models that require returns on investment, but do not curtail ramifications of climate impacts, a "blind spot" identified by the Presidential Climate Committee (CBI webinar, 2021, p. 19: 2444) that must be addressed through other means.

In very general terms, market actors require a certainty for their investments that transition endeavors of the envisioned complexity do not offer. A Nedbank capital market employee fittingly says in response to why the inconducive macroeconomic context had led to the failure of one of the bank's sustainability initiatives between 2012 and 2015, "unfortunately, there is never a right time for change: In good times, people say: 'Don't rock the boat', in bad times, they say: 'we have got to stop the bleeding, first'" (Banker 3, pos. 15). For green bonds, we thus need to differentiate between corporate bonds and public sector bonds, wherein the latter are likely to be more crisis resilient than the former.

Technical Shortcomings

Technical hurdles also inhibit green bond diffusion. The main technical challenge for issuers is to credibly prevent green bond proceeds from ending up in the issuer's general revenue pool (Service Provider 1, pos. 21). This challenge inhibits unexperienced actors from entering this space in the first place and evokes concerns of greenwashing in case issuers do not properly track and segregate proceeds on the other. This fungibility of proceeds certainly presents a gateway for criticism especially when the issuing entity operates in energy-intensive industries.

Another more technical limitation of the use-of-proceeds model is its lack of scalability. The anticipated returns are calculated up-front and up- and downside risks assessed. The sustainability chief of staff of one of the institutional funders argues:

> So, the project finance model, all of these things get dealt with *before* you actually go through financial close. By the time you go through financial close its like there is the runway. It's set, okay. But there are pros and cons, the pros are that you've managed a whole lot of risk upfront. The downside with project finance is that it is not scalable in other ways. There is no way of increasing your returns over time. You have already modeled your return for twenty years, that's going to be the return, okay. Whereas with other kinds of businesses that are on private equity capital, private equity guys go into them, and they say how can I scale this business so I am buying a software business, but I can actually scale it so there's a whole huge upside on the return. [...] So, in other words you know what the runway looks like already. (Fund Manager 2, pos. 190–192)

Thus, in their very setup, green bonds present hurdles for unexperienced issuers that may spook environmentally inclined investors and prescribe hard limits on the scalability of the green bond-funded projects. Both undermine green bond diffusion in very general terms.

The Lack of Sanctions in Case of a Green Default

One of the biggest conceptual limitations of green bonds deals with enforceability and oversight. Indeed, as the literature on green bonds (Mihàlovits & Tapaszti, 2018; Talbot, 2017; Wang, 2018) identified, sanctioning the issuer on missing climate goals, re-budgeting proceeds or not complying with reporting requirements can scarcely be addressed.

The leader of the green segment at the JSE provides an illustrative example:

> So, you have had an issuer, you have had a bond in the market now for three years. Come year 3, they don't report on the use of proceeds, or in fact they find that they haven't used the money the way they should have and they have gone and used it for something else. Now, what recourse does the investor have in that regard? And in fact, what is the issuing authority, the issuing regulator going to do about that? This is the question across the board. So, the basic thing is that right now you first sanction

that the JSE could apply is to remove the green status, to no longer list that bond on the green segment, because you're no longer applying the criteria. But we are not going to de-list the bond, because the bond is still functioning, still giving the return, still doing everything else it should do. But what it is not doing is fulfilling the green mandate. So, in terms of sanction, I think across the green bond market, it is quite limited. (JSE Representative 2, p. 9: 2348)

The JSE representative concedes the limited recourse for investors in the event of a so-called green default. By emphasizing that the bond will not be de-listed from the exchange, the representative readily rids herself of the only meaningful punishment in her armory. This lack of credibly sanctioning the issuers beyond reputation damage in sustainability circles powerfully underscores Bracking's critique of green bonds separating environmental from economic return (Bracking, 2015; Jones et al., 2020). It foreshadows the third conceptual limitation around the gulf between green label and sustainable outcome.

The Missing Impact from Green Bonds

The lack of outcome or impact generated from greening finance is bemoaned by most NGOs active in this realm. Asked whether she shares the widely held critique of investors focusing on attaining a green label more so than on green outcomes, the interviewee of an NGO advocating for the greening of the financial sector in South Africa answers:

Yes, definitely. People always take the easy way out and also the investor community in general is not trained or set up to care about the real-world outcome of their investment. They are trained to care about the investments that they get from them. So, there will always be a tendency to be happy with a box ticking regardless of the outcome and I don't think that it is possible to completely eradicate that ever because it happens with every single kind of attempt that has ever been made to improve these things. (Civil Society actor 2, p. 14: 7)

Similarly, another NGO's representative bemoans the lack of capacity to not only blend finance but also outcomes. He cites the example of plastic pollution on Tanzania's beaches, whose clean-up would benefit many parties, whether the local recycling industry, the tourism industry or the (local) government. Yet, "there is a lack of capacity to convene the table around this kind of issue. No one is blending outcomes. The same holds true for green bonds" (Civil Society actor 3, pos. 15–16).

Against the backdrop of looming construction risk and the lack of new bankable projects, the main opportunity for green bonds in South Africa lays not so much in funding projects up front but in refinancing loans once projects have completed construction. The head of the green segment at the Johannesburg Stock Exchange (JSE) says as much:

> The green bonds can equally be used for things like refinancing of solar or renewable energies. So that is another pocket where there is big opportunity potentially. And we have always been cited as having one of the most successful renewable energy programs in the world. And the green bonds, particularly provide one of the options for refinancing on REI4P [renewable energy tender] projects. (JSE Representative 2, p. 5: 3221)

If done correctly, refinancing, however, merely reduces borrowing costs for developers who constructed their project and now look for options to reduce capital costs—rightly so, since major risk concerns that were priced into the loan have not materialized. But, in the cases of refinancing, green bonds do not directly offer additionality (Jones et al., 2020; Schneeweiß, 2019) as no new products are geared as a direct result of listing the bond. It is merely recycling the developers' balance sheet, a reason for more adamant critiques to view refinancing with green bonds as mere "greenwashing" (Development Bank Representative 1, pos. 29):

> Why do I say that is all they're doing is they're taking existing projects, okay? And they're refinancing them through a green bond. So, tell me where is the benefit for South Africa Inc.? Where are we creating any new green projects? Because those projects are already funded. Okay? All they're doing is refinancing probably the lower rates and then the long tenure existing projects. In my mind, if you're going to issue a green bond, okay? Is to do new projects. Okay? Is to reduce carbon emissions or adapt to climate change or whatever. But to me to just issue a bond on an existing portfolio is just cynically a way of refinancing an existing portfolio. And in the process, those projects are done anywhere. The greening has taken place. (Development Bank Representative 1, pos. 29–31)

This lack of impact or additionality when green bonds are used for refinancing is certainly a concern (see, e.g., Schneeweiß, 2019). The fact that it frees up capital on the developer's balance sheet, which can then be re-invested into new and additional carbon-saving projects, is only a partial consolation that is contingent on factors outside of the direct purview of green bonds. That is the main reason why the IDC, for example, do not do refinancing, as they measure themselves against other social criteria such as job creation and want to expand the industrial base (IDC employee, pos. 118–122).

Green Bonds and Omnipresent Concerns Around Greenwashing

Concerns of greenwashing (Mihàlovits & Tapaszti, 2018; Talbot, 2017; Wang, 2018) have accompanied the market since its inception. It is a frequent overarching topic in the environmental finance analysis section, as remedies range from voluntary guidelines leaving it to investors to choose themselves to rigid standardization that would protect the label against more lenient interpretations (see next section 3 on the environmental finance coverage below).

Third-party accreditation of the bond is a standardized means to enhance the credibility of the offering. A key role in mitigating perception of greenwashing is played by second-opinion providers, such as the CBI, Moody's, McKinsey, Sustainalytics, CICERO and others. In order to make the decision to invest in their green bonds easier, one of the South African municipalities even got a double accreditation from CBI and Moody's, the latter of which merely assessing the "readiness to issue a green bond" giving the investors

something more in terms of that they have done their homework and their research that it is towards a green project. I think investors when we present them with the Moody's report, they were quite happy... [His colleague adds:] Because you see probably then a lot of investors do not have your CBIs, they all know who Moody's is. (Municipal representative 1 and 2, pos. 19–20)

This exemplifies the efforts issuers go through to bridge the nascency of the market and entice investors to enlist by referring to assurances of a reputable actor in this space (here Moody's).

When pressed as to why a(nother) developer solicited two external reviews, despite the additional costs, the respondent argued that they support market development:

> We went to them all and the big fund managers said, 'Just use Moody's because we understand them and we know they understand the market'. They've done rating before on renewables and the others were kind of still developing their strategies. [...] But what we wanted to do is prudent to the market on the auction basis so they could compete with it. (Developer 1, pos. 26–35)

Developers can, thus, leverage their rating through external revenues to sow competition among a wider array of institutional investors, thus opening up the green bond market and trimming capital costs. But they must signal their market readiness through third-party assessments.

This reliance on 'external experts' (Ferguson, 1994) to lend credibility to green aspects of a market-in-the-making is also practiced at the JSE. As the head of the green segment herself puts it:

> So, we at JSE recognized that we aren't experts on determining what is green. And we leave that to the experts. So in that regard, the requirements that are built into the list, there is a person who is providing that third party verification and assurance needs to have demonstrated a lot of work in that space, sufficient experience in order to be able to give a reliable opinion that they are now saying: We are of the opinion that this issuance and what it is going to be used for qualifies as green and is not something dodgy. So that is part of the verification. (JSE Representative 2, p. 4: 1650)

Still, third-party auditing and accreditation in the green finance realm is not sacrosanct, due to definitional vacuum of what is considered green and the prevailing conflicts of interests between sustainability officers and project managers at the fund's level and between second-opinion providers and issuers more generally. The imprecise definitions of what possibly denotes a green bond (see subsequent section) leave lots of room for discretion at the hands of third-party providers. Already in 2020, Christa Clapp, the CEO of the Norway-based second-opinion provider CICERO, admitted that though the environmental principles negotiated under the EU taxonomy at the time "is in alignment with our thinking. But as an external reviewer, we will be stretched in terms of some of the interpretation of this. It does require a fair amount of interpretation to meet this do no significant harm under this taxonomy" (C. Clapp podcast, 2020, pos. 15). One such set of criteria is CICERO's continuously updated so-called Shades of green approach (CICERO, 2021a, 2021b). Therein, it delineates different degrees of sustainability, measured against reaching a low carbon and climate-resilient future. These range from improving energy efficiency in fossil fuel industries on the lower and 'lighter' spectrum to plug-in hybrid busses in the medium-green and wind parks in the 'dark' green and most aligned segment. Through these forms of definitions, market actors contribute to categorizing the market and supplementing sustainability with a more nuanced meaning which ultimately contributes, once again, to 'translating' climate concerns into criteria readily understood by financial market actor (Tripathy, 2017). Though she predominantly cites the lack of available data as a key challenge in meeting the company's mandate (C. Clapp podcast, 2020, pos. 14), this discretion at interpreting data to drive the market mirrors the practices identified at the CBI, namely to come up with climate benchmarks and criteria transferable into the institutional investors' realm (Tripathy, 2017).

Beyond definitional sponginess, commercial interest trade off with environmental due diligence, whether at firm level or between issuers and second-opinion providers.

The lead in sustainability matters at one investment fund, for example, likes to externalize ESG due diligence because of lack of internal bandwidth (only three people on the team) and to minimize conflicts of interests as their salaries are paid upon making an investment. In his words, "we have to do deals to get a salary so that creates a conflict of interest" (Fund Manager 2, pos. 170). Still, he says, in board meetings when investments are signed off, he must act as a gatekeeper:

> I mean in these situations the ESG professional walks a slightly different line to some of the other professionals in the business so an ESG professional has to understand that they walk this link of being both player and referee okay and it's not an easy space to walk, you've got to be prepared that when there is a red flag and you say guys I now I have to put on my referee hat and say actually guys we either don't do the deal or we have to close this out otherwise the deal can't go through. So, you have to act as a gateway [...] you make sure that all the environmental, and social legal clauses are getting negotiated into those agreements and that's critical. (Fund Manager 2, pos. 170)

The role of the ESG manager exemplifies that pursuing environmentally friendly conduct can clash with business interests. His claim that externalizing due diligence "removes this conflict [of interest] completely" (ibid., pos. 14) does not necessarily hold up. As Christa Clapp of

CICERO explains, rating agencies walk this "balancing act" of facilitating "quick responses" (whether to Covid-19 or climate change) whilst making sure to not "do significant harm" (C. Clapp podcast, 2020, pos. 21). That these service providers differ in 'opinions' is apparent when a second-opinion provider rejects a firm's green bond proposal only to see its accreditation at another firm's monetary benefit, a conflict not only afflicting the green space, but any other sector within the rating industry space (see Viegas [2017] for an environmental finance critique and Sinclair [2010], for a more academic critique of rating agencies during the global financial crisis). That CICERO had in place exclusivity deals with SEB and HSBC up until 2016 as per environmental finance (Ludvigsen, 2016) adds additional concern regarding conflicts of interest of supposedly independent reviews.

Beyond conflicts of interest, the poor track record of verifiers in the carbon market had already set a precedent for distrust (Ludvigsen, 2016). Whether the intensifying concentration of the green rating market around Sustainalytics, ISS ESG, and CICERO (Environmental Finance, 2021a, 2021d) exacerbates these conflicts of interests and thus increase risks of greenwashing for the green bond market remains to be seen. What has been demonstrated is that increased competition among rating agencies benefits issuers and investors (Braun et al., 2018; Morkoetter et al., 2017), which will likely draw the shorter end of the stick at the end of these developments. Still, with Augusto & Co, a leading Pan-African Credit Rating Agency, was recently added to Climate Bond's list of approved verifiers (Climate Bonds Initiative, 2022a). The bourgeoning industry around certifying climate alignment exemplifies the struggles of the green bond market to assuage concerns of greenwashing. Given the limited impact and lack of sanctions in cases of a green default, there is certainly room to improve (for a more recent financial innovation, see next section).

This part of the chapter delved into the conceptual setup of green bonds. To advance and safeguard the expansion of the market, green bonds are deliberately kept simple to appeal to investors. Cushioned by second-order opinions of reputable rating agencies, they seek to signal credible investment opportunities for risk-averse investors. Still, their simple setup also carries limitations. I covered its limited influence on investment decisions, market actor limitations, a few technical hurdles, the lack of imposable sanctions (i.e. in case of a green default), the missing impact, and the limited assurance external experts can actually provide to investors.

SOUTH AFRICA'S TAXONOMY RISKS PERCEPTION OF GREENWASHING IN INTERNATIONAL MARKETS

Though Monk and Perkins (2020) did a great job in explaining the diffusion of the green bond concept by tracing developments globally, they ignored important aspects. The contested discourse accompanying these developments is fought out between different factions of the finance community around the definition of 'green' investments, its regulatory framework, and the eligibility of 'dirty' actors. We'll touch on these debates briefly to set the scene for and better understand the rationales underpinning South Africa's national sustainable bond taxonomy—and why these decisions will likely inhibit international buy-in into South Africa's green capital markets.

Contested Inroads in the Global Labeled Bond Market

Despite the success story of green bonds on the global stage and its unabated rise even amidst the Covid-19 crisis, the green bond discourse is not without its own controversies. Skimming through the Environmental Finance green bond updates and analysis sections (2014–2021) discloses some disagreements that green bond market actors publicly wrestle with. Globally, the debate of what counts as 'green' has been ongoing for quite a while (Environmental Finance, 2015) and recently reached a climax in the European context, when the European Commission published a proposed green EU taxonomy, that also includes labeling investments in gas and nuclear energy as green under certain circumstances, thanks to lobbying efforts by some EU member states (see Elsner, forthcoming, on the nuclear debate). Interestingly, these debates seem to gain steam whenever new sustainability-labeled bond issuances tend to threaten the integrity of the market.

As early as 2014, greenwashing became a major concern in the green bond market. 118 civil society groups including the CBI and BankTrack urged UN Secretary General at the time, Ban Ki-moon, in a letter that "green bond-funded projects must adhere to high social and environmental standards", in order to avoid "greenwashing private investment" (Robinson-Tillett, 2014, p. n/a). The letter came in response to green bonds being used to finance socially and environmentally destructive dams (ibid.). These concerns mirror the academic concerns evident in the financial practitioners' realm on ensuring market credibility.

Debates around greenwashing continued to flare up whenever controversial green bond issuances were floated. In 2015, Unilever used green bond proceeds merely to fund more energy efficient manufacturing plants in an otherwise sensitive industry. After critiques argued this behavior invited businesses to label business-as-usual investments as green (Environmental Finance, 2015; Holtedahl et al., 2015), it was removed from Barclay's MSCI green bond index. This was the start to a fierce debate about standardization versus voluntary guidelines, and a debate about stringent and exclusive 'pure-play' criteria versus more lenient interpretations of what should be considered green (Buchta, 2018; Claquin & Buchta, 2015).

In 2017, Repsol, the Spanish oil and gas giant raised eyebrows when receiving the go-ahead by Vigeo Eiris (the fifth largest second-opinion provider [Environmental Finance, 2021a, p. 36]) for a green bond, mainly because the bond would result in more investment in carbon-intensive production, albeit on a slightly more energy efficient footing (Viegas, 2017). That other second-opinion providers had declined verification, including Sustainalytics, did not stop the bond from being significantly over-subscripted, indicating investors' demand (ibid.). While the underwriting banks (including HSBC, NBP Paribas and Goldman Sachs) were faced with allegations of collusion around corporate greenwashing, the issuance spawned a debate about the direction of the market. Essentially, the controversy revolved around how much 'green' does a 'brown' company need to add to become part of the green bond community? A widely held compromise was reached by specifying the "ambition" that green bonds should align with the targets of the Paris Agreement, which is mirrored in the standards set by the Climate Bonds Initiative (CBI), among others. Due to prolonging the life of its refineries, the CBI ultimately red-carded Repsol's bond even though it funded a reduction of 1.2 million tons of CO_2 equivalent emissions, thus ending this episode (Cripps, 2017).

Still in 2017, the first SDG-linked bonds were issued. The World Bank raised US\$163 million in March with the HSBC following suit with a US\$1 billion bond in November (Environmental Finance, 2017). This time, concerns were raised around the proliferating labels that may inhibit issuers and investors entering the market given the lack of structure and oversight. By October 2018, Manulife insurers, for example, called onto market regulators to strike "a delicate balance not to obstruct [green bond market] growth through overregulation" (Hurley, 2018, p. 3); their refrain was to "keep it simple" (ibid., p. 1).

In 2019, Italian oil and gas distribution firm Snam and Marfrig, a Brazilian beef patty producer, issued what they termed a climate action bond, both of which divided opinion (Hurley, 2019). One fund manager opposing Snam's green listing referred to the energy efficiency assets in natural gas as a red flag, whereas Stephanie Sfakianos, the head of the sustainable capital markets at BNP Paribas argued it is "an enormously positive initiative" that encourages the oil and gas sector to reduce its climate impact (Cripps, 2019a). She went on to propose a new label for dirty industries, thinking of these kinds of bonds not so much as green but rather "transition bonds" (ibid., p. 3). In June of that year, AXA investment managers even produced a first set of guidelines for transition bonds taking a 1.5 °C world as their baseline (Takatsuki & Foll, 2019) in order to prevent the undermining of the green bond market. Their proposal was soon superseded by ICMA's handbook on transition bonds, last updated in December 2020 (ICMA, 2020). Sustainalytics even started its own separate second party opinion provision for transition bonds (Cripps, 2020). Beyond the controversies that accompanied the climate focused bond issuances of 'dirty industry' players, it did inaugurate a shift in market focus away from use-of-proceeds towards sustainability impact and performance. Issuers now have to prepare emission targets they will avail through the bond funding.

This shift marked a new milestone, when Enel issued the first sustainability-linked bond (SLB) in September 2019. Therein, their coupon was indexed to sustainability targets assessed half-way through the tenure, subjecting the bond's coupon rate to a hike of 25 percentage in case objectives are not met (Cripps, 2019b). Interestingly, the bond no longer uses the use-of proceeds model (the original innovation of green bonds) but is benchmarked against key performance indicators (KPIs) at company level, thus being more akin to equity than debt.

Advocates of these new kinds of sustainability-linked bonds, in turn, argue that they should be seen as complementary to traditional green bonds, allow for strategic alignment, do not diminish available green bond assets, and put greater emphasis on impact (Michaelsen, 2019). Under-pinning these restructuring of the labeled bond market is the idea to open up the market for 'brown' sectors, such as metal and mining, and to give them a roadmap to greener futures (see also CBI employee Manuel Adamini, 2019).

Still, given the increasing proliferation of bond labels raised concerns over labels infringing on each other's market shares and unduly fragmenting a still nascent market. As things stand, there are labels for transition bonds, KPI-linked bonds (also referred to as sustainability-linked bonds), social and Sustainable Development Goals (SDG) bonds, but names such as resilience bonds, blue bonds, circular economy bonds (Cripps, 2020) and even rice bonds (Marchant, 2019), Rhino (Sguazzin, 2022), and Masala or Biltong bonds (Banker 1, pos. 15) have also emerged—with an even greater array of social bond labels. By the end of 2020, ICMA had five different sets of bond principles and guidelines in place that had been updated no later than two years before (Lester, 2021b, p. 2).

With the labeled bond market maturing globally, issuances of transition bonds slacked in comparison with KPI-bonds (Cripps, 2021; Lester & Marchant, 2021). The Environmental Finance Transition Bond database covering the transition bonds until July 2021 lists 19 transition bonds having been issued globally for a combined US$8.75 billion. In comparison, the 'younger' sustainability-linked bonds raised US$9 billion in 2020 alone and attracted US$50 billion between January and August 2021. According to Environmental Finance's own database, transition bonds are very niche in comparison with the other sustainable bond labels, with transition bonds only garnered $4.3 billion in investment as opposed to $88 billion for sustainability-linked, $174 billion for sustainability, $188 billion for social, and $501 billion for green bonds (Lester, 2022, p. 2).

Many indeed argue that SLBs are better suited to drive transition dynamics than transition bonds, given the broader application, the better trackability of attained targets and the sanctions that could readily be implemented. Though certainly premature, Bram Bos at NN Investment Partners, averred "[Transition bonds] are really dying. We are all realizing vaguely-defined labels, like transition bonds, have no future" (Environmental Finance, 2021c, p. n/a).

Despite its significant growth in the last two years, sustainability-linked bonds (SLBs) are not bereft of greenwashing allegations either—far from it (see, e.g., Cripps, 2019b; Dupré, 2019; Lester, 2021b). When Indonesian food producer Japfa Comfeed issued its US$350 million SLB, it was three times over-subscribed and foresaw the company constructing eight water recycling facilities across its slaughterhouses. However, the KPIs were merely tight to installing the equipment rather than meeting a concrete reduction in CO_2 emissions—and neither was the coupon subject to a significant step-up were this target to be missed (Lester, 2021c). Why Vigeo Eiris opined the bond aligned with the SLBP is debatable and signals the conflict of interest of rating agencies in this realm (Sinclair, 2010).

I traced these issuances to underscore the contested nature of the green bond market-in-the-making (Asiyanbi, 2018; Hilbrandt & Grubbauer, 2020; Tripathy, 2017). Though plenty of new labels mushroomed since the inception of the market in 2007, each label heralds the same concerns for integrity, whether social or green. What exactly constitutes green remains hard to establish (Tripathy, 2017) and is subject to material interests (hence warranting a CPE lens found in Best and Paterson [2010] and Sum and Jessop [2013]), as the controversial issuances of energy-sensitive corporations and the debate about the EU Green Taxonomy (Elsner, forthcoming) powerfully underscore. Quite a similar debate of what is considered eligible under their green finance taxonomy simmers also in the South African context. We turn to South Africa's treatment of what makes a bond green in the next section and touch upon South Africa's need to incorporate energy-sensitive actors.

South Africa's Green Finance Taxonomy—A 'Living Document' for Transitioning Actors

Despite the recent focus on the tussle around the EU Green Taxonomy, the EU is by no means the only global actor to currently draft its standards for green investments, nor is it the first. China was the first country to adopt its own national green taxonomy (CBI & Agora Energiewende, 2021, p. 3) in 2015. The World Bank (2020) even launched its own guide to help countries develop their respective national taxonomies. Since launching its own green finance taxonomy on April 1, 2022, South Africa has entered an illustrious circle of countries with a taxonomy already in place (the EU, Japan, Malaysia, Mongolia, and, of course, China [Future of Sustainable Data Alliance, 2021]). The taxonomy is the latest development in a sequence of efforts to provide a green footing for capital market participants in South Africa (see also section "The Peculiarities of South Africa's Capital Markets Inhibit Green Bond Uptake" in this chapter). It is, nonetheless, the most interesting development and potential remedy to the hold-ups of green bond diffusion in South Africa. This section reiterates the journey the taxonomy has taken, charts out key rationales that underpin its creation, and briefly assesses its status quo.

Supported by the international Finance Corporation in partnership with the Swiss State Secretariat for Economic Affairs and the Swedish International Development Cooperation Agency (SIDA), and under the leadership of the National Treasury, the National Business Initiative and Carbon Trust developed and published a first draft of the green finance taxonomy in October 2020 (Carbon Trust/Treasury/NBI, 2020; National Treasury, 2022c). The initial impetus to draft a green finance taxonomy can be linked to a technical paper of May 2020 in which National Treasury explicitly recommends the creation and adoption of a domestic green finance taxonomy (National Treasury, 2020, pp. 6, 49).

In the GGKP webinar on green bonds in South Africa held in October 2021, Africa Director of Carbon Trust Christelle van Vuuren described the goal of this taxonomy as such:

> [T]his taxonomy sought to leverage the EU taxonomy development and there were various reasons around that we're an emerging market with significant FDI/ with the ambition to attract international capital increasingly. (GGKP webinar, 2021, pos. 1206–1213)

While the stated goal is to attract foreign investments into the country through a harmonized green framework, domestic capital market demands play a significant role, as the setup of the Taxonomy Working Group, which developed the draft, indicates. It features all the major domestic capital market associations as well as company heavyweights (National Treasury, 2022b, p. 14). The previous discussion of the global labeled bond market, furthermore, demonstrated that the devil lies in the 'green' details of the respective taxonomy. Quite analogous to the criteria at the green segment at the JSE (see section "The Peculiarities of South Africa's Capital Markets Inhibit Green Bond Uptake"), the balancing act between complying with international standards and carving out space for contextual flexibility has prevailed as Christelle van Vuuren infers when saying

> all of these standards developments, I think, at the end of the day, we're likely to quite strongly stick with what we see happening in the developed

markets, even as we contextualize it for our own needs. (GGKP webinar, 2021, pos. 1296–1301)

Given the fossil-based economic underpinning, it is unsurprising that the many capital market actors place hope on transition bonds. Shameela Ebrahim, a senior JSE representative, acknowledges that "the concept of transition [bonds] have come up a lot in the last few years" in the CBI webinar, simultaneously cautioning that investors perceive it as business-as-usual (CBI webinar, 2021, p. 7: 2855). Underscoring the Paris Agreement as a common goal, she emphasized the "different routes to get us there", flagging a JSE white paper in 2019 that sought to better capture the transition label (ibid.). This shift in moving from green use-of-proceeds bonds towards the more forward-looking bonds linked to reducing climate footprints of the issuers (CBI webinar, 2021, p. 8: 1341) is an understandable attempt which is also mirrored in graduating the green bond to a more encompassing sustainability bond segment (see subsequent section on the ambiguous role of the JSE in regulating this space).

Simultaneously, Ebrahim does note the increasing global concern around greenwashing which I outlined in the previous section as a key challenge, saying:

Issues around credibility, those are the things that are coming into vogue a lot more strongly now. One of the big concerns that we're seeing globally is the issues of greenwashing and so understanding the credibility of any of these anybody claiming to have green credentials, I think, is going to become more and more prominent. (CBI webinar, 2021, p. 11: 323)

Beyond dispersing fears of greenwashing, the interoperability of taxonomies is key. The EU-China Working Group (2021) addresses this concern in the China-EU context and epitomizes this need to enable frictionless green investment across taxonomies.[4] That is why CBI's Sean Kidney was pleased to announce in August 2021:

The good news is the taxonomy that the South African treasury put out for consultation is broadly in line with the European taxonomy. So, the

---

[4] Which, arguably, is lenient given China's taxonomy considers clean coal' investment solutions eligible under their green taxonomy (Ferrando et al., 2022).

interoperability looks very good which is going to make it much easier with international capital flows in terms of domestic capital flows. (CBI webinar, 2021, p. 19: 1037)

The interoperability thus renders green capital flows more commensurable (and probably also mobile) across jurisdictions, an important aspect for the growth of the market. For South Africa, interoperability would ensure the attraction of foreign investment, the stated overarching goal of South Africa's green finance taxonomy. Enhancing the mobility of green capital equivocally heightens the risk of investors shedding bonds during crises—the inherent instability is an important disadvantage to be borne in mind in emerging economies (Kaltenbrunner & Painceira, 2015; Karwowski & Stockhammer, 2017).

In preliminary terms, the draft (National Treasury, 2022d) that was launched on April 1, 2022, reflects the considerations outlined above in ingenious ways. According to one of four briefing documents (National Treasury, 2022b, p. 43) accompanying the launch of the taxonomy, the current draft taxonomy is a voluntary classification system that promises both a green taxonomy and a taxonomy for transitional activities. This latter taxonomy marks a new development globally, as none of the six taxonomies surveyed during the preparation of South Africa's green finance taxonomy offer a *comprehensive* dimension for transition activities, projects, or assets (National Treasury, 2022b, pp. 26–27). In this way, the Taxonomy Working Group skirts an important question: Whether the taxonomy shall be benchmarked against local policy or international best practice. By offering two taxonomies in one, the answer, apparently, is "both". In this way, the taxonomy tries to avoid an important trade-off. In the words of the policy brief:

> Should the taxonomy not be ambitious enough, then it risks deterring international investment; however, if the criteria and thresholds are too ambitious and stray far from local policy, then there is a risk that these will be challenging to implement, and economic activities become unachievable. (National Treasury, 2022b, p. 35)

The green taxonomy seems ambitious and in line with international best practice—though an intermediate verdict will only be reached when the IFC and the CBI complete their currently ongoing review regarding the taxonomy's alignment and interoperability with other taxonomies around the world. According to Sarah McPhail, the financial policy advisor at the National treasury who spoke at the launch event, roughly five percent of the current portfolio at the JSE would be considered green under the new draft taxonomy, making it rather ambitious (Author's Notes at Green Taxonomy Launch, 2022).

Simultaneously, by preparing a transition taxonomy, the draft incorporates domestic development and industry concerns raised in previously conducted surveys. These 'direct user surveys' compiled inputs from financial practitioners and other stakeholders regarding the scope, breadth, and depth of the envisaged taxonomy. Accordingly, there seems to be a strong user preferences for including transitional activities in the taxonomy and keeping those separate from green activities to avoid greenwashing (National Treasury, 2022b, p. 34). In this way, National Treasury safeguarded its position as a developing country and encouraged investments into 'transition assets', which treasury defines as "assets which might not be considered 'green' according to international best practice but form an important part of South Africa's development and decarbonization pathways" (National Treasury, 2022b, p. 36). This separate transition taxonomy targets activities that contribute to the

> phasing out of, for example, unabated fossil fuel-based activities, yet avoid activities that lock in such assets for fossil fuel purposes over the long term. This allows transition activities that have the potential to transform, for example, heavy fossil fuel industries such as energy. (National Treasury, 2022a, p. 43)

According to the policy brief, the six-week-long consultation process in June and July 2021 yielded more than 30 institutions submitted more than 440 comments, statements, recommendations, and queries during the drafting process (National Treasury, 2022b, p. 47). Along the drafting process, the taxonomy working group also received preliminary peer reviews from the CBI along questions of the draft taxonomy's usability, appropriateness, and coverage and from the European Union along questions of alignment and common approaches to its sustainable finance taxonomy (National Treasury, 2022b, p. 50).

According to the press release accompanying the launch (National Treasury, 2022e, p. 2), the current taxonomy should be understood as a "living document" that will be updated as the low-carbon transition of the economy more generally and the greening of the financial sector specifically progresses. This holds also true for sector-specific standardization of the taxonomy. So far, guidelines for buildings have been published to test market reception (National Treasury, 2022a); at time of writing (April through June 2022), a guidance for cement is in the making (Author's Notes at Green Taxonomy Launch, 2022).

This section demonstrated the careful balance South Africa tries to strike in order to ensure foreign investments. But it also showed how far financial regulators, chief among the National Treasury, go to incorporate the country's industrial base into a green finance taxonomy. The findings are thus in line with the context chapter's first main proposition that the persistence of the fossil dependence slows the development of green alternatives (see section "The Peculiarities of South Africa's Capital Markets Inhibit Green Bond Uptake" for further substantiation). As the taxonomy draft demonstrates, the re-engineering of domestic capital markets in global images (Gabor, 2021) comes with local strings attached. Two effects remain to be seen, one on investment and one on climate. Firstly, it will be interesting to see how investors will react to South Africa's double regulation and whether the goal of attracting foreign capital investments will be achieved. Secondly, regarding climate effects, it remains to be seen whether the transition taxonomy, in particular, can leverage change in energy- and CO_2-heavy industries or whether it will merely serve to bolster the status quo. With the transition bond concept not gaining steam globally, it seems questionable whether South Africa's transition taxonomy will make a difference or whether South African polluters are better advised to pursue KPI-linked bonds, instead. With a market on its toes and greenwashing widely perceived as the number one risk does at least justify a segregated approach. The green taxonomy mainly targets foreign investors whereas the transition taxonomy aims at domestic investors and issuers. Only after its adoption will detailed comparisons across different taxonomies make sense. These comparisons will yield concrete information on the different sets of criteria and the degree of flexibility pursued in the South African context. At least, the current taxonomy provides clarity on the direction the government wants its capital market to pursue and assures foreign as much as domestic interests are borne in mind. For interested investors and potential issuers, the taxonomy will be an important yardstick against to measure their investments and projects, respectively.

The Peculiarities of South Africa's Capital Markets Inhibit Green Bond Uptake

A discussion of green bonds is meaningless without delving into the particularities of the capital market in which these bonds are issued and traded. We will discuss the strengths of South African capital market first, namely its depth and mature legal framework, before delving into some bottlenecks that inhibit green bond uptake: The limited size of the market, its inherent fossil path dependence and risk aversion, limited understanding of green financial instruments, and the lack of regulatory incentives. As part of the latter, we take a concrete look at the JSE as a key actor in this space. I also zoom in on the country's renewable energy tender program, the major investment vehicle in the green transition, and discuss its merits with view to green bonds. In the end, we turn to (potential) green bond issuers and some attempts of DFIs to de-risk the market.

A Mature Regional Market at the Soft Currency Frontier

The former investment banker turned government advisor sums up the domestic capital market well: "We are a frontline soft currency emerging market" (RE Industry representative, pos. 34). The data second his assessment. As indicated in Fig. 5.1, South Africa is a unique case of emerging markets in that the vast majority (84%) of its bond issuances are denominated in South African Rands (ZAR). Emerging market actors more generally only issue about half of their green bonds in local currency. Excluding China, which heavily distorts the picture, it is even less than a quarter (see third column). South Africa is thus unique in its strong issuance of local currency bonds, which many emerging markets struggle with tremendously, and signals a strong local investor base (CBI webinar, 2021, p. 7: 1557).

By explaining his work, the senior capital market analyst of one major South Africa Bank charts out the values of this market:

We raise capital for our clients domestically in a very sophisticated debt capital market in South Africa. It is quite a unique system because it is a closed Rand-system. So, at any one time, any South African clearing bank holds the balance of Rand that is global. All comes back to Rand; all comes back to South Africa. We control a fishbowl. We are largely insulated, albeit

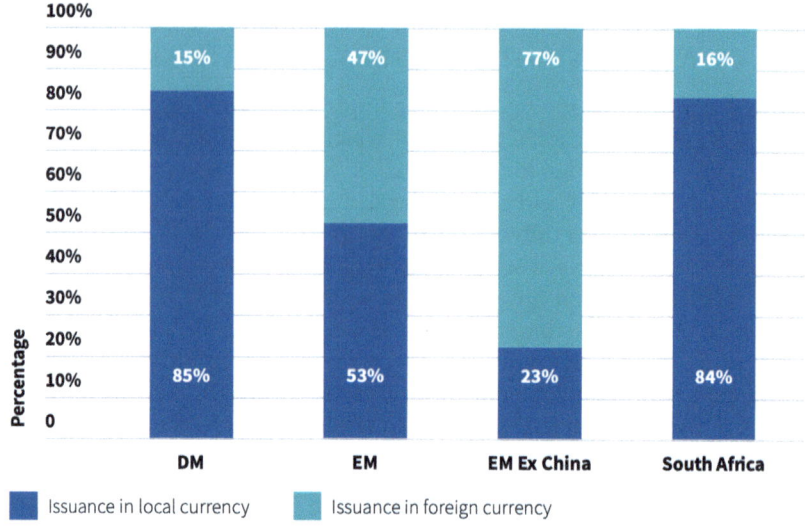

Fig. 5.1 Comparison of issuances in foreign and local currency (*Source* Climate Bonds Initiative and Agora Energiewende [2021, p. 7], own highlights)

increasingly less so, from the vagaries of Forex flows to the extent that we can control the Rand. However, to the extent that we get lots of foreign investment, like we have about 1.8trillion listed debt on JSE, which is primarily the channel to raise capital. Of that 1.3 trillion is government. Of that, around 32-40% is held by foreigners. What that means is, as an emerging market, we have a very liquid market serving as a proxy for other emerging markets. (Banker 1, pos. 4)

This is a defining difference in the wider region. Comparing South Africa to Zambia's ability to raise local capital, for example, a World Bank representative stationed in Pretoria argued:

The depth of the financial market in South Africa is a lot more mature. Debt instruments and security arrangements are in place, that are much more readily available. [Zambia] lacks that depth in financial markets. There is very limited opportunity to raise local capital. (World Bank representative, pos. 17)

This ability to raise local capital is "coupled with the fact that it's a jurisdiction with very highly and well-respected regulation you know cap and market regulation as well which plays an important part in credibility" as JSE representative Shameela Ebrahim argues (CBI webinar, 2021, p. 12: 110). South Africa, thus, represents a strong local currency bond market with sophisticated laws and regulations in place.

The Downsides of a Soft Currency Market—Demand Could Outstrip Funding Supply

Still, there are structural downsides to being an emerging market. Being a soft currency market, the investment banker explains, "places real constraints on us in terms of accessing [US]Dollar funding" (RE Industry representative, pos. 34). It also confines and makes issuances dependent on the sovereign's credit rating, because

> if you launch a Rand Bond in South Africa, you can't be any better than sovereign. You can't. The only way you can do it is launch a Rand Bond in London and then you can offer it at a cheaper rate. Why would someone come down here take a Rand bond and take it [to London]? (RE Industry representative, pos. 34)

After South Africa's second credit rating downgrade in 2020 (Civil Society actor 2, p. 7: 1953; Henderson & Naidoo, 2021), accessing cheap international capital has become more difficult. Though Moody's has changed its credit outlook from negative to stable following sustained efforts of fiscal consolidation in the meantime (Stoddard, 2022), these ratings nonetheless exemplify the volatility inherent to borrowing from international capital markets (Dafermos et al., 2021; Hall et al., 2018; Karwowski, 2019). And though the South African capital market is big in comparison with remainder of the continent, it is hardly big enough to muster the capital needed for a green transition, at least according to one of the big solar developers operating these markets:

> You need Enel, an EDF and all these big players, Uniper and whoever wants to come here. You need them really. I mean, you can get by with some South African but if you're going to grow, if you're going to grow renewables to 10-20,000 megawatts, you're not going to do it with South African money alone. So, you've got to be careful how you manage that. You need that funding base, I mean if you look at our Chinese partners,

what they invested in this process, I mean it's billions and you need them as customers. (Developer 1, pos. 70)

The former Investment banker turned solar industry advocate similarly argues with view to the financial sector overall:

> The question is: What is the capacity of my five commercial banks plus my three development banks – what is my depth of my commercial market to provide the debt required for normal-sized projects? You are starting to see Sanlam and others starting to move into potentially providing debt. A lot of the banks established investment and pension funds so Standard Bank has something called Stanlip. Sanlam used to be an insurer and build this investment house on the side. Old mutual has become a big investor in renewables. The question is if we suddenly get to a market where suddenly annual requirement for debt triples to R150-200bn per year, what is the capacity of our markets to keep lending under those conditions. (RE Industry representative, pos. 14)

As these two quotes exemplify, especially the renewables industry doubts that the country's domestic capacity will suffice to upscale the low-carbon transition in the country, particularly given the small banking sector that would fund the risky early project tranches. These industry actors would, indeed, welcome institutional investors, whether foreign or domestic, to channel funding into these developments.

A Market with Few Tradeable Assets

As already covered in the subsection on bankable projects, South Africa's capital market has few tradeable assets—it is characterized as a 'borrower's market' (Banker 3, pos. 38), meaning comparatively favorable lending terms for anyone willing to set up a bankable project. A former JSE sustainability representative seconds the banker's earlier observation that most listings on the JSE are government bonds with corporate bonds having not really taken off thus far (JSE Representative 1, p. 6: 2791). For the green economy consultancy representative, these are some of the cross-cutting issues afflicting the domestic capital market:

> [T]he lack of a VC [venture capital] market in South Africa is quite a big one in the green economy. And there's very little money flowing into that innovation space, into that risk space. Working capital and the availability

of working capital seems to be quite a big gap as well, across the board. That sort of R&D [research & development] and feasibility of money also seems to be really hard to find. (Civil Society actor 1, pos. 73)

The lack of bankable (green) projects equates to very little secondary trading. In one development banker's words:

Well, that's the problem it's because, so that's one of the big concerns of a national treasury is that there's no depth in our debt capital markets. There's no secondary trading. So, the people that work the Cape Town green bond, I bet you not one of them has sold one Rand of that. Because what are they going to replace it with? But the thing is that's not the fault of the debt capital markets. That's the fault of the fact that there's no projects to fund through the debt capital markets. You're going to create liquidity in the market, you got to have a lot more to fund. (Development Bank Representative 1, pos. 306)

Despite sophisticated regulations and tremendous market capitalization, South Africa's capital markets seem largely dependent on sovereign issuances with little dynamism in innovative and riskier investment realms.

The Role of Reputation Within a Small and Risk-Averse Capital Market

The small number of actors in the market, additionally, heightens reputational risks and forces members to take conservative decisions. One asset management consultant observes:

And I think South African investor market is traditionalist, you know, like a corporate bond market has never really ever taken off in South Africa. And there's been good corporates in South Africa obviously, you know? Very good corporates and there's never really taken off, you know because it's expensive, the JSE systems make it difficult to list corporate bonds [...] So, anything new they can't. You know either it doesn't form part of the mandate or it's too risky for them to be doing that because they could get punished you know if it doesn't perform or it's not classified correctly. (Asset Management Consultant 2, pos. 62)

Another consultant in the ESG space, similarly, emphasizes the reputational risks attached to new instruments in a conservative environment:

We, again, we're a very small investment community in South Africa. So, if you're going to do something, you better make sure that you succeed, because if you don't, there's almost not a second chance for you. So, people are very/ fund managers, if they are fund managers of a certain standing and stature, they're not going to risk losing mandates. So, the status quo remains. It's more your emerging managers who are actually incentivized to take risk, to make a name for themselves, to be different, because that's why you should give them a mandate. (Asset Management Consultant 1, pos. 88)

One investment manager who prematurely proposed a green bond platform in South Africa's domestic markets was turned down across the institutional investor spectrum as well as governmental bodies. As one developer comments:

His program was flawed because we spoke to people in the World Bank and they said they weren't actually backing it. And they didn't believe that it was the right way of doing it. So, we didn't. He said, he had it, but he didn't have it and he was very/ when he produced that document, it was very early stage. If you drill down into the document, it's/ he hadn't done his homework. (Developer 1, pos. 41)

To introduce innovative new asset classes like green bonds can be quite difficult, especially when this space is likened to a "pedestrian" market (Banker 1, pos. 12) where asset creation is slow and everybody knows everybody. Those with innovative ideas stand a lot to lose from miscalculating, misreading market developments, and overplaying prevailing mandates. As one government advisor says tongue in cheek: "South Africa is a strange financial market. It has some of the worlds most sophisticated tools, but, actually, I wouldn't say the most sophisticated investors" (RE Industry representative, pos. 13).

A Knowledge Gap Inhibits Green Bond Uptake

That few green bonds are listed on the JSE's sustainability segment is also to do with the lack of understanding around the instrument, according to several domestic investors. For one institutional investor, this knowledge gap spans from the supply to the demand side:

But I don't think the international market actually understands local markets efficiently to participate in the local green bonds... I just think that the local market doesn't understand green bonds efficiently. And there's been— there's not been a lot of offering also in the South African market. But understandingly, it's a new sort of area and a new offering in the South African market. So, we can understand there's been a slow build up. But it's new and I think it all needs to gain some traction. (Futuregrowth employee, pos. 44, 46)

For the Old Mutual investor, the domestic capital market lacks an "awareness around the overall characteristics of green bonds. [It] is not well understood in the context of South Africa" (Old Mutual Representative, pos. 151). For the head of the sustainability segment at the JSE, this lack of knowledge around green bond presents a major impediment to green bond uptake. For her, educating investors and issuers about the benefits of the instrument needs to improve in order to resolve misconceptions about the added costs of green bond issuances:

And we need a lot more education within the market as to the fact that this is actually a great instrument to use, this is how you can use it and that is the education. The other thing – with that education part and parcel – is the fact that people perhaps are under the impression that it costs a lot more to issue a green bond because of you know the necessity to have third party verification on the green characteristics of the bond, the ability to earmark on the spending and being able to report on that separately annually – and they see that as a cost. So, the cost factor could potentially be an impediment. (JSE Representative 2, p. 6: 723)

The representative of the finance NGO points to a more abstract knowledge deficit relating to green bonds; namely, the ability of directing fund into low-carbon infrastructure is missing, due to the complex nature of it:

And so then as I say, this very poor understanding within the financial sector of how you actually direct funds to green infrastructure and renewable energy, just transition stuff. They don't understand how they can do it and to be fair it's not that easy. It's not as easy as investing in the JSE and I know that there a lot of people working on trying to make it easier to do that. But because it's not an area they are familiar with and because it's not transitional listed equities. You know the South African renewable energy IPP project was so successful because it was kind of presented on a plate, right? The banks didn't have to do anything. It was all there for them; it was all easy it was all packaged the way they understood things to be packaged. So that's really what we lack I think in kind of finance and energy financing and all of the financing. (Civil Society actor 2, p. 5: 864)

Apart from the subordinate position in the global capital landscape, it is the lack of size, inherent risk aversion as well as missing know-how that characterizes the slow growth of the green bond market domestically. Capital market regulations further complicate the picture.

The Prevailing Regulatory and Policy Vacuum

Beyond the structural disadvantages of the capital market, current regulation and lack of policies is another key bottleneck in the sector. Stringent mandates to drive green investments at banking or institutional investor level are absent and change hard to come by given some hidden gatekeepers of greening finance. I first touch on some regulations currently carved out in South Africa's capital markets, before discussing the role of regulatory gatekeepers in this space. Thereafter, we turn to the supply-side policies and the opportunities it carves out for green bond issuances.

The Regulatory Framework—Disclosure Trumps Prescribed Assets
According to the former head of the Principles for Responsible Investment in Africa and CRISA secretariat, the regulatory debate around green bonds picked up pace with the public consultation process on updating the Pension Fund's regulation 28 in 2019 and circled around the two poles of prescribed assets and reporting disclosure (Asset Management Consultant 1, pos. 14–16). The major regulatory weakness of green bonds, according to a fund manager specializing on rooftop PVs, is that they are not a prescribed asset, but ultimately depend on investors' special purchasing interests: "Now if there were a prescribed asset class of green bonds, that would change everything" (Fund Manager 3, pos. 63). The regulator, in this case the Financial Sector Conduct Authority, could require pension funds to acquire a share of its portfolio to be green bonds. This approach represents the heavy-handed government approach which has infamous historical precedents in South Africa. The Government Employee's Pension Fund (GEPF), for example, used to have prescribed assets, but they have been done away with (JSE Representative 1, p. 4: 1622). Two private sector concerns underpin the reservations against

prescribed assets, namely poor government record and the country's Apartheid past.

This asset consultant links the poor government's record to liberal market premises:

> So, there's a fear that government, when push comes to shove, because of our economic conditions presently, because of corruption, because of the difficulty for a lot of our state owned companies to raise money in the public market [...] issuances, etc., there is this kind of concern that there will be this prescribed asset requirement where domestic South African pension funds would be forced to invest five or ten percent of the portfolio into specific, let's call them state owned entities, to prop them up almost artificially. And of course, nobody from a private kind of liberal capitalism perspective would want that. (Asset Management Consultant 1, pos. 16)

Beyond the present predicament of the political administration and its state-owned entities, another institutional investor also refers to the dark legacy of Apartheid as a dangerous precedent for prescribed assets and draws comparisons to corrupt practices within contemporary state-owned enterprises (SOEs):

> I think in the context of prescribed assets and the way in which prescribed assets was abused in the Apartheid era, I don't see it ever being actually, I don't see it ever really actually being sort of a palatable or acceptable solution. [...] What will happen is you know, department of agriculture would issue an agriculture bond, and then the government says, right, every single pension fund in the country [...] must have 15 percent of its assets in the newly issued agri bond, and then everyone has to buy their agri bond. The agri bond gets lots of capital and then you've got a couple of corrupt individuals inside there that just plunder the pot. That's the way it's abused, you know.
>
> And so, to go through that cycle again, in the context where already the government has got governance issues inside of those state-owned entities, so if Transnet [the SOE dealing with large-scale transportation infrastructure] were to issue a rail bond, is anyone really going to believe that Transnet can properly distribute the proceeds given their recent history[5]? No. (Old Mutual Representative, pos. 261–265)

---

[5] As the Zondo Commission inquiry has affirmed in the meantime, Transnet was deeply embroiled in 'state capture', the shorthand for the corrupt practices during the Zuma administration (Cohen & Vollgraaff, 2022).

These reservations against prescribed assets also dominated the reform process of the pension fund's regulation 28. Originally, this regulation yielded the first major breakthrough in greening pension funds in 2011 with a new stipulation enshrining in its preamble the support of

> the adoption of a responsible investment approach---[giving] appropriate consideration to any factor which may materially affect the sustainable long-term performance of a fund's assets, including factors of an environmental, social and governance character. This concept applies across all assets and categories of assets. (National Treasury, 2011, p. 5)

In other words, the provision required pension funds to consider ESG criteria when investing and enforcing ESG compliance onto their respective clients (Asset Management Consultant 1, pos. 16–20).

A key component of this regulation is the ensuing sustainability reporting directive born out of the investment Industry Association of South Africa (ASISA) called the Code for Responsible Investing in South Africa (CRISA). Alongside the King Code, which sets best practices for companies and corporate bodies around ethical conduct, good corporate citizenship and compliance (Johannesburg Stock Exchange, 2021, pp. 16–17), CRISA provides responsible investing disclosure guidelines. According to Asset Management Consultant 1 (pos. 16), it serves as "a defense mechanism against prescribed assets" and by placing hopes in market principles to "achieve a lot of these social and national outcomes without needing the prescribed assets approach". Punitive measures for non-compliance apply on a case-by-case basis, but only after a grace period. They range from imposing a fine to putting the pension fund under public administration. As a CRISA representative and institutional investor explains, "the view was that simply the sustainability lane should be entrenched across all asset classes" (Old Mutual Representative, pos. 127).

The effects of the Code for Responsible Investing, however, have been disappointing. As the Old Mutual investor goes on to say:

> CRISA is quite narrow in its application, and it only applies to a list of assets. It largely mirrors what the UNPRI [the United Nation's Principles of Responsible Investment reporting guideline] says. And I would say that there's a fair amount of lip service given to its application in South Africa. I mean, it simply says exactly what the UNPRI says, and you should report and disclose on an annual basis. It's used quite effectively I think

by the media and others to push companies to be accountable because it's a voluntary industry standard that must be applied. And if you don't apply it, you must explain why you don't apply it. (Ibid., pos. 131)

The sustainability representative at the JSE doesn't consider this regulatory to be incentive enough for climate alignment, concluding that "[u]nfortunately, CRISA has not seen the traction in implementation it was intending", but pointing to "efforts to boost that again" (JSE Representative 1, p. 4: 1622), with a reformulated directive. Other green institutional investors were less optimistic:

So even with this new directive, I don't think it's necessarily going far enough, or it's still very much the industry needs to self-regulate, self-govern, and they will come in when there are really bad examples or incidents, like Steinhoff,[6] where we had close to 200 billion Rand of shareholder money value destroyed. We don't need more examples like that of what can happen. Again, hindsight is always 2020, but we don't need more examples of Steinhoff to demonstrate why we need to be better stewards of our retirement fund capital. (Asset Management Consultant 1, pos. 22–24)

That CRISA has been ineffective is also linked to its governance setup inviting conflicts of interests that prevent proper checks and balances. Ultimately, its purpose is to purse shareholders' interests. Given the absence of an institute of shareholders in South Africa, it is, instead, housed within the Institute of the Directors:

And so, for example, if, you know, CRISA says 'You must go and take on directors because of excessive pay issues', it's kind of difficult because CRISA is secretariated [sic] inside the Institute of Directors. And the Institute of Directors, of course has the interest of directors at heart you know? (Old Mutual Representative, pos. 135)

Regulation 28 remains the only non-voluntary obligation for pension funds. But it lacks precision, as the sustainable index representative at JSE

---

[6] The incident refers to Steinhoff, a multinational mattress firm, and its shares crashing after kickbacks, inflated forecasts, and personal enrichment for executives of the firm became public, wiping out more than ZAR200 billion off the JSE. Millions of ordinary South Africans' pensions were adversely affected (Kew & Vecchiatto, 2021; Rose, 2018).

argues: "[I]t has no indication how that finds expression in your investment, whether that means you have to follow a sustainable index, or you have to invest in a green bond" (JSE Representative 1, p. 4: 1622).

The little progress achieved lately in greening the mandatory regulatory framework has to do with the general overhaul of the capital market model in South Africa being implemented in 2019, which took up and essentially blocked wide-ranging capacities. The "Twin Peaks model, the regulatory model that splits prudential regulation from market regulation" has tied up many regulatory bodies in those processes, leaving little capacity for broader climate concerns (JSE Representative 1, p. 4: 3335). Another institutional investor supports this assertion, arguing that this corporate restructuring of the Twin Peaks model, "people have had to reapply for jobs, some people have left, new people are coming in. So, it's a very messy business, and unfortunately, things as important as this directive have kind of been important, but not urgent" (Asset Management Consultant 1, pos. 12).

In fact, during the latest iteration phase of the adaptation of Regulation 28 in October 2021 (National Treasury, 2021c), no prescribed green assets were inserted. Quite the contrary, as per follow-up announcement by National Treasury (2021b, p. 1) in November, reporting requirements on infrastructure purchases were further diluted after feedback raised concerns about this requirement being "too onerous". The reporting was restricted to the top 20 infrastructure investments of the pension fund (ibid.). It is, thus, likely that a light-touch approach such as currently enshrined in the regulation 28 of the Pension fund's act will prevail.

On instilling a mandatory demand push for climate-aligned assets (which could be funded through green bonds), the regulator, thus, opted for a light-touch approach. This seems reasonable given the lack of bankable projects to quell the resulting demand for green (prescribed) assets and complexity of prevailing requirements and ceilings on investments for pension funds. These concerns are also mirrored in the voluntary green finance taxonomy, which guides and standardizes green investments in South Africa (see section "South Africa's Taxonomy Risks Perception of Greenwashing in International Markets"). Yet what role does the Johannesburg Stock Exchange play in all this? After all, it is the regulatory venue where green bonds are listed and traded.

The Ambiguous Greening Drive of the Johannesburg Stock Exchange

The Johannesburg Stock Exchange plays a pivotal role in South Africa's capital market. I will shine a light on both its inroads in greening finance as much as its endeavors to balance its approach in order not to jeopardize capital market returns over climate alignment. Therein, I substantiate the critique of environmental, social, and governmental (ESG) criteria as an investment framework of limited use to attain sustainable outcomes and discuss these findings in light of the capital market dependent on fossil energy.

The most noteworthy institutional innovation was the setup of a so-called Green Segment at the Johannesburg Stock Exchange (JSE) in 2017 which has since evolved into a broader 'Sustainability Segment' so as to enable not only green bonds but also other labeled bonds, be that transition, social, or sustainability-linked bonds to also be featured there (JSE Press, 2020). The idea behind this sustainability segment is to enhance the visibility for climate-aligned investments in the country. The JSE readily portrays itself as a frontrunner in sustainability, pointing to the fact that it was the first exchange globally to introduce a sustainability index in 2004 (JSE Press, 2020). The JSE was also a founding partner and has a "strong presence" (GGKP webinar, 2021, pos. 595–596) in the Sustainable Stock Exchanges initiative, a global platform of exchanges trying to align and enhance ESG performance (UNEP FI, 2022a). Speaking of the sustainability index instated in 2004 and geared towards capturing listed company's ESG performance, the former JSE sustainability lead plauded the leading role the JSE has played for years:

> It was the only exchange for many years until very recently. The new exchanges don't do anything on sustainability as yet, so the JSE is still the leader. That index was the first of its kind in an emerging market. And it was the first in the world to be run by an exchange. So, it was pioneering at the time. Brazil followed suit just a year after the JSE index was launched. From then on, it was kind of the two leading exchanges in terms of this phase in emerging markets. It has changed a lot. But that length of experience has meant a lot. (JSE Representative 1, p. 3: 1937)

Regardless of pushing environmental concerns in a media-savvy fashion on the global stage, the question remains as to whether the Johannesburg Stock Exchange is actually a driver or a spoiler of greening finance. As per green segment representative, the JSE is the biggest exchange in Africa by size at domestic market capitalization of US$1,356,590 million (UNEP FI, 2022b). The Exchange demutualized into a private trading entity in 2005 started listing its own shares in 2006; bonds started trading after the JSE gobbled up the Bond Exchange of South Africa in 2009 (ibid.; JSE, 2022a).

According to Petry (2020) and Petry et al. (2021), the JSE is an exchange governed by a neoliberal logic. With its main shareholders steeped in fossil fuel dependence, it is questionable whether greening efforts will yield quick climate benefits. In the prescient words of the NGO representative, I interviewed in 2020:

> I don't know about that in detail but I can tell you that nothing the JSE does is robust or stringent when it comes to climate or environment or anything like that so you know. They are, more than anyone else, able to lobby and they want to make it like easy for issuers right so they will do the least possible. I think we have a big lobbying situation in South Africa and nobody talks about it. Strong industry associations that have a lot of influence on these kinds of things [...] I certainly wouldn't look to the JSE for leadership on this. (Civil Society actor 2, p. 10: 668)

The NGO representative, thus, heavily disputes the JSE climate intentions beyond creating labeled investment opportunities for the domestic markets. Following up with a question on who could propose binding commitments for ESG criteria, she responds:

> [A]gain that would be the JSE; it should come from the JSE, no sign of that. When we asked the JSE at its AGM [Annual General Meeting] a few months ago whether they are considering making TCFD [Task Force on Climate-related Financial Disclosures] reporting a listings requirement, they said that they might launch a consultation process in about 18 months. I think it's more likely to come from government, actually. There are, the reserve bank it started to say/ the reserve bank financial stability review says additional reporting by financial institutions is required to accurately attract and transition the physical risk associated with climate change. So, they are starting to get it and I think that might happen sooner than we think. But again, it won't come from the JSE at all. It will come from the government. (Civil Society actor 2, p. 11: 979)

These two quotes demonstrate the NGO's doubts about the JSE credibly pursuing climate objectives at the detriment of incumbent returns. The

JSE, according to her, speaks green while safeguarding returns in practice. It is yet another example of the separation between creating sustainable investment opportunities for issuing companies and investors as opposed to creating positive environmental impact (Bracking, 2015; Jones et al., 2020).

More stringent climate sensitive measures, however, are difficult to implement, such as a negatively screened index,

> Whereby companies that were in certain sectors would be excluded. Those kinds of ethical indices existed, and they do exist. But in the South African environment the sense was based on our consultation with the marketplace that if you were to do that, from a practical perspective, you would end up with a non-sense financial product because the mining companies are the heart and soul of the listed environment so you wouldn't have anything to invest in. (JSE Representative 1, p. 2: 2853)

The capital market's path dependence thus precludes exclusionary or punitive listing measures. Beyond this criticism, the JSE's conduct underscores the limited usefulness of ESG criteria on creating climate-aligned investment outcomes. Instead, a social and responsibility index was initially set up, as the sustainable index representative of the JSE explains, which ranked companies according to their (climate) risk identification, its management, and disclosure. Before it was rolled up into a FTSE index in 2015, it consisted of the top 40 companies, "mainly the large mining corporations and then later on the large banks and a few others that ended up in the high-performing category" (JSE Representative 1, p. 2: 2296). She goes on to explain:

> This is the conundrum in the sustainability environment which I am sure you are familiar with, that the guys that are most exposed and are probably most frowned upon in terms of their activities are the ones that quickly do well in these kinds of indices. (JSE Representative 1, p. 2: 2596)

The ICMA representative at Old Mutual and the Sustainability lead at one major investment fund in renewables see ESG as conceptually limited. The ESG framework is only "helpful from a risk/return perspective" (Old Mutual Representative, pos. 53) without focusing on strategic outcomes (Fund Manager 2, pos. 118). The sustainable city representative says upon prompted about the focus on procedure at the detriment of ESG outcome: "Yes, the initial argument was for ESG to gain traction first and then grow teeth later" (Civil Society actor 3, pos. 20). But,

> lots of dirty big companies should be red-carded on the basis of ESG in South Africa, but they are not. Historical examples include companies around the Marikana massacre, the housing issues, exploitation. ESG reporting has not been influential enough to address these issues. (Civil Society actor 3, pos. 20–22)

As previously alluded to, the directionality of physical risks associated with climate change is often deliberately left unclear. There is a tremendous difference between reporting the companies' *exposure* to climate-related (physical) risks than to present ways to reduce the companies' own *contributions* to climate change (Simpson et al., 2021). At the time of the interview in 2020, the JSE had merely set up a consultation process to deepen the former.

Regarding disclosure and reporting, however, incremental change is imminent. The JSE's disclosure guidance document out for public comment until the end of February 2022 (JSE, 2022b, p. 18) includes provisions for the so-called double materiality perspective that considers not only ESG risks and opportunities *for* the company, but also the company's effect *on* society, the economy, and the environment. It, thus, addresses criticism about one-directional ESG disclosure in favor of the company's financial interests (Simpson et al., 2021). But, in its provisional form, these disclosure guidelines remain voluntary. And whether the JSE will implement this guidance against the resistance of industry bodies who, according to Climate CEO at Just Share Robyn Hugo (2022), likely argue to wait for global standards before local guidelines should take effect remains to be seen.

Beyond the limited ability of ESG criteria to set incentives for reducing climate impacts, the JSE's regulatory framework for green bonds specifically also proved very lenient. Referring the City of Johannesburg issuing its self-declared green bond before the JSE even had listing requirements in place, the same former JSE representative concedes:

> But the JSE has designed rules that are quite broad, they did not want to ascribe to a particular standard, so they are not specific. They use the Climate Bonds Initiative's green bonds principles as a basis, but I don't

think there is a prescription that you have to apply those. It was quite a conversation, I think. (JSE Representative 1, p. 4: 883)

And quite a conversation it has been. Striking a balance between credible climate safeguards and economic growth aspirations is a difficult task at the JSE's green segment as much as the overarching green taxonomy. Quite analogous to the green finance taxonomy developments, the JSE representative working in the sustainability segment recalls:

> So, what we have done in the South African context, is to allow a certain flexibility around what and how you can be certified as a green bond because we realized that there are certain local context issues, that we need to pay cognizance to. So, we are a developing economy, we are still very much a coal-based economy in South Africa. And so, the transition and the types of things that we might need to fund could maybe for example not strictly speaking be able to fall within the CBI framework, which is a very science-based framework. [...] And while we completely consider that to be the gold standard and aspirational, we found that initially we couldn't limit issuers to a very narrow framework or a very tight framework in relation to green. But we do allow, at the same time, as to how to balance that with the credibility of what is really green, right. 'Cause we don't want somebody to come tomorrow and say I am going to fund the making of a coal-fired power station more efficient – and that is green. So, we do take cognizance of the fact that it is a transitional economy, we are on a transitional pathway in terms of the energy mix in the country. And how do we accommodate that, how do we do that? And of course, remember, that any market is on a willing-buyer – willing-seller basis. (JSE Representative 2, p. 3: 2407)

With her statement, the JSE representative raises four important issues: Firstly, she argues that the criteria to list a green bond need to be less stringent than those by the CBI or ICMA, the two main standardizing institutions that rely on science-based or Paris Agreement aligned assessments. Secondly, the need for 'flexibility' arises from the structural hurdles in the domestic capital market that need to be considered. This flexibility, in turn, is justified by South Africa still being a developing economy that is steeped in coal, signaling competing socio-economic development priorities and fossil path dependence. Conversely, were the JSE to apply the gold standard, hardly any issuer would be able to issue a bond in the segment. To account for the structural path dependencies, the listing criteria are thus watered down to enable businesses to issue and purchase debt labeled 'sustainable'.

In the CBI webinar, Shameela Ibrahim reiterates this argument in an attempt to justify the flexibility in codifying green and transition bonds for domestic needs:

> [W]at we did with green bonds was we looked at the [...] green bond principles and then codified the recommendations into listings require-ments which then helps with bringing credibility to the market and then looking at those and allowing for a level of flexibility within that. And the thinking behind that was even before there was the word transition or the notice was actually that we need to look at context. And every jurisdiction has contact specific considerations and so there's a level of flexibility that might be required in an economy like South Africa that doesn't mirror a European economy where there's multiple different energy sources and open markets and things. So, what would be the kind of issues that we might face in this market? And what sort of flexibility do we need to bring in at the same time helping to ensure that credibility is maintained in the market? And so our framework, it ultimately was a little bit more flexible but still had certain reporting requirements that were not negotiable and then the expansion of that to reflect on where the market is going was that last year that was expanded to include social bonds and sustainability bonds with a similar perspective of codifying certain principles to allow for that to change. (CBI webinar, 2021, p. 11: 1335)

Concerns around greenwashing in the South Africa context seem to loom large when scientifically established climate rigor is diluted in favor of business industry concerns. So far, they have not destabilized the JSE's sustainable segment. But that is for a simple reason: The JSE's segment has not been challenged by an outright 'fossil outlier' as the JSE representative I interviewed concedes:

> So far, we haven't had our framework tested with big outside cases or outliers that could be for example – you know the same example I mentioned – of the more efficient coal-fired power station. And I honestly don't think we would be faced with such a requirement of people coming to the market to fund such a thing. So, our framework is saying that there is flexibility should it be needed, but the reality is that we don't expect in practice that it is going to happen. (JSE Representative 2, p. 4: 344)

As the previous section on the controversial debate around what constitutes green in the global labeled bond markets aptly shows, it is exactly these contentious issuances at the sustainable margins that herald criticism for tarnishing the market's green integrity. That the JSE's green segment has not been confronted with such controversy is, I argue, not so much an achievement of striking a balance between conflicting interests (business versus climate). Rather, the segment will likely be subject to intense scrutiny once the likes of Eskom or Sasol seek to place a bond (whether green, transition, or KPI-linked) at the JSE's sustainability segment. Whether they will attract interested investors remains to be seen.

As emphasized in the first section of this chapter, South Africa offers few projects investor identify as green and bankable. In combination with a capital market deeply embroiled in energy-intensive production and social policy trade-offs, the policy space to draw up a regulatory environment that aligns climate concerns with domestic conditions is quite a narrow lane. These quotes powerfully drive home the fact that the country's fossil path dependency slows climate alignment (confer Hypothesis 1).

As these two subsections have shown, both the public regulatory bodies as much as the JSE are hesitant to materially tilt the capital market towards greener futures. But what about pension funds and managers themselves? Against the backdrop of CBI specifically and green bond market advocates more generally emphasizing the business case of green bonds as low-risk, profitable long-term investment opportunities, what prevents them from upping their stakes in the green transition?

Asset Consultants as Hidden Gatekeeper of Greening Finance

Beyond the stringent regulatory framework within which pension funds maneuver, pension funds make investment decisions according to their individual mandates. This subsection dwells on the hold-ups in greening mandates at the fund's level.

An investment banker concluded after embarking on an ultimately unsuccessful roadshow for a green bond platform that there is a lack of ESG mandates, few green performance criteria, and little accountability for asset managers outside of economic considerations (Fund Manager 4, pos. 14). Instead, pension funds often refer to their fiduciary responsibility as the stewards of capital of hard-working people to avoid excessive risks—though moral hazard exists in the South African corporate and public capital market landscape not least since the Steinhoff case and the corruption at the Public Investment Corporation (Kew, 2020; Kew & Vecchiatto, 2021, more on the PIC below). Institutional investor references of fiduciary obligations seem to serve as a justification not to engage with green bonds. This holds particularly true in emerging markets with higher risk profiles (Haag & Müller, 2019; Volberding, 2021; Waissbein et al., 2013)—another structural inequality preventing emerging markets from accessing cheap capital to drive a low-carbon transition (Bigger, 2017; Bigger & Millington, 2019; Caprotti et al., 2020). To refute this justification, ClientEarth and JustShare solicited a legal opinion (ClientEarth & Just Share, 2019) and sent it to the largest pension funds arguing that climate change should be considered a material risk and thus be part of fiduciary obligations (Asset Management Consultant 1, pos. 30). Still, referring to the fund's fiduciary responsibility and its respective mandate largely serves as an argument against investing in green bonds. One important question, thus, is who sets these mandates and how can those possibly be turned green?

As the sustainable index representative at the JSE argues, there is misalignment of interests coupled with—again—an educational gap among key stakeholders:

> You get the same story that is the global challenge for asset managers: The asset managers are mandate-takers they are not mandate makers. So, the mandate makers are the asset owners, which are the pension funds mainly, the other institutional investors, and their asset consultants. So, we still [after] ten years, we have heard the story: 'oh the asset consultants are the gatekeepers'. The pension funds are starting to wake up to it, but there is an educational gap that has to happen [sic]. There is a strong reliance on professional advisers who may not necessarily be kind of supportive of green investment or responsible investment in whatever form it takes. (JSE Representative 1, p. 5: 3838)

Indeed, the asset owners, particularly the board of trustees, don't necessarily understand capital markets well, but rely on consultants' expertise. She goes on to say:

> For those asset managers that are really pro-active in driving it, it is frustrating because they can develop products, but unless they have clients to take up their products, it won't help. And the JSE is in a similar conundrum: if they don't have anyone issuing green bonds, they don't have

anything to list. But even if there is something to list, if there is no invest-ment interest, then there is no liquidity in the product, which means it doesn't really make it viable for the longer term to have a signifier there. But I think there is enough evidence globally on the impact that green bonds are making and the growth of green bonds, that people should start sitting up and taking notice. (JSE Representative 1, p. 6: 988)

The institutional investor at Old Mutual expands on this criticism of asset consultancies. Regarding the recent uptake of sustainability concerns in South Africa, he argues:

And even then, the large asset consultants that really are the gatekeepers between the asset managers and the asset owners are very slow to the party. Because it's just extra work for them and you know, they don't know a lot about it. [...]They're the ones that are doing the asset liability modelling, and they are supporting them around drafting mandates. (Old Mutual Representative, pos. 103–121)

Asset consultants, thus, wield tremendous power in shaping investment trajectories at pension funds although the decisions ultimately rest with the respective board of trustees and the principal officer. The former CRISA member combines both arguments of the lack of understanding on the part of the government and asset owners and mis-incentives on the part of the asset consultants:

So, unfortunately, I don't think the regulator is going to really drive the uptake of the green economy in South Africa. It has to be driven by product innovation and by customer demand. I think somebody said to me once or quoted in a message, 'the best regulator is your customer'. Because then that's private sector motives, it's the profit motive, it's the commercial motives. And so, you really want a more educated, informed client base who demand these types of changes. Now, unfortunately in South Africa, your trustee community, your asset owning community is not empowered with the same level of knowledge and financial acumen as their service providers. And so, there's this inordinate benefit to all kind of entities in the investment value chain, except for the ultimate beneficiary. And so, until we start to put power back in the hands of trustees, I don't think we're going to really see the change that we want in all aspects of getting good value for money, by the ultimate beneficiaries, pensioners, members of funds. Yeah. And it's just as true for the green economy and the transition to a green economy. (Asset Management Consultant 1, pos. 34)

One interviewed institutional investment consultant (IIC) sees a mutually dependent bind of new asset classes that lack definitions, asset managers cannot fit it into their portfolio:

> [IIC]: So, basically, they can't fit it in in there… so automatically it is not there. And you know to change mandate requirements is a process because then you know you have to go back to the clients and say, "Well, listen, here's the new asset class" and so, there's a procedure, it's not easy, and it doesn't just happen.
> [author]: So, it has to be the clients driving a bit?
> [IIC]: Well, in this, the managers should actually be informing their clients you know, this is what's happening in the market and these are the opportunities da, da, da. And then they should open up that opportunity, but basically you know when the market is small, it's undefined, you're not going to get that motivation. It's not how it's going to be.
> [author]: But isn't that a chicken and an egg problem then?
> [IIC]: It is. It is. Yeah, it definitely is. That's why someone's got to start it. Someone's got to do it. And that's where the opportunity lies, you know? (Asset Management Consultant 2, pos. 66–70)

Essentially, asset managers should inform asset owners about new climate-friendly opportunities but do not market them due to their definitional imprecision. Clients, in turn, could demand climate alignment more rigorously but rely on managers to provide financial background for an informed decision. That is why NGOs like JustShare seek to empower shareholders and inform them about effects of investment decisions. The domestic development banker also sees investment managers responsible "to educate people through alternative investment funds, through their broker network […] because you know it's very important that we do try and, you know, save the planet. So […] It's not an easy process" (Development Bank Representative 1, pos. 41–47).

More work needs to be done to increase political pressure on greening mandates, as the former investment banker turned government advisor pinpoints with an important question: "[C]an we start to wake up savers in South Africa to say: I want to see a percentage of my portfolio in sustainable investments?" (RE Industry representative, pos. 34). The domestic development banker also singles out millennials as customers that need to put pressure on pension funds to increase positive social and environmental impacts by "forcing the mandate" (Development Bank Representative 1, pos. 41–47). Ultimately, again, it is the people's pensions that are at stake (Economic Development Department representative, pos. 41; WWF representative, pos. 54; Sean Kidney in CBI webinar, 2021, p. 3: 2697).

Green bonds could safeguard pension funds' returns and simultaneously meet climate alignment. But creating the demand for these solutions through regulation and mandates is significantly lacking in South Africa. There is little political pressure from the regulator and customers to force changes in mandates and instill this additional demand. We will turn to regulation and policies encouraging supply of green investment opportunities next.

Supply-Side Regulation, Its Artificial Ceilings, and a Stuttering Rollout of Renewables

As previously established in section "The Purported Opportunities of Green Bonds Hardly Transpire in Emerging Markets" of this chapter, South Africa lacks green bankable projects. This shortcoming also hinges on the lack of regulations and policies in place to expand on green investment opportunities.

Even after the country updated its nationally determined contributions (NDCs) to reduce its carbon emissions in March 2021, the CBI refers to the Climate Action Tracker deeming them "insufficient" that is "not yet likely to be in line with the Paris Agreement 1.5 C temperature goal" and recommending "much greater ambition" (CBI & Agora Energiewende, 2021, p. 4). In October 2021, South Africa registered updated NDCs at the UNFCCC with revised limits from 398–440 $MtCO_2e$ to 350–420 $MtCO_2e$ by 2030 (IASS/IET/CSIR, 2022, p. 1). Though these incremental steps signal a transition, the government seemed to have lacked leadership and assertive action for quite a while. Beyond lukewarm demand-side regulation, a key inhibiting factor for greening finance still is the government, according to an interviewee of a financial sector NGO: "They are not making it easy policy-wise to invest" (Civil Society actor 2, p. 5: 1844). I focus here on supply-side policies the government has enacted in the energy sector as the greening of other sectors, particularly electrifying the domestic car industry and pipelining a green hydrogen value chain, is in its very early stages (Sguazzin & Prinsloo, 2022; Vecchiatto, 2022).

The energy sector accounts for the largest amount of CO_2 emissions in the country and offers the quickest means to decarbonize (CBI & Agora Energiewende, 2021, p. 10), due to three auspicious pull factors: Geophysical ones like solar radiation and strong winds; an aging fossil fleet slowly decommissioning (Civil Society actor 4, pos. 5–6, 11–12); and frequent power outages adversely affecting economic growth (banker 2, pos. 23). But, the Integrated Resource Plan (IRP), the national energy planning tool, has significantly inhibited the expansion of solar and wind over the last years, be that by resurrecting a debate around nuclear energy (Service Provider 2, pos. 13–14, RE Industry representative, pos. 5), applying artificial ceilings on renewables' expansion (CBI & Agora Energiewende, 2021, p. 6) and stalling its bi-annual updating (see also the context chapter). Whether the IPP office, the investment community, or external technical expert, my interviewees agree that though the Integrated Resource Plan is supposed to be a technical document offering least-cost scenarios (Service Provider 2, pos. 7–8), it is politicized by the National Economic Development and Labor Council and the cabinet for policy adjustment (IPP office representative, pos. 23). That is not necessarily wrong from a political economic perspective, as efficiency rationales often ignore distributional components or second-order effects (like environmental effects) that need to be considered (Bayliss & Van Waeyenberge, 2018, for example, illustrate this in discussing the narrow focus on efficiency gains that underpin many public–private-partnerships). As the solar industry representative and government adviser argues, every deviation from the least-cost scenario must be politically justified (RE Industry representative, pos. 7). When the IRP was finally updated in 2019, it was after a longer hiatus in which Eskom's financial position deteriorated further and its ministerial board significantly reshuffled (IPP office representative, pos. 25, see also Chapter 4). The IRP was finally updated when President Ramaphosa closed the door on nuclear option, citing excessive cost concerns (RE Industry representative, pos. 7). Though provisions for additional renewables and the decommissioning of the country's old coal fleet are included, the updated IRP of 2019 is still neither net-zero aligned nor least cost (CBI & Agora Energiewende, 2021, p. 6). And since it also includes provisions for new coal stations, banks finance these projects pointing to their alignment with the government's energy plans (Civil Society actor 2, p. 3: 120). The government, thus, misses out on creating a credible roadmap to shift the energy sector towards greener futures.

This is also to do with competing interests within the governing party, some of which favor a transition whereas others support conventional mining (WWF representative, pos. 13–15). Even the current Minister of Mineral Resources and Energy, Gwede Mantashe, who is considered to belong to Ramaphosa's centrist faction, ostensibly backed the coal industry lobby when Ramaphosa's Presidential Climate Committee negotiated the just energy transition partnership fund with European countries and the USA (Davies, 2021; Njini, 2022; see also section "Other Crises Overshadow and Compete with Climate Policies"). It comes as no surprise that even the CBI refers to him as 'King Coal' (CBI & Agora Energiewende, 2021, p. 6). For the representative of the World Wildlife Fund (WWF), it is the new entrants disconnect to the old fossil power elite and its interconnection with faction within the governing ANC that presents a bottleneck in advancing a green transition (WWF representative, pos. 12–13). To capture these internal power plays, my theoretical framework offers little insights—the WWF representative (pos. 11, 16) referred to the political settlement theory as potentially insightful here (see, e.g., Frederiksen, 2019; Hickey et al., 2020; Khan, 2010). But we can still draw the preliminary takeaway of conflicting policy stances within the governing party, which contested the updating of the IRP and thus the trajectory of the energy sector. This plan also includes the targets for renewable energy upscaling and thus provisions for supply of green investment opportunities eligible for green bond financing.

The Renewable Energy Independent Power Procurement Program
The Renewable Energy Independent Power Procurement Program or REI4P for short presents the very exception to this dearth of investable climate-aligned investment opportunities in the energy sector (Development Bank Representative 1, pos. 114). Undergirded by government guarantees covering for various sets of risks in case of the off-taker (Eskom) not paying for electricity generated, the program enables renewable energy developers to bid for projects on a competitive least-cost basis (though social factors also apply, see Chapter 4). These renewable energy projects can be financed and refinanced via green bonds.

The REI4P was set up by the Treasury and the Department of Energy and institutionalized in the IPP office in 2008 (IPP office representative, pos. 6). It superseded the RE-Fit program which incurred excessive fiscal burdens by subsidizing renewable energy generation trough a feed-in tariff. The RE-Fit had also heightened concerns over abuse and corruption for people close to government, according to the Economic Development Department representative (pos. 6–9). The REI4P, in turn, was perceived as the cheaper and more efficient market-inducing alternative (ibid., RE Industry representative, pos. 7), an important fiscal consideration given limited fiscal space for maneuver. In the words of a senior representative of the Department of the Environment: "We [South Africa] do not have the luxury of a coal commission as in Germany" (Environmental Ministry representative, pos. 13). By enabling the private sector to contribute funding for renewable energy projects through competitive bidding, the IPP office can well be described as a market-led institutional innovation (Arent et al., 2017; Sum & Jessop, 2013) in a space with little prior experience (IPP office representative, pos. 8).

The program was mainly driven by the national treasury, which repositioned itself as the lead institution (Economic Development Department representative, pos. 9) in governing the transition. It relied heavily on consulting with financial sector actors. By prioritizing their investment concerns around a nascent space like renewables (IPP office representative, pos. 10) and by heeding their need for bankability, other transition concerns took a backseat. Though the Environmental Ministry representative argues that the ministries collaborate on an issue-by-issue basis, with various ministries being in charge depending on the policy to be formulated (Environmental Ministry representative, pos. 8), the most important decisions seem to be made in the halls of the treasury. Indeed, weighing in on decision making does not seem to stretch far beyond financial and energy industry lobbyists. At ministerial level, collective decision making seems mostly absent in the governance of the transition. As one former ministry employee who was part of the carbon tax negotiations recalls, "[t]here is not much. The national treasury calls the shots" (Economic Development Department representative, pos. 53). We, thus, witness the upgrading of the national treasury as the key institution to oversee the transition. The treasury is the major vehicle to impose financial logics into the transition endeavors (Pagliari & Young, 2020).

These financial logics introduced in the program were key to attracting institutional investors. According to its representative, the engagement of Old Mutual, "the biggest player in the debt and the equity side of the

REI4P program" (Old Mutual Representative, pos. 197), was not driven by environmental concerns:

> I don't think that was necessarily driven by an asset register transition discussion, I don't think it was driven by any kind of green or altruistic. I think it was driven by an opportunity to pursue commercial returns. It just so happens that there were lots of other ancillary benefits around it, you know? (Ibid., pos. 197)

Beyond the primacy of economic over environmental parameters in investor's decision-making processes (see Bracking, 2015), this statement also alludes to the state guarantees that de-risked these investments (Dafermos et al., 2021; Gabor, 2021; Volberding, 2021) and made them even more lucrative. As a sustainability lead at the JSE and the CBI put it, the REI4P is the investment opportunity for green bonds (CBI & Agora Energiewende, 2021, p. 15; JSE Representative 2, p. 5: 3388) and offers the low-risk profiles institutional investors would crave—especially once construction risks are overcome. State-led de-risking endeavors were, thus, key to attracting institutional investors into the renewable energy sector. Due to being ultimately backed by state guarantees and providing set expectations on returns due to fixed pricing enshrined in the respective purchasing power agreements, this program ticks all requirements of green bond investment profiles of most institutional investors:

> And yeah, again, if you look at your breakdown of where most of your retirement funds invest, fixed income or bond type investments, especially if they are government guaranteed or inflation linked, ideally both, long-term investors like pension funds can't get enough of that stuff. So, if it's investment grade, you've got the downside protection, that's inflation linked. It's a no brainer. (Asset Management Consultant 1, pos. 50)

Why have green bonds not seen a surge in issuance then? Well, that is because the program did come with a set of downsides. I will focus on regulatory challenges, namely lack of due diligence and little competition over loan provision, the consolidating oligopoly of developers as the rounds advance, the ramifications due to persistent discontinuities of the program, its incomplete business case, and the missing social benefits.

Some academics and especially the IPP office representative celebrate the program variably as "a victim of its own success" (Researcher, pos. 29), which capitalized on the "downward trend in renewable energies" by "breaking the program into different bid windows [...] one of the success factors of our program" (IPP office representative, pos. 23). These factions see in this program a successful driver of the renewable energy sector.

Domestic fund managers and energy experts, however, are a bit more critical. According to an energy consultancy representative, REI4P created moral hazard problems due to the public backstop, with people now "gotten used to filling in documents" rather than focusing on proper risk due diligence (Service Provider 1, pos. 30–33). He goes on to cite the failure of a waste-to-energy project in the Cape Town area as a pertinent case for failed due diligence (Service Provider 1, pos. 34). Another PV fund manager and the chamber of commerce representative, similarly, contest the REI4P's role in driving down generation costs domestically. They attribute the decrease in generation costs more directly to landscape developments around uncertainty in the US market, drops in EU subsidies, and knock-on effects for technical appliances in the Chinese markets, which the South African market harvested (Fund Manager 3, pos. 55; Chamber of Commerce Representative, pos. 90).

Especially in the early bidding rounds, however, the program did come with more downsides than just improper due diligence. As the aforementioned fund manager argues, the renewables sector quickly turned into a regulated space with lots of unexperienced actors:

> The REI4P program is very different to what project finance has been historically, in that it created a moment where the demand for funds far outstripped the capacity to process those applications – which meant that the banks found themselves in a position where they were market-makers and price makers in the negotiation with clients. There was no real competition between the banks. The clients couldn't really get any competitive positions from the banks. So, you ended up with Banks dictating what went into those projects (terms) and that distorted the market completely, because it was entirely bank-friendly, everybody descended to the common denominator from a risk perspective. (Fund Manager 3, pos. 5)

The banking sector, thus, turned into the main beneficiary of a policy envisioned to drive private investments into the renewable energy space. Given their lack of internal competition (Development Bank Representative 2, pos. 17; see also Neumann & Elsner, forthcoming; Simatele, 2015), banks could set their loan conditions relatively independently and inordinately benefited from investing into these early bidding rounds.

Though the state guarantees safeguarded the banks' returns on investment, it led to ballooning contingent liabilities (Development Bank Representative 2, pos. 39, see the subsection on actors driving market development below). And to reform, let alone phase out state guarantees, the 'gold standard of guarantees' is politically difficult, like "stealing the Porsche", according to one Development Bank Representative (ibid., pos. 62). The program, thus, brought about due diligence problems as well as state-guaranteed investment returns largely harvested by the banking sector. We will return to a key distributional conflict around these returns and the role of green bonds therein in the last section of this chapter.

The high tariffs and the resulting lucrative returns for developers and lenders in the early rounds drew in international actors in the later rounds. As the solar industry representative put it,

Look particularly solar, is building Lego energy. What global players are now looking at is global deployment of capital. It is more about how much capital will I deploy to South Africa or Sub-Saharan Africa, to South America. If I am at Enel, it is a portfolio play. Why is REI4P great? Because it is mechanistic, it gave me great protection by entering into a market that was owned by a monopoly. A monopoly that openly disliked any competition. It allows you to bring a large amount of capital in. You are coming into a jurisdiction that has good laws, good banking system, good engineering system. It allows me to deploy that capital through the building of a solar PV plant with a PPA [power purchase agreement] that is backed by government. And after three years, it allows me to sell and take my capital. What is not to like?! And geopolitically, it puts me also in a place that has the potential to be probably the largest regional market. Those are the things that I think an Enel or ANG are here. (RE Industry representative, pos. 43)

As many of my interviewees emphasized (Fund Manager 1, pos. 54; RE Industry representative, pos. 37; Old Mutual Representative, pos. 219–231), the bidding rounds three through five were increasingly decided upon developers being able to access capital, structurally putting big multinationals like Enel and Eni at an advantage (Müller & Claar, 2021). These multinationals can finance these projects off their balance sheets and do not need to raise additional money in the capital markets. Profits for domestic funds halved to about 12–14% in the later rounds, according to one domestic investor (Fund Manager 1, pos. 46), suggesting increased competition. Still, according to one developer, it is the same group of six actors that dominate the independent renewable energy producer's space, not only in South Africa, but beyond:

> It's the same group. It's always the same group. So, it's gated by them [...] Mainstream, Enel, EDF, ENG. It's always the same. You know, the sort of top six or seven. We see them everywhere, even when we're going within Africa they are there. So, during this period where we focused on Africa, everywhere we went was the same group building energy, same bunch. (Developer 1 and 2, pos. 148–152)

In the latest fifth round in 2021, Mainstream, whose majority is owned by the Norwegian Industrial investment group Aker Horizons, again secured roughly half and thus the lion's share of the 2.6 GW auctioned out by the IPP office (Renewables Now, 2021a, 2021b). We, thus, see a growing consolidation of a few transnationally active developers (see also Müller & Claar, 2021 to substantiate this finding). For the solar industry representative, the challenge is to make sure "that this doesn't become a market that is owned by six foreign players. [...] But how do we make sure that it doesn't become a feast for the few?" (RE Industry representative, pos. 41). One of his answers is to scale up domestic ownership programs, develop domestic energy champions, and create spaces for municipals to partake (ibid.).

This brings us to the next shortcoming, the program's mediocre size and longer hiatus. The limited size of the auction windows and the frequent discontinuity of the program overall have squandered hopes of quickly scaling up industrial capacities in the wind and solar sector. One developer identified the program itself as the "biggest bottleneck" (Developer 2, pos. 244). The developers went on to characterize the program as very "disruptive" in its persistent stops and restarts, costing the company an estimated two years of net revenues due to the delay of the REI4P (Developer 2 and 1, pos. 244, 257). Asked how they managed the dry periods resulting from the hiatus in the REI4P program that was ongoing for three years and (would eventually come to an end in 2020), they said:

> We were lucky we had operational projects, so we had revenues from operational projects. So, people like Mainstream really battle in this market now simply because they don't hold on to their assets. They sell them down a lot, so they end up with no revenue, no, you know, no annuity revenue, whereas we do. We hold everything. (Developer 1, pos. 162)

The longer hiatus of the program that resulted from the delay in upgrading the Integrated Resource Plan, thus, prevented an industry to form which would also require significantly more ambitious renewable targets that the ones currently auctioned. The solar industry representative argues "25,000 MW of solar PVs over the next 5–6 years" (RE Industry representative, pos. 41) would be a proper signal to the market rather than the 2600 MW currently auctioned in round 5. The same amount of MWs is also envisaged in round six, which will take place later in 2022 according to President Ramaphosa's 2022 'State of the Nation Address' (Cohen & Cele, 2022).

That the renewable energy sector has not expanded more quickly is also to do with the incomplete business case renewables yet provide. The Council for Scientific and Industrial Research (CSIR), a government-funded think tank, made headlines when they found that generation costs for both solar and wind appliances had outperformed conventional energy sources (interview with CSIR in February 2018).[7] The drop in generation costs finally provided the 'business case' renewable energy and green bond advocates were waiting for.[8] It also defeated those voices (particularly from the coal lobby) complaining about the renewables excessive cost structures. Due to the depreciation in pricing for renewable energy generation, "there is no trade-off between the cheapest and most environmental solution any longer" (Civil Society actor 4, pos. 17). Still, as Christophers (2021) demonstrated in a recent paper, there are more components than just generation costs that make up the profit structures of incumbent as well as nascent energy industry members.

What is more, due to the small size of the program, the fall in generation costs for renewables has had no meaningful effect on prices for end consumers (Energy & Finance Journalist, pos. 34). Against the anticipated 45% hike in electricity prices for consumers between 2019 and 2022, the price of energy is a key socio-economic criterion for society or as the chamber of commerce representative put it a "social question" (pos. 115). This social question of access to cheap or even free electricity collides with business interests (Municipal representative 3, pos. 17–19).

---

[7] This interview was conducted with colleagues during a scoping visit to Johannesburg in February 2018 and is not included in the set of interviewees on pp. 8–9.

[8] In the fifth bidding round, six of Mainstream's projects achieved the lowest tariff to date in South Africa at ZAR374.79/MW hour (Burkhardt & Prinsloo, 2022).

Indeed, municipalities had opposed the demands of the Energy Intensive User Group, which accounts for about 40% of the nation's power consumption and also includes Eskom, to hike tariffs by over 21% for 2022–2023 (Burkhardt, 2022a); NERSA, the energy regulator, eventually approved a 9.61% hike in consumer tariffs, still a major bone to swallow for less affluent parts of society. To date, the savings in generation costs of renewables seems too marginal to significantly weigh in on tilting consumer prices in favor of the less well off.

In all, despite serving as a blue-print for the introduction of competitive renewable energy bidding across the continent (Müller et al., 2020), the REI4P has several downsides that I elaborated above. For the rollout of green bonds, in a nutshell, the program has thus far proven insufficient to create regulatory support on the supply side of the investment equation despite all references to the contrary. Regulation to support the expansion of green bonds remains largely voluntary on the demand side and unambitious on the supply side. As gatekeepers, asset managers prevent a more aggressive tilt towards climate-aligned investment mandates. And even the JSE seems caught too deep in the fossil dependence of the capital market to unapologetically set its sails towards greener futures. Who, then, could step up to the plate and signal a greening of the domestic capital markets? The next subsection takes a look around.

Actors That Could Drive Market Development

First and foremost, the sovereign could step up its green credentials. It is telling that the green bond market has not really taken off when the main bond issuer in South Africa, the sovereign itself, has not issued a green bond as a market signal as yet. CBI CEO Sean Kidney, for example, cites Canada, France, and Germany (who set the record single green bond issuance in 2020 at US$13.6 billion [Environmental Finance, 2021a, p. 3]) as providing great examples as to how the sovereign can offer liquidity and benchmark pricing in the green bond market (CBI webinar, 2021, p. 18: 966). Shameela Ebrahim insinuated discussions taking place (as of August 2021) between the JSE and the sovereign and that the JSE would generally support the sovereign were it to consider issuing a green bond (CBI webinar, 2021, p. 17: 1105). As an important signal and trajectory for the market, a sovereign bond engenders an important financial practice (Chiapello, 2020) to expand the green bond market— despite the Nigerian sovereign setting a counterproductive example.

Given the abysmal track record of South Africa's state-owned enterprises (see context chapter), this bond would be closely scrutinized by market actors and civil society alike. As of the latest available budget report by treasury, gross loan debt is expected to increase to ZAR4.38 trillion or 71.6% of GDP by 2022/2023 (National Treasury, 2021a), which is still below thresholds considered worrisome mainstream economists. Still, contingent liabilities arising from backstopping private investors through state guarantees were already a headache for development banks in 2019 (Development Bank Representative 2, pos. 39). These exposures are expected to further increase from ZAR979.9 billion in 2019 to 1.16 trillion in 2022/2023 (National Treasury, 2021a). The country's weak infrastructure record tarnished by corruption has prompted Futuregrowth to announce its divestment from SOEs in 2017 (Fund Manager 1, pos. 18). As the Futuregrowth employee I interviewed noted, the investors' divestment move yielded a media backlash "we didn't expect" (Future-growth employee, pos. 94–112). But after suspending lending to two SOEs for a couple of months, information provision and transparency were greatly enhanced for the boards of the capital market, something she considered a "great outcome" (ibid., pos. 110). It, nonetheless, exemplifies the unease of market actors with government and SOEs intervening in markets which also guided the corporate governance restructuring favored by the financial industry. Though some NGOs see the government responsible for leveraging the transition (Civil society actor 2, p. 11: 1411, 1836), the recurrently invoked concerns around state capture that guided responses against prescribed assets and the widespread unease adds credence to the second hypothesis which states that the governing party faces a governance and legitimacy crisis which inhibits their ability to drive the transition.

Municipalities as sub-sovereign units have already been discussed in the first section of this chapter. Their lack of creditworthiness inhibits their active participation in the green bond market beyond the few with a clean audit, such as Johannesburg, Cape Town, or the City of Tshwane, which according to its municipal financial analyst Monene Mathiba is currently looking into issuing a green bond (GGKP webinar, 2021, pos. 198–275).

The Government Employee's Pension Fund (GEPF), the biggest pension fund on the continent, is another key actor that could fund a low-carbon transition through green bonds as various civil society actors suggest (Civil Society actor 4, pos. 27; Civil Society actor 2, p. 4: 1230, p. 11: 1935). Unfortunately, due to its embroilment in state capture

(Civil Society actor 2, p. 12: 309; Asset Management Consultant 1, pos. 8; see also context chapter) that afflicted its main investment arm and largest asset manager on the African continent, the Public Investment Corporation (Janice, 2020; Kew & Wessels, 2019), its reputation suffered tremendously. Add to that the fiduciary obligations or lack of mandate to take on construction risk (see first section of this chapter), it is yet to become a fitting actor to front-load financing (Civil Society actor 2, p. 4: 901). Still, the GEPF currently seeks greater alignment with the government's development agenda (Old Mutual Representative, pos. 91). Were the government to take more direct action, other actors would indeed fall in line. In comparison with the banking sector, the government pension fund could bring the necessary money power to the market.

ASISA, the Association for Savings and Investments South Africa, a representative body of the institutional fund managers in South Africa could also play a bigger role as demanded by the solar industry representative (RE Industry representative, pos. 14). The same holds true for BATSETA, the former Office of the Directors and official council of retirement funds in South Africa, which was instrumental in setting up the Code for Responsible Investing in South Africa (IoDSA, 2022). However, BATSETA is sponsored by domestic and international capital market heavyweights (BATSETA, 2022) whose priority remains safeguarding returns, whether aligned with climate objectives or not. And also ASISA's Board of Directors is staffed with the same domestic heavyweights (ASISA, 2022). Whether they take an active stance on climate issues, thus, depends on whether they see returns deriving from this shift in the longer term.

In the banking sector, Nedbank has been praised a "pioneer" in the green bond market (CBI webinar, 2021, p. 4: 841). Initially, they issued a retail green bond backed by its balance sheet. They used this retail bond to test the bank's green monitoring system which was "piggy-backing on *existing* flows and processes" (Banker 1, pos. 29). Since then, they issued several green bonds under their ZAR75 billion domestic medium-term note program (CBI & Agora Energiewende, 2021; JSE, 2021) with *new* RE projects lined up, thus creating additionality. Standard Bank, in turn, issued its first green bond in London before following up with a ZAR1.4 billion green bond on renewable energy projects as part of their sustainable bond framework they had established in February 2020 (Businesslive, 2021). Aligning the banks with climate goals isn't smooth sailing, however, as JustShare can attest to. The finance NGO had been pushing for shareholder resolution at Standard Bank to publish a climate change policy which the banks management itself requested its shareholders to oppose on grounds of it being too onerous (Asset Management Consultant 1, pos. 28). In the end, Standard Bank bowed under pressure and came out in May 2021 promising the publication of a climate strategy by summer 2022 (Buthelezi, 2021). More generally, domestic commercial banks increasingly divest from fossil fuels with recent coal IPPs struggling to get funding. The major banks' commitment to greening the sector, however, predominantly exists on paper and still awaits significant capital restructuring (see Neumann & Elsner, forthcoming). At the same time, the banks benefit tremendously from the current disposition of the market, particularly in the energy sector, where they gauche tremendous revenues for lending into the early phases of new projects (more on that in the last section of this chapter). And as the solar industry representative pointed out on a more general level, the domestic banks are too small to muster the necessary capital for the overhaul of the economy as a whole.

Of course, domestic and international development finance institutions (DFIs) could also take the lead in expanding the green bond markets by bridging bank- and market-based markets through de-risking measures. For example, the Kreditanstalt für Wiederaufbau (KfW), the German development bank, provides technical assistance to roll out green bonds through its local currency market bond scheme (Asset Management Consultant 2, pos. 26), set up an indirect first-loss facility for a small-scale solar PV fund (Fund Manager 3, pos. 12), and considers creating a bundling platform for smaller-scale municipalities to eventually fund an infrastructural overhaul through this portfolio approach that would also possibly include green bonds (Development Bank Representative 2, pos. 49–50). Complementary to that and as part of the German-South African Energy Partnership, the German Development Agency (GIZ) advises the ministry of energy on technical aspects of integrating renewables into the grid and supports municipalities in the restructuring process. Technical support ranges from reports, i.e. on electricity distribution and grid capacity (Voss et al., 2018), to mitigating the lack of technical know-how at local municipal level, a consequence of the public sector management crisis (Butler, 2012; Southall, 2016). As the development agency representative argues, many communal energy suppliers "often do not know what assets they dispose of" (Development Partner, pos. 29). By supporting them in cleaning their balance sheets, the development agencies support a vital step towards making these municipals bankable and, thus, eligible for pooling green bond issuances.

The French development bank AFD, in turn, provides subsidized lending rates through its SUNREF program funding in the RE space (Chamber of commerce, pos. 42). The international DFI's roles, however, are politically mandated and depend on foreign policy strategies devised in their respective home countries. And especially in the small solar market, the development bank's de-risking measures tend to compete rather than complementing each other, especially between AFD and KfW (Chamber of Commerce Representative, pos. 42–509).

Domestically, the Development Bank of Southern Africa (DBSA) could more actively de-risk investments to provide entry for institutional investors. They have also issued a couple of green bonds already, though the latest one merely refinances renewable energy projects across Africa (DBSA, 2021). However, due to their own lending stakes in South Africa's REI4P rounds, they would hurt their own balance sheet if they were to actively support efforts to expand the role of green bonds as means of refinancing the program (more on that in the last subsection).

As this brief overview on the actor's landscape underscores, South Africa's green bond ambition is still in their nascent stages, an observation seconded by domestic institutional investors (Old Mutual Representative, pos. 84–85; Futuregrowth employee, pos. 46). Many actors carry significant baggage, whether a reputation tarnished by corruption or portfolios steeped in fossil fuels, which prevent them from more aggressively penetrating the green bond market.

This fifth section spelled out the idiosyncrasies of the South African capital market. It touched on the unique role of the country's Rand (especially in comparison with other emerging markets outside China) and the sophisticated and mature capital market framework. It went on to highlight the bottlenecks the market presents vis-à-vis increased green bond uptake. Especially, the fossil-based disposition of the main capital market actors inhibits quicker advancements into greener futures. The lack of tradeable green assets is a major result deriving thereof. I touched on risk aversion and lack of understanding of green bonds and took a closer look at the green regulatory framework which offers few incentives on both supply side and demand side. This section dealt with the limits of financializing South Africa's transition through green bonds. That green bonds have not been more successful in South Africa also hinges on other maladies, especially socio-economic ones that require attention. We turn to these concerns next.

OTHER CRISES OVERSHADOW
AND COMPETE WITH CLIMATE POLICIES

The fourth hypothesis I derived in Chapter 4 states: Climate change faces competition from other (developmental) policy priorities. Most interviewees provide supporting evidence for this assertion. I first recap a few perceptions of the climate crisis in South Africa before touching on the other crises and how they interfere with green bond diffusion. I discuss the notion of the 'right to develop', governmental errors, especially relating to energy provision, and the perception of green projects being considered elitist. I then discuss the financial sector's fear of a political backlash and finally zoom in on some of the main pillars in South Africa's just transition discourse and how they affect the rollout of green bonds.

In the CBI webinar, Sam Ashman, Professor of Economics at the University of Johannesburg, underscores the severity and uneven ramifications of climate change, referring to "the multi-year droughts that have afflicted Southern Africa, which is getting hotter and drier. Temperatures in the region have risen at twice the global rate of the last 60 years" (CBI webinar, 2021, p. 13: 975, see also Engelbrecht et al., 2015; McBride et al., 2022). The floods in Durban and surrounding KwaZulu-Natal which killed at least 453 people most of which living in informal settlements were made twice as likely through climate change (Carrington, 2022). But, according to an independent renewable energy activist and consultant, the urgency of climate change is not properly appreciated in the South African context: "We are running out of time, as plans to replace mines is [sic] running too slow" (Civil Society actor 4, pos. 17). Given the "layers of corruption and incompetence that took place at Eskom, people aren't even thinking [of] climate change" (ibid.).

In line with this activist's position, the DBSA development representative argues, South Africans have not "woken up quick enough" (Development Bank Representative 1, pos. 331–338) to be optimistic about greening the financial landscape in time to avert climate ramifications. He explains that in the developing world, other more immediate challenges are on people's minds, like education, health, and housing (ibid. 1, pos. 338–340). A key argument around the limited climate action within South Africa also circles around the question of who is responsible for the climate crisis in the first place:

> There's a lot of conscience as well that they know that the developed world is responsible for most of the carbon emissions. The deterioration of the climate is because of the developed world, not the developing world. So, you know, four percent of the world's carbon emissions come from the African continent. But the whole of the African continent is paying the price because the developed world is spewing out a lot more. So, I think there's also a conscience factor as well to be honest. You know that it's not Africa's/ Africa is not responsible for you know the global carbon emissions, you know where we find ourselves [with respect] to the global warming. It's largely, what is China, India, and the U.S.? You know I think between them, they're close to 60 percent. (Development Bank Representative 1, pos. 53)

The limited contribution of the African continent to global CO_2 emissions is certainly true. And it is a widely held position. According to the former chief Director in the Economic Development Department,

> The dominant view is that climate change is real. The only few disagreeing have vested nuclear/coal interests. South Africa's greenhouse gas emissions are huge in comparison to the rest of Africa, but at 1.17% of the world, relatively negligible in comparison to China. Even if Eskom were to cut its emissions by half, climate change is not averted. South Africa struggles with cutting emissions, since it is a developing country that will have to live with the negative economic externalities. (Economic Development Department representative, pos. 23)

Beyond the limited relative contribution to the problem, being an emerging economy—with all its other accompanying and mutually reinforcing crises—further complicates the discourse around climate action. As the representative of an NGO contemplates:

> I don't know how much people believe this versus how much it is an excuse to delay action. But the idea that Africa must be given the time and we haven't contributed to the problem, we have to catch up. This transition stuff is not our problem, so don't tell us we can't exploit our coal our gas because we are going to do it any way. And if you don't want us to do it then you must pay us for doing something. That narrative is

becoming stronger and stronger, I think, as the threat to these operations get bigger and bigger. (Civil Society actor 2, p. 3: 805)

The perceived lack of responsibility for the climate crisis (the inverse polluter pays principle) complements well with the 'right to develop' argument (see Sengupta [2002] for a general legal perspective and Bos and Gupta [2018] for a discussion on climate change-related exploitation of natural resources in the global South). Both provide a powerful discursive smoke screen and ethical justification against climate action—which is still required not least since South Africa ranks 12th in the list of largest carbon emitters worldwide (European Commission, 2020, p. 11). That these arguments have salience is likely to do with the limited development outcome derived from energy-intensive production. Yet, it is not the only differentiating discursive factor for an emerging economy in global comparison.

Beyond justifiably pointing fingers at the Global North as responsible for the climate crisis and referring to the right to develop and exploit one's own resources to defer climate actions, another major global event resulted in differentiated responses, namely the global financial crisis. In his introductory remarks on Day 2 of the 6th OECD Forum on Green Finance & Investment in 2020, Hugh Wheelan, the CEO Responsible Investor, quoted Laurence Boone, the OECD's chief economist as saying with view to the Covid-19 crisis: "We missed the green recovery in the financial crisis, we can't afford to miss it again" (Wheelan, 2020, min. 2:35–2:45). He, thereby, alluded to the 'green' opportunity to repair the reputational dent many financial sector practitioners suffered from enriching themselves at the cost of public economic stability (Monk & Perkins, 2020; Paterson, 2010). As I emphasized in the context chapter, however, the global financial crisis had variegated effects on the South African economy. Asked whether South Africa's financial sector jumped at the opportunity to regain legitimacy as actors 'doing good for society' just as many in the Global North, one NGO representative retorted:

It's actually the opposite because the South African financial sector was remarkably unscathed by the crisis and so it was just another ego boost for them, like 'Look how well we did!'. The whole world's financial systems collapsed, and we were so strong and resilient' and that kind of thing, you know. So, it almost *reinforced* the way that they were doing things already because they didn't suffer that crisis. (Civil Society actor 2, p. 6: 2100)

Because they fared well through the global financial crisis, domestic financial market actors don't seem to see the need for a green overhaul of the sector. As the subsection on the South African taxonomy and the ambiguous role of the JSE, similarly, demonstrate, the impetus to shift into greener gears is limited, in large part due to the perceived risks that accompany these shifts into only partially chartered territory. Though the financial sector is increasingly influencing the governance decisions (Pagliari & Young, 2020), whether regarding the taxonomy or the market-led energy sector reform (see also the subsection below on depoliticization), it is mainly to ensure the status quo is maintained.

* * *

The context chapter delineates the various socio-economic challenges the government—itself caught in a legitimacy crisis—struggles to maneuver. Sam Ashman refers to the rampant social crises, particularly (racial) inequality, that undermine state capacity and need to be rebuilt (CBI webinar, 2021, p. 15: 663). All financial actors and NGOs I asked about the government crisis invariably made Jacob Zuma responsible for the erosion in government legitimacy (Civil Society actor 2, p. 7: 285; RE Industry representative, pos. 7; Fund Manager 1, pos. 66), prompting one fund manager to proclaim: "[Our] Fund stays as far away as possible from government entities since [our] projects are small and need to be up and running quickly. Once you start engaging with government entities, it takes too long" (Fund Manager 3, pos. 28). That governments alone cannot solve the climate crisis rings even louder in the South African context. The lead in sustainability of one institutional fund even justified his career move into the financial sector in light of government shortcomings:

> [P]ersonally that's one of the reasons why I joined the financial sector as an ESG professional. I felt that the finance sector provided a real leverage in making decisions and actually making them happen and I think [...] the reality is since the late sixties, we have relied on government, and they have gotten us nowhere. (Fund Manager 2, pos. 116)

With the start of Ramaphosa's administration in 2018, many in the financial sector and beyond placed hopes on him rooting out corruption (RE Industry representative, pos. 5–7; Futuregrowth employee, pos. 138–42), one of the main tickets of his campaign (see Chapter 4). He put a stop to debates around nuclear expansion, one of the epicenters of corrupt practices, citing costs as the main binding constraint (RE Industry representative, pos. 5–7). But he has yet to act on the Zondo Commission's reports that were published by June 2022 and investigated state capture. That money earmarked for pandemic relief during the Covid-19 pandemic was siphoned off and let to the dismissal of Health Minister did not help either (Bloomberg, 2021; Cohen, 2021). And even his riches he attained in cattle trading and as a businessman (Hartley, 2017) raise eyebrows:

> I would say that Ramaphosa is also a beneficiary of rigging the state and economy in favor of particular elites. But he did it under the law. [...] How do people get so rich, immediately? (WWF representative, pos. 16)

And competing interests within the party are palpable particularly with regard to the trajectory of the energy sector. This is evident in the delay of the Integrated Resource Plan and Energy Minister Gwede Mantashe launching the Energy Council of SA[9] right at the time President Ramaphosa's Climate Committee negotiated the just transition deal with the EU, the UK, and the USA (Davies, 2021; Njini, 2022). Due to its tripartite setup (see context chapter), the ANC government seems hamstrung by internal divisions that explain some of the contradictory policy decisions that stall the unbundling of Eskom and safeguard coal while expanding renewables.

* * *

Load shedding is still a common feature in the country's energy landscape, resulting from severe mismanagement of Eskom's coal fleet (Civil Society actor 4, pos. 5–6) *adversely* affecting economic growth trajectories (Banker 2, pos. 23). According to the WWF representative I interviewed, the transition discourse then shifted from a purely environmental to an energy security concern (WWF representative, pos. 9). This was evident in the Democratic Alliance, a liberal opposition party, to deploy "Keep the lights on" as their campaign slogan in 2019 (Maimane, 2019). That load shedding has persisted throughout 2022 is also to do

---

[9] A lobby group comprising the four fossil fuel companies Sasol, Eskom, Exxaro, and Total Energies as well as Anglo American Platinum, the Industrial Development Corporation, the Central Energy Fund and Automotive Business Council Naamsa.

with Eskom's abysmal financial record, the main spoiler of the transition efforts, according to one development banker. He describes Eskom as a

> monolithic autocratic domineering institution that controls distribution and transmission and generation. Or even control the licensing NERSA [the energy regulator]. [...] I mean they control everything. And now they just buried themselves into a hole because of Medupi and Kusile [the two biggest coal-fired power plants in the country, both of which don't operate at full capacity]. Medupi and Kusile, the history books are written, will be the cause of Eskom's failure. Nothing else. Absolutely nothing else. (Development Bank Representative 1, pos. 352–358)

South Africa's energy sector is somewhat uniquely caught in the double bind of urgently required transitions: One being induced by the climate crisis and the other being its legacy system which has prevented the liberalization of the sector (Chamber of Commerce Representative, pos. 113; Development Partner, pos. 67). The unbundling of Eskom, which has been more and less aggressively debated for decades, has gotten new impetus under President Ramaphosa. Especially given persisting load shedding, the governing ANC needs to make positive headlines. As one developer observes:

> The ANC are in deep trouble because of load shedding. If they don't seem to do something now, they're really going to be in trouble. I think for the first time they're really worried about losing votes because of load shedding and it's real, and so. And they're kind of going into recession soon unless they fix the problem. So, they've got a lot of you know a lot of issues there and that sort out. (Developer 1, pos. 290–292)

The government made slow progress slowly in recent months, with legislature being waved through cabinet that would pave the way for transmission to be separated into its own entity (Burkhardt, 2022b), quite along the lines as former CSIR head Tobias Bischof-Niemz has suggested (Bischof-Niemz, 2019). Particularly among trade unions, according to the NGO representative, there is a deep-seated fear of the green transition leading to privatization and ultimately the loss of not only jobs in coal but also the lucrative Eskom salaries at three times above market rate (Civil Society actor 4, pos. 16). We return to this issue when discussing the just transition below.

* * *

The rampant social crises overshadow efforts at greening the financial sector evident in the likelihood of funding to be geared more towards social rather than climate concerns. An institutional investor explains:

> There's definitely been more of a focus on the social element in South Africa simply because there's a big social need in around upliftment and economic development into social areas, like the infrastructure, like your housing and so forth. Okay? I mean that speaks to the immediate need of South Africans - the lack of infrastructure. So, obviously, first, if you know, and therefore the bigger focus on projects that provide a green sort of social outcome and social upliftment. The green sort of climate element, I think South Africans are realizing and South African investors are realizing that you know we can't ignore the climate risk that is here and is affecting everything here now. But definitely, there's been more focus on the social side. (Futuregrowth employee, pos. 56–58)

An investment consultant agrees with her statement adding that the widespread social crises have shored up resentments against green projects perceived as luxurious and elitist. He explains:

> So, if you were to pose a scenario to a retirement fund board of trustees, and you said, 'Here's a couple of investments, a green bond without much detail, a low cost education provider, private, not government, a low cost private healthcare provider, low cost, not government, anything that's going to lead to job creation or an improved living standard for your rural black South African', it's probably more likely to get funding than a lot of these green bonds, which are seen as, and again this is my view, it's an armchair view, it's a kind of a fancy investment instrument to almost make the rich richer, the poor poorer. Without [unclear], again, education, awareness raising, what is a green bond? What is it trying to achieve? (Asset Management Consultant 1, pos. 76)

These elitist perceptions are ground in some anecdotal evidence. Growth-point Properties, which issued the first corporate bond, used its green bond to upgrade its high-end office spaces. As the asset management consultant goes on to explain:

Green building is very popular in South Africa, but again, it's seen as this nice to have, because we're talking about A grade office, corporate head-quarters. We're not talking about neighborhoods, suburban neighborhoods or schools. It's still very much seen as this elitist, first world. It's almost this benchmarking for the top one percent of society, and the rest of us we need to, whatever, survive from one day to another. (Asset Management Consultant 1, pos. 78)

The treasury I interviewed described a similar problem. Their attempt at procuring electric buses to 'green' public transport turned out 5 times as expensive as conventional fossil-run buses; they opted for the cheaper fossil-based quote (Municipal representative 2, pos. 153–154). That 'green' connotes 'expensive' and 'nice-to-have' is a widely held belief that also green bonds anecdotally support.

Financial Sector Fear of a Populist Backlash

The uneven developments not least since the global financial crisis have thrown social crises around unequal access and poverty into sharp relief. Many financial actors fear a populist backlash premised on aggravating inequality. To the Old Mutual representative, "rising popularism" exudes a "big level of threat" possibly leading to "the green economy agenda" to be "seen as something that's the purview in the domain of the elite" (Old Mutual Representative, pos. 279). The ICMA representative suggests inclusive growth strategies as part of the green economy to pay cognizance to the injustices of South Africa's Apartheid past (ibid., pos. 271).

The capital market specialist at one of the big banks derogatively refers to the "uninformed uneducated majority who don't understand all effects, work themselves up in a frenzy […] you can often get the public to make a wrong call. And then you are guilty by public auction" (Banker 1, pos. 47). An ESG consultant even uses a counterfactual anecdote to make the same case:

So, an anecdote from my last Namibia trip, second to last Namibia trip, we went to a solar farm, and I kid you not, in less than a kilometer away there is an informal settlement without access to electricity. And yet a kilometer away you have a ten-megawatt solar farm, which could easily supply that community with power, but those kinds of dots weren't joined in the, in the development of the solar farm.

It's not South Africa. But in South Africa we would have the inhabitants of that informal settlement going and burning down, or destroying the solar farm, because they're not benefiting from it. Which is not the case in Namibia, but that just shows you some of the, some of the challenges, what/ to South Africa's credit, there are very strong social requirements in terms of having a community development trust and economic development benefits to local communities around these various project sites. (Asset Management Consultant 1, pos. 64–66)

The third hypothesis stating that 'the uneven aftermath of the global financial crisis bolstered South Africa's financial sector', thus, faces conflicting evidence. The NGO representative's comments on the financial sector's emboldened position due to surviving the global financial crisis unscathed support the hypothesis as does the lack of impetus in greening finance through regulation. Simultaneously, concerns for popular resistance to 'green' projects seems widespread in the financial sector community, which themselves raise concerns over 'elitist' perceptions of green projects.

A 'Natural' Transition with Self-Fulfilling Properties

A popular argument among technical proponents of the transition, whether institutional investors, the solar industry, or the IPP office, paints the transition as an inevitable outcome of 'natural forces'. An institutional investor argues that "mine workers jobs are ultimately at risk but it's not because of renewables, it's because those projects are going to come to a *natural* end of their life" (Fund Manager 1, pos. 68). The IPP office representative, similarly, uses the term 'natural transition' to variously connote market forces around supply and demand, i.e. "if you run out of capacity on the grid in the Northern Cape, where else do you go" (IPP office representative, pos. 37) to choices between coal and renewables which should not be put as "opposing to each other" as it is more "about information, about benefits, about training and reskilling activities, it is about getting manufacturing up" (IPP office representative, pos. 47). It is an attempt to depoliticize the transition discourse by trying to brush over trade-offs inherent to each energy technology and instead focus on the 'common' goal of ensuring energy provision. To the IPP office representative, the political elements merely include considerations to "direct that transition earlier" (pos. 37). This statement is also echoed by the CBI report on South Africa, wherein the transition carries a self-fulfilling element: They see, "investors all around the world are no longer questioning if a shift will happen but rather how quickly it will happen and how it will play out" (CBI & Agora Energiewende, 2021, p. 2).

Quite unique for a sector that is dependent on future returns, actors vested in green financial products invoke a self-fulfilling prophecy of a green overhaul of the sector. The head analyst for capital market developments at one major bank argues with view to their maiden green bond:

> Because there is no observable benefit in the funding as yet, the asset guys aren't particularly fazed, because they are borrowing money at the normal cost as they would when they price their projects and so on – internal transfer price mechanism just like in any other bank. There is going to come a time when maybe those green bonds are more cost-efficient and Nedbank is raising capital, because they are green, at a cheaper price. And the guys in the asset unit are going to say, 'If I want to have the benefit of that cheaper funding, I can pass it on to my client and be more competitive'. So, when I pitch for the deal, I come in at a more competitive price, I'll have a better chance of winning that transaction. That is where it is going to end up. (Banker 1, pos. 33)

One developer shares this confidence in its green bond opening up the market (Developer 1, pos. 21). The hope that, one day, green projects "will far exceed yield on coal and all the rest of it" (Banker 2, pos. 49) is grounded in some fact. That firms active in heavily-emitting industries increasingly struggle to get funding is exemplified by the recently announced domestic coal IPPs, that struggle to reach financial close as more banks are refusing to fund it, fearing reputational backlash (IPP office representative, pos. 51; Developer 2 and 1, pos. 200–207; Energy Capital, 2019; Yelland & Lilley, 2019).

The appeal to 'naturalize' the transition by calling it a "natural movement away from the fossil fuel industry" (IPP office representative, pos. 48), thus, appears sensical given the ailing 35GW in fossil fleet planned to be decommissioned by 2050 (Mkhize & Radmore, 2021) and the price differential between conventional and renewable energy sources increasingly tilting towards renewables (CSIR, 2016). To speak of a self-fulfilling prophecy of a green overhaul of capital markets based on global investor demand for green assets underpins the hype (Knuth, 2018) around the product that shall safeguard its growth trajectory. One bank representative likens her bank's innovative push for green bonds to the tech giant Apple, who "need to create the demand" (Banker 4, pos. 44) for a product like green bonds. One way to get there is by hyping it up.

However, to favor a "disinterested" view to drive the transition (Old Mutual Representative, pos. 281) depoliticizes the effects of a transition and excludes the interests of stakeholders affected by these changes (Best and Paterson, 2010). Ridding the transition off its political economic elements by portraying it as natural has not really worked in the South African transition discourse. I argue that precisely this technical attempt at guiding the transition has contributed to its limited success as it ignores the vested interests of incumbent industries. Still, repoliticizing a transition neither necessarily renders it more democratic or just. As one academic familiar with the matter argues, there is a cacophony of opposing voices to a low-carbon transition ranging from Eskom staff to nuclear advocates, those wary of foreign (green) takeover as well as trade unions fearing privatization and seeing renewables solely as a capitalist tool (Researcher, pos. 60–61). Still, in defiance of all efforts at painting the transition as a natural and inevitable process, socio-economic concerns persist and are best embodied in the debate around the just transition.

A Contested Just Transition

South Africa was the first country to enshrine a 'just transition' in its NDCs (Civil Society actor 5, pos. 34; Department of Environmental Affairs, 2016). President Ramaphosa even launched a so-called Presidential Climate Committee and assigned it with the task to advance a just transition concern which resulted in a framework for a just transition that is currently out for public comment (Presidential Climate Commission, 2022). Beforehand, the National Planning Commission had toured the country for a year to device a stakeholder dialogue on just transition pathways (National Planning Commission, 2019). Many initiatives like the Trade and Industrial Policy think tank or GreenCape try to "get the government to understand the opportunities, the economic opportunities inherent in this concept of a just transition" (Civil Society actor 2, p. 8: 498, see also Civil Society actor 1, pos. 13–15).

A representative of the International Labor Organization (ILO), who used to work in South Africa for most of her life before moving to organize just transition networks at global stage, comments:

We don't really get the synergies going with the messages that come from the ground and civil society, from workers' organizations. [… By contrast], you have this really high-level debate that is a bit detached from reality. (ILO representative, pos. 19)

In South Africa, there is no common understanding on the just transition. The key slogan that is invoked is the 'just transition' though the term is used strategically by diametrically opposed camps. Environmental groups like *Earthlife* used it to rally against the coal mega projects in Kusile and Medupi only to be framed "unpatriotic" (Civil Society actor 5, pos. 48). Standard Bank uses it to justify its persistent investment in coal (Neumann & Elsner, forthcoming). Trade unions use it to safeguard jobs in the mining sector and the government uses it ambiguously to justify the status quo *and* appeal for change. As a climate NGO interviewee explains, many unions do not align with the climate justice movements' transition demands, considering it an attack on workers, thus "driving a wedge between these unions and climate justice movements" (Civil Society actor 5, pos. 26). She still considers these conflicts vital spaces for deliberation and understanding "environmental justice issues and its links to jobs" (ibid.).

According to a solar industry representative, however, the challenge around the just transition arises from a lose-lose situation of environment and jobs lost due to mine closures:

The issue is really about how do we find an outcome from a lose-lose situation for mines and government that says 'Ok, I am going to give you a very clear exit task ok and you get to walk away with mine closure license. I get you to help set in place a new legacy for these areas'. (RE Industry representative, pos. 24)

Concerns for an equitable and job-creating transition are justified in the face of rampant unemployment and poverty (see Chapter 4). That an additional 70,000 jobs in coal mining will be lost needs to be properly mitigated (RE Industry representative, pos. 24; see also IASS/IET/CSIR, 2022 for green job estimates in the hardest hit regions). Trade unions, in particular, fear that a privatization of an electricity sector largely dominated by Eskom would exacerbate the employment crisis (Chamber of Commerce Representative, pos. 113).

Unfortunately, the renewable energy projects—one of the key investment vehicles for green bonds—have not cashed in on the job promises
originally made (Energy & Finance Journalist, pos. 5, 32, 35; Economic
Development Department representative, pos. 14; RE Industry representative, pos. 24, 26; WWF representative, pos. 5–6, 31). According to
NERSA, the country's energy regulator, 300,000 new jobs in generation, and manufacturing were targeted by 2020 (NERSA, 2017, p. 3).
By 2020, the target figures had completely narrowed to merely targeting
direct employees at the respective IPPs and significantly lower benchmarks—it is therefore no surprise that these have been successfully met
(NERSA, 2020, p. 19).[10] More ambitious plans for labor to transition
to renewables have been tabled but were contested and lost pace due
to the lack of a clear roadmap in the REI4P program. The government's
hesitancy to scale up renewables arguably exacerbated the issue of employment creation. Indeed, local content requirements and local shareholding
have not yielded immediate returns (Fund Manager 1, pos. 50; Asset
Management Consultant 2, pos. 90–91).

To the representative of one NGO active in this realm, the employment
situation has been abysmal, even before the Covid-19 pandemic worsened
the scene:

> The number of people who have lost their jobs, unemployment in South
> Africa is such absolutely horrendous. Inequality poverty, all of those things
> and state capacity to act and do what's necessary to get the economy better
> going again I mean I don't like to say that, but you know what I mean but
> do all what the economists want you to do. And I think that that is also
> an opportunity and sort of build better thing many would. [...] There is a
> tendency now in some circles to say well, let's just focus on/ what are you
> talking about, you can't get rid of coal, we've got to grow the economy,
> you can't be losing jobs, we can't be doing this. We've got to be better
> at framing the just transition as a mechanism to get us out of this [...] I
> mean it was exacerbated by Covid, but it wasn't caused by Covid. We were
> in a terrible slump long before Covid hit you know. (Civil Society actor 2,
> p. 7: 1953)

Framing the just transition in advantageous terms has, thus, been not
garnered enough support. To the solar industry representative and

---

[10] One academic also pointed out the difficulty to audit job creation, as numbers are
just passed along from developer to the Department of Energy (Researcher, pos. 50).

government advisor, the solution is a massive expansion of renewables. He drafted his own Solar Industry Development Plan:

> [RE industry Representative]: So, in very crude terms what I want to say is, if I now know that I am going to build 5100MW PV plants over the next 10 years, around Classdorpe or Wittbank, we create maybe 400-500 jobs per site for a 9-months period for unskilled workers. But if I keep rolling over and over, I start to create some jobs.
> [author]: Rolling over meaning constructing more plants?
> [RE industry Representative]: Constructing more plants. So, if I say in 10 years, I am going to build 5 plants so that means I am going to create on a wider basis probably 4-5000 jobs. It does not solve the issue, but it starts to absorb some of that labor. But the most important thing is the following: the SIDP [Solar Industry Development Plan] is about how do I create a framework that then allows the state, the mining companies in particular Mpumalanga over the 5-10 years that you want to close and get mine closure licenses. You have Eskom that needs to close some 16 coal-fired power stations over the next 20 years in that area and we are going to build a sh*tload of IPPs. The first thing is: Can we get alignment of our strategy that says over the next 20-30 years I want to transition a dying mining economy into a mixed green economy? And I am using the deployment of large-scale renewable energy as the catalyst – This morning I sat with one of South Africa's largest reverse-osmosis plant builders. What is the second biggest problem in the West Rand and Mpumalanga? It is mine wastewater. The way you treat mine wastewater is reverse-osmosis. Anywhere between 25% and 40% of the cost of the water reverse osmosis is due to electricity. So, now I want to start using renewable IPPs to start retreating water. (RE Industry representative, pos. 24–26)

Unfortunately, his proposal was vetoed by the National Union of Mineworkers, who said "they couldn't stand the idea of IPPs in the energy sector" (RE Industry representative, pos. 29). The just energy transition in the country is caught in a paradoxical double bind of trade unions blocking the expansion of independent power producing for the lack of current job creation and fears of privatization on the one hand. And the solar industry cannot upscale production and create jobs due to the lack of an ambitious roadmap to expand renewables on the other. There is a strong case to be made that this resulted less from the private element that competitive bidding for independent power producing heralded than the lack of continuity in the program which would have provided clear investment horizons for companies that heavily invested in the early phases of the program only to suffocate and go bankrupt over the hiatus. The change to aggressively grow the domestic industry was missed.

There have been interesting global developments, however. Unlike a country like Germany that can churn out €69–93 billion for its coal commission to cushion the phase-out of its coal sector by 2038 (Agora Energiewende, 2019, p. 8), South Africa cannot fiscally afford such an economy-wide transfer (Environmental Ministry representative, pos. 13).[11] But it remains to be seen what comes of the just energy transition partnership fund endowed with US$8.5 billion in grant and concessional funding, the Presidential Climate Commission negotiated with Germany, France, the United Kingdom, and the USA at COP26 for its coal phase down and Paris alignment (Pilling et al., 2022; Sguazzin & Prinsloo, 2022). At its current magnitude, however, it will do little to overcome rampant and worsening unemployment rates (Naidoo, 2021) and provides—at best—a start towards funding a national energy transition requiring an estimated US$250 billion over the next three decades, according to a recent study (Blended Finance Taskforce & Centre for Sustainability Transitions, 2022).

As the previous paragraphs demonstrated, social concerns, particular around job creation, and retention loom over the transition and are captured under the just transition umbrella. To many green institutional investors, however, the just transition debate impedes the transition to greener pastures. They perceive trade unions as one impediment to their low-carbon transition endeavors, citing misinformation campaigns around coal being cheaper than renewables (Old Mutual Representative, pos. 280–281) and the expensive early round tariffs of the REI4P as responsible for Eskom's dire financial position (Researcher, pos. 40). As the IPP office representative laments, the REI4P has become the false "scapegoat" for Eskom's mismanagement (IPP office representative, pos. 14). It highlights the political economic nature of transition endeavors from which lots of stakeholders standing to gain or lose.

This chapter recapitulated my interviewees' perception of the multiple crises that magnify and simultaneously deter from the climate crisis. They

[11] Although the levels of inequality (Chancel et al., 2022, pp. 217f) would justify more heavy-handed redistribution from top to bottom, i.e. via wealth taxes.

unanimously mirror the concern for competing policy priorities. These either slow—if not outrightly block—or at least complicate efforts at aligning with the Paris Agreement. The variegated debate around the just transition embodies these difficulties. Green bonds are by no means equipped to address this multitude of demands. On its own, a financial fix like green bonds cannot accommodate the myriad of different and divergent needs nor remedy *all* the multiple crises afflicting South Africa. Their application serves narrow climate-conscious investment decisions.

These mutually incommensurable positions at various ends of the economy trying to weigh in on the transition trajectory of the country demonstrate its politically contested nature. This section demonstrated that depoliticizing the transition by painting it as pursuing a natural course has yielded popular opposition. This is unsurprising, given the structural overhaul and distributional ramifications that transitions of this magnitude entail (Kern & Markard, 2016; Swilling & Annecke, 2012). The financial sector's technical approach and incomprehension of other socio-economic criteria necessarily clash with industrial and job-centered approaches as favored by trade unions. Green bonds, per se, are too narrow a financial instrument to decisively disrupt this deadlock. In the last section, we also stay within the politically charged terrain of the low-carbon transition endeavors but focus more directly on the political economic apples of discord ripening around green bond market expansion.

Green Bonds—A Political Economic Question Over Sharing of Benefits and Public Support

As the previous subsection on the just transition demonstrated, the trajectory of the low-carbon transition in South Africa is politically highly contested, despite financial sector and external advisor pleas to pursue a "disinterested" (Old Mutual Representative, pos. 281) or "technical–economic" (Service Provider 2, pos. 8) approach. This last subsection looks more concretely at the attempts to depoliticize *finance-led* transition endeavors. I zoom in on efforts to disguise trade-offs in South Africa's green finance taxonomy debate, the reliance on 'apolitical experts', and the depoliticizing elements in the taxonomy's governance setup. In a second step, I will lay bare the limits of attempts to depoliticize a finance-led transition by foregrounding the distributive elements that are invariably contained in the financial setup of this transition. This will be illustrated along the battle over refinancing REI4P projects through green bonds, which the Independent Power Producers office (IPP office) has opposed. This example powerfully demonstrates not only the limited take-up of green bonds due to political economic reasons. It also demonstrates that the depoliticization of South Africa's transition endeavors has been largely unsuccessful. Thirdly, it exemplifies the limited success of a finance-led transition that is blind to redistributive concerns. Lastly, it provides insights into the tug-of-war between market and bank-based lending provisions.

The Depoliticizing Elements of South Africa's Green Bond Taxonomy

Standard-setting organizations such as the CBI are vehicles through which (green bond) market expansion can garner legitimacy and political support (Hilbrandt & Grubbauer, 2020; Tripathy, 2017). The ongoing deliberation around South Africa's green taxonomy is one such attempt to agree on a green standard that simultaneously aims to foster market growth. In my research, I stumbled across efforts to depoliticize this debate around the taxonomy and ridding it off the contradictory interests. I supplement these findings with other observations painting the market expansion of green bond in ethically intrinsic terms.

In the GGKP webinar on green bond diffusion in South Africa, Christelle van Vuuren, the Associate Director of Carbon Trust and a key driving force behind the South African green bond taxonomy, describes efforts to do away with the trade-offs of what constitutes green. After making a strong case to attract international capital, she argues for the necessity to coalesce

> views and policy perspectives on what constitutes green and all of the conflicting uh well in the past conflicting but now increasingly um cooperative issues around social environmental and trade-offs that used to be but we're seeking to no longer have that kind of narrative um in the long term. (GGKP webinar, 2021, pos. 1214–1226)

With her statement, she acknowledges conflicts in the debate around what constitutes green as much as the inherent economic and environmental trade-offs—be that the environmental procedures perceived as cumbersome for market actors or the anticipated adverse economic effects of being excluded from the taxonomy. But she brushes these concerns aside by focusing on the benefits of a taxonomy, whichever guise it will get in the end. This statement openly calls for ignoring social and environmental trade-offs to make way for a market to operate. At the green finance taxonomy launch, she doubled down on this argument, averring, that the taxonomy "is without trade-off. There isn't social attribution or climate ambition brought around at the detriment of the other" (Author's Notes at Green Taxonomy Launch, 2022, roughly 67 minutes into the event). It is, thus, a prime example of what cultural political economists term efforts at "depoliticizing" (Best & Paterson, 2010, 2015) the effects of a key regulatory instrument to finance the transition, a deliberate blind spot widely criticized in Transition Studies (Geels, 2014; Köhler et al., 2019). Interestingly, this depoliticization not only occurs at the level of *negotiating* the taxonomy, but is also the *result* of a taxonomy that can then—as a standard—be referred to when justifying investments (Hilbrandt & Grubbauer, 2020).

This tendency to ignore trade-offs is also palpable in the JSE's sustainability lead leaving the assessments of what is green "to the experts" (JSE Representative 2, p. 4: 1467). She, therein, infers an apolitical and impartial notion of how external advisors (Ferguson, 1994) or rating agencies like Moody's or Sustainalytics reach their assessment, despite evidence to the contrary (see subsection on the green taxonomy above and Sinclair, 2010).

One commercial banker is very frustrated with the conflicting sets of interests inhibiting the low-carbon transition. Like the institutional investor's hunch for a disinterested pursuit, this banker argues in favor of leaving the transition to experts that have the overarching goal of addressing climate change in mind:

> But until everybody realizes that we got one common cause and one vested interest and we actually have to operate under a mandate like a project player or any other thing we build. When we build something, we get the builder in to lay the bricks, we get the steelworker in to get the steel, we get electricity – why don't we do that in climate finance? The researching guys want to all understand credit. They want to be an expert in credit. The credit guys want to understand the community aspects, the environmental aspects. Why? Why? Why? Why? I should be coming to you as the expert and you should be 100% liable for that. When I lose money, 'cause you gave me sh*t advice, you should lose money with me. And if you lose money because I made a sh*t credit decision, you should be protected from it. Now it is game on. (Banker 2, pos. 51)

This ostensible reliance on external expertise seeks to bolster credibility of this nascent market, which is also palpable in the academic style in which market reports are written (Tripathy, 2017). This notion of expertise, however, risks elevating technical know-how above wider concerns for socio-economic consequences that may follow. It also risks ignoring vested interests supposedly apolitical expert may harbor. This is not to discredit expertise but to understand it in a political economic context in which this knowledge is created.

Beyond the reliance on external expertise, South Africa's green bond market is complemented—somewhat counter-intuitively—by the celebration of its community as a community of learning (Monk & Perkins, 2020). This emerging community seems driven by an intrinsic motivation as Christelle van Vuuren describes in the webinar in early November 2021:

> There is a lot that's happening in South Africa over the last two years especially, I mean preceding that also but it's really uh the momentum has built so much. And there's been such a lot of coalition work that it's really an extremely exciting place to be at the moment. Also, emails are jammed and people are stretched but it's a /there's such a lot of cooperation that's also happening between private sector and public sector and industry bodies and others so a lot of momentum but that also comes with a lot of work to keep sort of ensuring that you're aligning, aligning, aligning. (GGKP webinar, 2021, pos. 815–830)

The community of learning is evident in one major South African institutional investor sharing its impact measuring platform with competitors in the industry "to raise the level of reporting and thinking about how people do [impact reporting] properly" (Fund Manager 2, pos. 138). Turning a privately financed framework into a public good for competitors is a remarkable facet of mutual learning in the market other studies already noted (Monk & Perkins, 2020). Nonetheless, this particular fund stands to benefit from the standardization effect were other industry players to adopt the same metrics.

CICERO's Christa Clapp summarizes the inroads of the labeled bond market by describing it as "a learning process. So, I very much welcome that we are trying these new financial products, and then we have some learning to do along the way" (C. Clapp podcast, 2020, pos. 23). The green bond community seems to be learning fast. Some still need to get used to green bond's new hype. Bridget Boulle, similarly, looks back:

> I used to do my first job at climate bonds was analyzing all these bonds and I had a quite an easy job because it was you know a trickle if one or two would come in a month maybe uh sometimes got two or three a week and now I see emails from my colleague who's taking my place and there's 100 a week to look at so you can see that the uh the growth has been enormous. (CBI webinar, 2021, p. 4: 2514)

The community of learning, thus, surfs on a hype it helped create that deliberately seeks to sideline trade-offs arising in the roll out of the market.

* * *

The regulatory overhaul of the capital market in South Africa carries both functional and depoliticizing elements. The major functional effect (Ferguson, 1994) is the increased financialization of capital market regulations by shifting regulatory responsibility to capital market actors (see also Pagliari & Young, 2020). This is evident in the taxonomy working group setup that negotiates the taxonomy and its consultation process and is significantly slated in favor of capital market interests and the setup of the green segment at the JSE.

This taxonomy working group is part of the umbrella of the Climate Risk Forum Steering Committee, chaired by the National Treasury and hosted by the Banking Association South Africa (BASA). The financial regulatory bodies South African Reserve Bank, the Financial Sector Conduct Authority (FSCA), and the South African Reserve Bank Prudential Authority are also members of the committee, as are capital market lobby groups like the Association for Savings and Investment South Africa (ASISA), the Council of Retirement Funds for South Africa (BATSETA), and the South African Insurance Association. With the Department of Environment, Forestry and Fisheries, another government ministry is present though in a subordinate position to the National Treasury. Lastly, the JSE is of course also part of the committee (South Africa Sustainable Finance Initiative, 2021). The very setup of these working groups or consulting workshops, however, is political, comprising both elected representatives of ministries as much as industry lobbyists, whose vested interests should not be ignored. And though more than 30 institutions submitted more than 440 comments, statements, recommendations, and queries during the drafting process (National Treasury, 2022b, p. 47), it remains to be seen to what extent NGO demands have been incorporated.

Similarly, the launching of the green segment in Johannesburg was preceded by consulting and awareness campaigns. The former sustainability lead at the JSE remembers:

> The JSE did a number of workshops with people, even before the segment was launched also when they were developing the rules, so there are regulatory processes that they have to follow by law in developing rules. Before that there was a lot of consultation. I was not that close to it, which was the right approach. It was run by the market and business development product specialist side, talking to the potential issuers and potential people to provide the verification and opinions and so on. They had a whole marketing campaign that was run around the time it was launched, events and so on. I am not sure what the take up has been since, but certainly there was lots of effort to make people aware of it. (JSE Representative 1, p. 7: 686)

Far from being mere technical endeavors, consultations, thus, not only serve to gather feedback but are also a means to promote a new product and raise awareness among potential issuers and investors: It is a key ingredient for the establishment and successful take-off of financial innovations.

That the debate around the low-carbon transition can seamlessly shift away from contentious elements and be depoliticized is questionable, given the ongoing debates at global stage that constantly reflect on the latest development of this market-in-the-making. Nonetheless, as Hilbrandt and Grubbauer (2020) show, adopted green standards put to rest political tug-of-war over definitions. They just haven't concluded yet.

The myriad of financial practices (Chiapello, 2020) underpinning the ramp-up and hype (Knuth, 2018) of financial innovations in the climate sphere underscores that transitions are political endeavors and no technicality. These examples paint the emerging labeled bond market actors as an innovative community that strives for the alignment of investment criteria for a climate-aligned future. Trade-offs are perceived as undue hurdles along the way. Unfortunately, these political economic trade-offs are inherent aspects of transition endeavors that reallocate burdens and benefits across markets and society. The mere effort to exclude them from discussions around green bond taxonomy and its market expansion can be uncovered using a CPE lens (Best & Paterson, 2010). They help explain why the green bond market has not expanded significantly in South Africa. This claim is probably best substantiated by describing the tussle over refinancing proceeds, which we will turn to next.

The Right to Refinance—A Battle Between Market- and Bank-Based Lending

The domestic renewable energy landscape was caught in a major upheaval in February 2019 when then Minister of Public Enterprises Praveen Gordhan proclaimed that the government will "renegotiate" contracts with companies that won the first two rounds of the REI4P program (Businesslive, 2019; Creamer, 2019; Banker 2, pos. 23). The high tariffs at the time had led to a controversy around 'undue profits' for the financiers of the renewable energy projects. Beyond inaccurate rhetoric around the claim that these tariffs are responsible for Eskom's dire financial position, this controversy, however, yielded interesting insights into the inherently political nature of transition governance. Not only the finance industry, but also developers had opposed the earlier statement. Brenda Martin, the CEO of the South African Wind Energy Association (SAWEA), publicly stated:

> 'Renegotiation, besides raising the specter of breach of contract, would require extensive and careful process to ensure fairness to affected investors while also providing sufficient assurance to prospective investors', says Brenda Martin, CEO of SAWEA. (Creamer, 2019, p. 3–4)

The South African Photovoltaic Industry Association also put out a public statement commencing with a similar argument:

> To stimulate and grow the SA economy, these five elements are critical: predictability, consistency, lower risk, and policy certainty. A simple and blanket tariff renegotiation alone does not achieve this. (Creamer, 2019, p. 4)

Shortly after his statement, Minister Gordhan backpedaled, stating in a public press conference that existing contracts will not be touched (Fund Manager 1, pos. 66–69). The IPP office representative I spoke with conceded that tariff renegotiations as initially proposed by Praveen Gordhan were a "wrong signal to the market"; they complicate contracts which is "not what we want to achieve" (IPP office representative, pos. 30). Indeed, the vast pricing spread of ZAR4 per kilowatt in the first rounds versus ZAR0.5 per kilowatt in the latest round has been a major "headache" for the IPP office under pressure to show positive headlines, thus, looking "at ways of optimizing those tariffs going forward" (IPP office representative, pos. 12, 13).

Instead of renegotiating the old contracts, the IPP office proposed to revamp its refinancing regulations, targeting the first three bidding rounds. In the IPP office representative's own words:

> So, the response to that is rather to say and the Minister of Energy also specifically said that we are looking at *refinancing*. These projects are very ripe to refinance now. And that has been the one element that has not really happened. And when you look at the financial markets, maybe that is also what the markets need to get ready for the next rounds. Maybe the banks need to unload some of these assets and institutional investors should be coming in. And through that process, there should be a benefit in terms of a tariff reduction. (IPP office representative, pos. 30)

Conflicts over the means to refinance those early rounds were ongoing since early 2018 (Fund Manager 1, pos. 4–8). At the time of the interview in April 2019, the IPP office had received 20 applications or requests for refinancing, according to its representative (IPP office representative, pos. 31). This shift in the IPP office away from renegotiating tariffs to negotiating refinancing conditions hinges on a contract clause forcing developers to request permission from the Department of Energy in case they look at refinancing loans (IPP office representative, pos. 31). Given the lack of competition, the domestic commercial banks were the main beneficiaries if not price makers in the early rounds (see the REI4P discussion in section "The Peculiarities of South Africa's Capital Markets Inhibit Green Bond Uptake"). Refinancing enables developers to offload these expensive loans onto institutional investors balance sheets once those have reached lower levels of risks at the end of the construction phase. What looks like a mere technical procedure, however, has turned into a tug-of-war over the loan proceeds and resulted in a major refinancing hold-up. A hold-up, I argue, that can best be explained through a combination of literature around financialization and political economy. I'll present the different positions to this refinancing conflict, namely that of the IPP office as the government representative, a development bank's perspective, an institutional investor perspective, a developer's perspective, and an asset manager's perspective.

Backed by state guarantees and endowed with foreseeable returns, the IPP office considered these uncontested early round projects as "very good assets to the lenders" (IPP office representative, pos. 31). Given the lack of social-economic benefits through the REI4P program, whether through job creation or lower tariffs for end consumers, the IPP office was bulging under pressure to produce positive socio-economic results (IPP office representative, pos. 47). Therefore, the IPP office demanded a share in the benefits to be reaped over refinancing those loans:

> A simple principle: 50:50 share in refinancing gain, which is a general accepted principle in terms of PFI [Public Finance Initiative]. Whether you look at the PPPs [in] the UK, it is accepted in the PPP regulations of the national treasury. So that is what needs to come about. As I said these are very good assets. The banks are always incentivized – they have a good stream of income into the future [...] However, we have not been able to find each other in terms of how the refinancing gain flows through to another tariff. It makes no sense to reduce the tariff by 2 cents or 3 cents. So, there is not a – how can I say in this moment in time – the refinancing that we have been looking at are not of such a nature that it makes a big difference in tariff. (IPP office representative, pos. 31)

As alluded to above, the IPP office representative defended the office's stance on sharing the benefits of refinancing equally by referring to the need to deliver socio-economic results, in this case embodied by lower electricity prices for consumers. In her words:

> Why it is so important to us is really that one needs to understand that: In South Africa there is a big coal industry lobby, that always used the argument that the IPPs are too expensive as a way – that is the conversation that they used in the media etc. It is not always correct. But it is very emotional and then saying that renewables is [sic] going to cause job losses in the coal sector and is responsible for this and that and everything that goes wrong, you know. To roll out future programs, you will need to be able to show that you are bringing a contribution to the economy, you are bringing job creation, you are supporting just transition. But you also have

to show that you are levelling out the cost of electricity to the consumer. (IPP office representative, pos. 35)

She went on to argue that there has been no harmonized set of rules for refinancing yet since "we have not been able to find grounds of rules that would be acceptable to the market and that would give us the outcome we want" (IPP office representative, pos. 43). The negotiation over this 'outcome' is a classic political economic question about the redistribution of benefits, namely capital cost savings for developers on the one hand and lower tariff for the IPP office on the other. The IPP office deemed its demands justified because "[t]he returns on those (first) projects for the developers, for the banks, for whatever, is [sic] crazy" (IPP office representative, pos. 45). For the IPP office, an agreement—whether enshrined in a set of rules or negotiated individually—could only include major concessions on the developer's tariff demands. Through the backdoor of negotiating refinancing options for developers, the IPP office, thus, attempted to reach the same old goal: To renegotiate tariffs.

One development bank I interviewed lobbied for a harmonized approach to refinancing, best enshrined in a harmonized set of documents applicable to all developers, domestic or foreign. Such a document would have spelled out the conditions to bridge the markets between bank-based and (capital) market-based lending (Gabor, 2021; Karwowski & Stockhammer, 2017; Knafo, 2022). The Development Bank Representative advocated for "transparent refinancing guidelines in order to explain to every market participant how refinancing works – many developers are not aware of this – and, on the other hand, to enable a port-folio approach" (Development Bank Representative 2, pos. 22), which would have bundled risks and yield lower risk premia on the part of the investors. This foreign development bank was planning to co-create a green bond platform to make refinancing rules transparent for developers and institutional investors. As per prevailing de-risking practices, the development bank would have shouldered the high-risk tranche and garnered the residual returns. As the bank representative went on to explain, it would have undergirded the platform with its balance sheet and cushioned payment defaults (Development Bank Representative 2, pos. 18). The envisioned partner on a domestic level, however, jumped ship at last minute, seeing its own business in the tender jeopardized by a common platform. Given the limited competition among banks, this platform would have re-engineered domestic capital markets (Gabor,

2021) and driven competition for capital provision. Transparent refinancing guidelines, in turn, would have set clear conditions and represent an important step in conjoining banking and capital markets. According to the development bank representative, these proposals (the platform and the refinancing guidelines) did not seem to reap enough political support. She presumed this also resulted from the complex technicalities of these markets "which some politicians do not understand and therefore don't support on a political level" (Development Bank Representative 2, pos. 45). Other than that, she saw "no rational reasons against introducing guidelines" (ibid., pos. 45). The development bank even issued a "seriously worded letter to the Department of Energy" (ibid., pos. 23), emphasizing the importance of transparent refinancing guidelines and a portfolio approach to creating a green bond platform. The development bank, thus, favored a solution to bridge markets and end the refinancing impasse. It wanted clear market-inducing guidelines that would benefit developers (who would be able to offload expensive capital), institutional investors (who would be able to invest in de-risked projects), and consumers (who would benefit from a better price down the line). In their scenario, the domestic commercial banks were the only ones to lose out on their lucrative revenue streams going forward.

The institutional investor I interviewed actively rallied for a green bond refinancing platform and provided important contextualizing figures. According to him, the first three bidding rounds of the REI4P accumulated ZAR90 billion (US$5.85 billion) in which commercial banks and DFIs account ZAR60 billion and ZAR25 billion whereas institutional investors only underwrote ZAR5 billion (US$325 million) (Fund Manager 4, pos. 5). As he put it, "most of the debt is still sitting there and is very expensive for developers to finance [...] these debts sit on the four big banks' balance sheets and yield tremendous amounts of profit" (ibid., pos. 5). To him, the IPP office was the last hurdle to refinance. He argued that providing a transparent framework for refinancing would invite international investors to come in and gobble up the debt depending on their appetite (ibid., pos. 16). He presumed it is exactly the anticipated "larger foreign holding of debt and equity" that explained the reluctance of the Department of Energy to issue transparent guidelines (ibid., pos. 22). That is why, to him, the IPP office had been adamant to negotiate on an individual basis to avoid fiercer competition from abroad, while reducing tariffs nationally. Due to the lack of competition within the banking sector, this had not really worked out. Still, he averred that refinancing via a green bond platform would offset the capital outflow by bringing down prices and thus resulting in better electricity tariffs for the country. He estimated that were a green bond platform to launch, "banks would lose R2bn in profits over night" (ibid., pos. 22). This institutional investor's position, thus, largely mirrored that of the foreign development bank with the same winners and losers and the same key bottleneck—the IPP office's reluctance to produce common guidelines.

Developers, in turn, stood to gain significantly from offloading expensive debt in domestic and international capital markets. To one developer heavily invested in the REI4P project and supported by a development bank in creating their own internal green bond framework, the Department of Energy acted as a gatekeeper and predominant bottleneck to refinancing their projects since developers needed the Department's approval (Developer 1, pos. 8). Confronted with the demand to reduce tariffs, the developer recounted:

> So, we looked at that quite actively and we spent quite a lot of money modelling different scenarios which we presented to the Department of Energy. And the reduction in tariffs wasn't enough for that. They wanted much more. (Ibid., pos. 9)

The representative of the domestic development bank added credence to their concern, commenting the IPP office may have been "too aggressive" in demanding their "pound of flesh" from developers and banks, when considering the price differential of ZAR2.40 as in the first rounds as opposed to ZAR0.60 now (Development Bank Representative 1, pos. 136). The developer I interviewed preferred green bonds as means to lower their capital costs. Rather than handing out their project pipeline to one investor, they wanted "to open up the market, we want people to bid for those because that way we can really get raised up" (Developer 1, pos. 35). This developer was thus staunchly in favor of having institutional investors compete over refinancing their loans and did not mind foreign investment either as "you're not going to do it with South African money alone" (ibid., pos. 70). The competition over capital provision would have ultimately reduced their capital costs and rendered their operations more profitable.

One asset manager I interviewed collaborated closely with Mulilo, a major solar developer in South Africa, and helped them refinance their portfolio (Asset Management Consultant 2, pos. 18). The manager explained their sale's pitch through refinancing as such:

> So, what we do is we basically see, you have a project company, you'd set up a subsidiary of that project company. So, the project still remains owned by the project companies. They set up a, let's call it a refinancing company, that's from their company. And then the refinance company would issue the green bond and the proceeds of that would be rooted into the project company to settle the existing models. So, now you've got a new profile. But that requires the consent for DOE and that's where the sticky points is [sic]. (Ibid., pos. 33)

Refinancing, to him, untaps the "cash trapped" in debt service accounts (ibid., pos. 34). He was quite frustrated recalling his attempt to kick-start refinancing:

> And where we came short is at the Department of Energy, [they] just aren't ready for entertaining these kinds of things, because they're in a bit of a conundrum as you know Eskom is in quite a lot of trouble, financial trouble. And so [...] they want to cut tariffs by like ridiculous levels, make [sic] uneconomic for all those projects for it to make sense. (Ibid., pos. 20–22)

He alleged the IPP office made a political decision not to engage with developers on refinancing given the dire macroeconomic situation with Eskom (ibid., pos. 36)—again emphasizing the impeding competition from other socio-economic policies preoccupying government capacities as much as the impossibility of technical decisions being void of political rationales (Best & Paterson, 2010). Drawing a global comparison, the asset manager argued for the need of the Department of Energy to allow for refinancing, since "the rest of the world is doing it and you need to give these developers the ability to grow their portfolios" (Asset Management Consultant 2, pos. 42). He, thus, not only invoked the need for South African developers for competitiveness (Sum, 2009) as a concern. He also considered green bonds to be an entitlement for developers, given the hard work they put in in the first place: "Why subject them to extremely stringent terms forever?" (Asset Management Consultant 2, pos. 50).

The IPP office largely settled this refinancing impasse in a stalemate when issuing its 'Evaluation of Seller Refinancing Notices – Refinancing

Protocol/Guideline' in June 2020 (IPP Office, 2020). None of the demands on the side of the developers, development bank, or institutional investment sphere were incorporated. Instead of providing transparent guidelines for refinancing for *all* market participants as the development bank proposed or enabling developers to refinance their portfolios to reduce capital costs (which could be channeled in new developments to create additionality), the IPP office held firm on its role as a gatekeeper. Every request for refinancing still requires the IPP office's approval. The IPP office retains its prerogative to negotiate its share in the benefits individually. As passage 2.1. in the refinancing protocol explains:

> Refinancing may be of benefit to both the Seller and the Department and, as such, a Refinancing may be proposed by either the Seller or the Department. [...] Furthermore, the Department have [sic] the right to consent or to decline any proposed Refinancing and where necessary in the exercise of this right of consent the approval of National Treasury pursuant to the PFMA if required may be sought. (Ibid., pp. 4–5)

Interestingly, the IPP office differentiates between increases in returns to the Seller from "improved performance" and improved returns deriving from "changes in the nature of or the terms governing the financing structure" (ibid., p. 5). While the former should exclusively benefit the developer, the latter must be split between developer and IPP office "at least on a 50/50 between the Department and the Seller however higher percentage sharing may be negotiated on a case-by-case basis" (ibid., p. 5).

Despite seemingly restructuring the energy sector along market rationales, the inherent politics of these processes *cannot* be rendered technical (Swyngedouw, 2017). As this example, powerfully, underscores, the political economic questions of distribution of benefits and burdens remain at the core of these market-based restructuring processes. Without these political economic vantage points, these conflicts cannot be fully understood. And as a Development Bank Representative argues, the IPP office, an embodiment of market-oriented institutional innovations, is still party to political tug-of-wars:

> You have the national treasury, the department of environmental affairs, the department of energy, DBSA, the unions, the political parties, I mean, [...] that's who you're talking to every single day of your life. And you

can't get more political if you tried it. (Development Bank Representative 1, pos. 454–456)

By refusing to grant the market 'laisser-faire' in refinancing, the ministry effectively blocked its expansion. The lack of new issuances of green bonds as vehicles for refinancing these early round projects suggests that many developers have not reached a mutually acceptable settlement with the IPP office. The banks, thus, continue reaping the benefits of this stalemate. The IPP office, further, exemplifies that regardless of the achievements in driving generation costs down, they struggle to fulfil their wider socio-economic mandates. Green bonds can only play an indirect role *subsequent* to a refinancing agreement. In short, to reap the benefits of green bonds through refinancing requires prior political consent.

The conundrum over refinancing also illustrates the struggle accompanying the shift from a bank-based to a market-based provision of lending (Gabor, 2021; Knafo, 2022). As this section demonstrated, the Department of Energy seems to retain a preference for bank-based lending, for a myriad of reasons that do not fully align. It is, thus, yet another example of the messiness of vested interests that, by necessity, accompany transitions of this complexity. It also emphasizes the limits of the toolbox of a de-risking state (Gabor, 2020, 2021) that tries to meet socio-economic targets by inducing private investments.

To summarize this entire chapter, I delineated seven arguments that contribute to explaining the lack of green bond diffusion in South Africa. In a first step, I argued that some of the promising capacities of green bonds, so astutely promoted in the green bond community, have not yet materialized in an emerging country context like South Africa. I specifically touched on the lack of bankable projects for investors and the mixed record of the so-called *greenium*, the key motivation for issuers to list a green bond. In this first section, I established the non-negotiable condition of profitability that underpin investors' interests in purchasing green bonds. The need for profitable returns overrules any other consideration, whether social or environmental. Secondly, I juxtaposed Cape Town's green bond success story with Nigeria's failed green bond splash, arguing that both elucidate reasons why potential issuers decide or hesitate to embark on a green bond listing. In this section, I also delineated how the market is bolstered through the provision of market-ready information and reliant on success stories for credibility. In a third step, I derived some of the conceptual flaws of green bond as a product deliberately left 'simple' to be a marketable product to investors, citing the lack of innovation, structural and technical hurdles, the missing leverage in sanctioning a green default, a focus on use-of-proceeds or input factors at the detriment of impact and outcome, and concerns around greenwashing. All these shortcomings can be linked, again, to the need for positive returns to be safeguarded against practical infringements or environmental trade-offs. In an important fourth section, I traced the controversial issuances of sustainability-labeled bonds in the global market to demonstrate the contested terrain of what counts as 'green' and, therefore, as part of the market. I, then, delved into the deliberations of South Africa's own green finance taxonomy, which will likely dilute environmental criteria in its transition taxonomy to account for the fossil-based path-dependent economy. As the controversies around energy-intensive issuers wanting to tap into the green market disclose, it will be interesting to see how resilient South Africa's green finance taxonomy will be when faced with criticism of greenwashing, a key concern among green bond market proponents worldwide. In the fifth section, I dwelled on the idiosyncrasies of the South Africa capital market, namely its mature and sophisticated setup which lacks tradeable assets, its conservative risk-propensity and limited understanding around green bonds, and the regulatory bottlenecks which inhibit green bond take-up. In the latter, I differentiated between lack of stringent regulation on the demand side, identified regulatory gatekeepers, and scrutinized the few policies that drive green bond expansion on the supply side. I focused specifically on the REI4P tender program, the exception to the dearth of supply-side policies, but also spelled out its own respective difficulties. In the sixth part of this chapter, I contextualized the climate crisis with other rampant crises in South Africa to bolster one of my hypotheses around competing policy priorities. I deciphered efforts to paint the transition as natural and counter this narrative with ongoing just transition debates, which themselves at times draw on populist rhetoric bereft of factual footing. That section drives home the politically contested environment green bond advocates specifically and the green economy in South Africa more generally, maneuver. This is also demonstrated in the last section of this chapter, wherein I first delineated the depoliticizing tendencies of market-oriented restructuring efforts of South Africa's low-carbon transition. Given the distributional questions inherent to these structural changes, depoliticizing the transition has not been successful. Far from it, the battle over the 'right to refinance' the loans of the early bidding rounds of the REI4P program, powerfully, disclosed the distributional tug-of-war between the ministry, the banking sector, developers, institutional investors, and a development bank. That the IPP office prevented transparent refinancing to be institutionalized is one of the latest and largest pieces to the research puzzle, which explains why green bonds have yet to decisively fund transition endeavors in South Africa. Their bearing on the governance and the contested discourse around the transition endeavors, however, is already palpable. A transition premised on technical-financial innovations like green bonds is unlikely to succeed. The reliance on profitable returns significantly narrows the instruments' applicability and ignores political economic aspects. In South Africa's politically contested transition, redistributive and participatory elements will have to be significantly foregrounded to make a climate-aligned transition a reality.

References

Adamini, M. (2019, October 25). *Talking transition with metals and mining companies.* Environmental Finance. https://www.environmental-finance. com/content/analysis/talking-transition-with-metals-and-mining-companies. html

AfDB. (2022). *African Economic Outlook 2022.* https://www.afdb.org/filead min/uploads/afdb/Documents/Publications/African_Economic_Outlook_ 2018_-_EN.pdf

Agora Energiewende. (2019). *Die Kohlekommission. Ihre Empfehlungen und deren Auswirkungen auf den deutschen Stromsektor bis 2030* [The coal commission. Its recommendations and their effects on the German energy sector until 2030]. https://static.agora-energiewende.de/fileadmin/Projekte/2019/Koh lekommission_Ergebnisse/167_Kohlekommission_DE.pdf

Arent, D., Arndt, C., Miller, M., Tarp, F., & Zinaman, O. (2017). *The political economy of clean energy transitions* (D. Arent, C. Arndt, M. Miller, F. Tarp, & O. Zinaman, Eds.; 1st ed.). Oxford University Press.

ASISA. (2022). *Board of Directors.* https://doi.org/10.18061/bhac.v5i2.8704

Asiyanbi, A. P. (2018). Financialisation in the green economy: Material connections, markets-in-the-making and Foucauldian organising actions. *Environment and Planning A, 50*(3), 531–548. https://doi.org/10.1177/030851 8X17708787

Author's Notes at Green Taxonomy Launch. (2022). *Launch of the Green Finance Taxonomy for South Africa,* 1–9. via Zoom

Baker, L. (2015). The evolving role of finance in South Africa's renewable energy sector. *Geoforum, 64*(July), 146–156. https://doi.org/10.1016/j.geoforum.2015.06.017

BATSETA. (2022). *About Batseta Board of Directors.* https://www.batseta.org.za/aboutus

Bayliss, K., & Van Waeyenberge, E. (2018). Unpacking the public private partnership revival. *Journal of Development Studies, 54*(4), 577–593. https://doi.org/10.1080/00220388.2017.1303671

Best, J., & Paterson, M. (2010). *Cultural political economy* (J. Best & M. Paterson, Eds.; 1st ed.). Routledge.

Best, J., & Paterson, M. (2015). Towards a cultural political economy—Not a cultural IPE. *Millennium: Journal of International Studies, 43*(2), 738–740. https://doi.org/10.1177/0305829814557063

Bigger, P. (2017). Measurement and the circulation of risk in green bonds. *Journal of Environmental Investing, 8*(1), 273–287.

Bigger, P., & Millington, N. (2019). Getting soaked? Climate crisis, adaptation finance, and racialized austerity. *Environment and Planning E: Nature and Space, 3*(3), 601–623. https://doi.org/10.1177/2514848619876539

Bischof-Niemz, T. (2019). *South Africa' s IRP and Eskom restructuring* (Issue March). https://energytransitionsa.files.wordpress.com/2019/03/irp-and-eskom-rmb-investor-forum-tbn_6mar2019_final.pdf

Blended Finance Taskforce, & Centre for Sustainability Transitions. (2022). *Making climate capital work: Unlocking $ 8.5 billion for South Africa's just energy transition.* https://static1.squarespace.com/static/5acdc066c258b4b d2d15050b/t/628e373f28dafe216b114042/1653487452874/Making+Cli mate+Capital+Work+-+FINAL+REPORT.pdf

Bloomberg. (2021, June 11). *Next Africa weekly newsletter.* Bloomberg. https://www.bloomberg.com/news/newsletters/2021-06-11/next-africa-bad-time-for-south-africa-to-lose-a-health-minister

Bos, K., & Gupta, J. (2018). Climate change: The risks of stranded fossil fuel assets and resources to the developing world. *Third World Quarterly, 39*(3), 436–453. https://doi.org/10.1080/01436597.2017.1387477

Bracking, S. (2015). Performativity in the green economy: How far does climate finance create a fictive economy? *Third World Quarterly, 36*(12), 2337–2357. https://doi.org/10.1080/01436597.2015.1086263

Braun, B., Gabor, D., & Hübner, M. (2018). Governing through financial markets: Towards a critical political economy of Capital Markets Union. *Competition and Change, 22*(2), 101–116. https://doi.org/10.1177/102 4529418759476

Buchta, S. (2018, December 5). *The argument for green bonds from "pure-plays."* Environmental Finance. https://www.environmental-finance.com/content/analysis/the-argument-for-green-bonds-from-pureplays.html

Burkhardt, P. (2022a, January 21). *South Africa's big power users want more predictable tariffs*. Bloomberg. https://www.bloomberg.com/news/articles/2022-01-21/south-africa-s-biggest-power-users-want-more-predictable-tariffs

Burkhardt, P. (2022b, February 11). *South Africa takes legal step to open power grid to competition*. Bloomberg. https://www.bloomberg.com/news/articles/2022-02-11/south-africa-takes-legal-step-to-open-power-grid-to-competition

Burkhardt, P., & Prinsloo, L. (2022, February 28). *Cheap South African solar projects challenged by cost surge*. Bloomberg. https://www.bloomberg.com/news/articles/2022-02-28/cheap-south-african-solar-projects-face-cost-challenge-to-close

Businesslive. (2019, February 15). *Pravin Gordhan seeks new deal for old IPPs*, 4–5. https://www.businesslive.co.za/bd/national/2019-02-15-pravin-gordhan-seeks-new-deal-for-old-ipps/

Businesslive. (2021, December 10). *Standard Bank issues green bonds for renewable energy and housing*, 1–2. https://www.businesslive.co.za/bd/companies/financial-services/20...tandard-bank-issues-green-bonds-for-renewable-energy-and-housing/

Buthelezi, L. (2021, May 27). *Standard Bank commits to adopt climate strategy in 2022*. Fin24, 1–3. https://www.news24.com/fin24/Companies/standard-bank-commits-to-adopt-climate-strategy-in-2022-20210527

Butler, A. (2012). The African National Congress under Jacob Zuma. In J. Daniel, P. Naidoo, D. Pillay, & R. Southall (Eds.), *New South African review* (1st ed., pp. 164–183). https://doi.org/10.18772/22010115164.12

Caprotti, F., Essex, S., Phillips, J., de Groot, J., & Baker, L. (2020, April). Scales of governance: Translating multiscalar transitional pathways in South Africa's energy landscape. *Energy Research and Social Science, 70*, 101700. https://doi.org/10.1016/j.erss.2020.101700

Carbon Trust/Treasury/NBI. (2020). *Developing a national green taxonomy: Project briefing report* (Issue October). https://sustainablefinanceinitiative.org.za/wp-content/downloads/Stakeholder_Briefing_Document_9_October_2020.pdf

Carrington, D. (2022, May 13). South Africa's April floods made twice as likely by climate crisis, scientists say. *The Guardian*. https://www.theguardian.com/environment/2022/may/13/south-africa-floods-climate-crisis-global-heating?CMP=Share_iOSApp_Other

Cassim, A., Radmore, J.-V., Dinham, N., & Mccallum, S. (2021). *South African climate finance landscape 2020* (Issue January). https://www.climatepolicyinitiative.org/wp-content/uploads/2021/01/South-African-Climate-Finance-Landscape-January-2021.pdf

CBI. (2019). *State of the market report: The Nigerian green bond market development programme.* Climate Bonds Initiative (Issue November). https://www.climatebonds.net/files/reports/nigerian-green-bond-market-development-programme-state-of-the-market-final.pdf

CBI. (2021, August). Green bonds in South Africa: How green bonds can support South Africa's energy transition. *Climate Bonds Initiative.*

CBI & Agora Energiewende. (2021). *Green bonds in South Africa: How green bonds can support South Africa's energy transition.* https://www.climatebonds.net/files/reports/cbio_sa_energytrans_03d.pdf

CBI webinar. (2021, August 10). *Financing South Africa's energy transition: Unlocking viable economic investments for an African New Deal.* https://www.youtube.com/watch?v=RmzgqQ32BQ8

Chancel, L., Piketty, T., Saez, E., & Zucman, G. (2022). *World inequality report.* https://wir2022.wid.world/www-site/uploads/2021/12/WorldInequalityReport2022_Full_Report.pdf

Chiapello, E. (2020). Financialization as a socio-technical Process. In P. Mader, D. Mertens, & N. van der Zwan (Eds.), *The Routledge international handbook of financialization* (1st ed., pp. 81–91). https://doi.org/10.4324/9781315142876-7

Christophers, B. (2021). Fossilised capital: Price and profit in the energy transition. *New Political Economy, 27,* 146–159. https://doi.org/10.1080/13563467.2021.1926957

CICERO. (2021a). *Best practices 2021.* https://static1.squarespace.com/static/5bc5b31a7788975c96763ea7/t/61375b3479b49020400fc5d7/163101779 5351/CICERO+Shades+of+Green+Best+Practices+2021.pdf

CICERO. (2021b). *Factsheet—Shades of green.* https://static1.squarespace.com/static/5bc5b31a7788975c96763ea7/t/60b75a72af17a60e035fd4d6/1622628980614/CICERO_SHadesofGreen_factsheet_v5.pdf

City of Cape Town Media Office. (2017). *Green pays: City's R1 billion bond a resounding success in the market* (Issue July). https://www.capetown.gov.za/media-and-news/Green%20pays%20City

Claquin, T., & Buchta, S. (2015, October 6). *The big debate: Pureplay green bonds.* Environmental Finance. https://www.environmental-finance.com/content/analysis/the-big-debate-pureplay-green-bonds.html

ClientEarth & Just Share. (2019). *Pension funds and climate risk.*

Climate Bonds Initiative. (2017). *Sovereign briefing.* https://www.climatebonds.net/files/reports/sovereign_briefing2017.pdf

Climate Bonds Initiative. (2022a). *Climate Bonds Standard Board award Agusto & Co the approved verifier status.* https://www.agusto.com/climate-bonds-standard-board-award-agusto-co-the-approved-verifier-status/

Climate Bonds Initiative. (2022b). *Our funders our partners.* https://www.climatebonds.net/about/funders

Cohen, B. M. (2021, May 29). *Scandal clouds South African health chief's political ambitions*. Bloomberg. https://www.bloomberg.com/news/articles/2021-05-29/scandal-clouds-south-african-health-chief-s-political-ambitions

Cohen, M., & Cele, S. (2022, February 10). *Ramaphosa extends grant for poor amid jobs-or-welfare tussle*. Bloomberg. https://www.bloomberg.com/news/articles/2022-02-10/ramaphosa-gives-south-africa-s-poor-income-grant-reprieve

Cohen, M., & Vollgraaff, R. (2022, February 1). *South Africa graft panel finds racketeering occurred at transnet*. Bloomberg. https://www.bloomberg.com/news/articles/2022-02-01/south-africa-graft-panel-finds-racketeering-occurred-at-transnet

Creamer, T. (2019, February 15). *Gordhan's IPP renegotiation proposal triggers 'breach of contract' warnings*, 1–11. https://www.engineeringnews.co.za/article/gordhans-ipp-renegotiation-proposal-triggers-breach-of-contract-warnings-2019-02-15

Cripps, P. (2015, April 1). *Results: Environmental Finance's 8th annual deals of the year awards*. Environmental Finance. https://www.environmental-finance.com/content/news/results-environmental-finances-8th-annual-deals-of-the-year-awards.html

Cripps, P. (2016, December 15). *Poland issues green bond market's first sovereign bond*. Environmental Finance. https://www.environmental-finance.com/content/news/poland-issues-green-bond-markets-first-sovereign-bond.html

Cripps, P. (2017, August 2). *Lessons from the Repsol bond*. Environmental Finance. https://www.environmental-finance.com/content/analysis/lessons-from-the-repsol-bond.html

Cripps, P. (2019a, March 6). *Green bond comment, March 2019: What role should green bonds play in the energy transition?* Environmental Finance. https://www.environmental-finance.com/content/analysis/green-bond...9-what-role-should-green-bonds-play-in-the-energy-transition.html

Cripps, P. (2019b, October 18). *Enel's sustainability bond was greenwashing, says Nuveen*. Environmental Finance. https://www.environmental-finance.com/content/news/enels-sustainability-bond-was-greenwashing-says-nuveen.html

Cripps, P. (2020, June 3). *Green bond comment, June 2020: What use is use of proceeds?* Environmental Finance, 1–5. https://www.environmental-finance.com/content/analysis/green-bond-comment-june-2020.html

Cripps, P. (2021, June 2). *Green bond comment, June 2021: Are oil and gas firms still locked out of the sustainable bond market?* Environmental Finance. https://www.environmental-finance.com/content/analysis/green-bond...nd-gas-firms-still-locked-out-of-the-sustainable-bond-market.html

CSIR. (2016). *Wind and solar PV resource aggregation study for South Africa* (RFP No. 542-23-02-2015). Fraunhofer IWES. https://www.csir.co.za/sites/default/files/Documents/Wind%20and%20Solar%20PV%20Resource%2020Aggregation%20Study%20for%20South%20Africa_Final%20report.pdf

Dafermos, Y., Gabor, D., & Michell, J. (2021). The Wall Street Consensus in pandemic times: What does it mean for climate-aligned development? *Canadian Journal of Development Studies/Revue Canadienne d'études Du Développement, 42,* 238–251. https://doi.org/10.1080/02255189.2020.1865137

Davies, T. (2021, November 11). *There's good reason to be suspicious of Mantashe's latest brainchild,* 11–13. https://justshare.org.za/media/news/theres-good-reason-to-be-suspicious-of-mantashes-latest-brainchild

DBSA. (2021). *DBSA launches a second green bond* (Issue January). https://www.dbsa.org/press-releases/dbsa-launches-second-green-bond

De Lille, P. (2017, June). *City commences investor road show to promote inaugural R1 billion green bond,* 1–7.

Department of Environmental Affairs. (2016). *South Africa's Intended Nationally Determined Contribution (INDC).* UNFCCC (Vol. 1, Issue April). https://unfccc.int/sites/default/files/NDC/2022-06/South%20Africa.pdf

Dupré, S. (2019, October 31). *In response to accusations that Enel's SDG bond was greenwashing.* Environmental Finance. https://www.environmental-finance.com/content/analysis/in-response-to-accusations-that-enels-sdg-bond-was-greenwashing.html

Elsner, C. (forthcoming). *Alleviating or institutionalizing greenwashing: Nuclear energy and the EU taxonomy.* Working Paper, currently under review.

Energy Capital. (2019, April 17). *Standard Bank withdraws funding of new coal IPPs in South Africa.* 58, 1–3. https://energycapitalpower.com/standard-bank-withdraws-funding-of-new-coal-ipps-in-south-africa/

Engelbrecht, F., Adegoke, J., Bopape, M. J., Naidoo, M., Garland, R., Thatcher, M., McGregor, J., Katzfey, J., Werner, M., Ichoku, C., & Gatebe, C. (2015). Projections of rapidly rising surface temperatures over Africa under low mitigation. *Environmental Research Letters, 10*(8). https://doi.org/10.1088/1748-9326/10/8/085004

Environmental Finance. (2015, April 15). *Some discussions should be public.* Environmental Finance. https://www.environmental-finance.com/content/analysis/some-discussions-should-be-public.html

Environmental Finance. (2017, December 13). *The SDGs and the bond market.* Environmental Finance. https://www.environmental-finance.com/content/analysis/the-sdgs-and-the-bond-market.html

Environmental Finance. (2021a). *Sustainable bonds insight 2021.* https://www.environmental-finance.com/assets/files/research/sustainable-bonds-insight-2021.pdf

Environmental Finance. (2021b). *Sustainable debt roundup: Q3 2021*. www.bon ddata.org

Environmental Finance. (2021c, September 16). *Transition bonds "have no future whatsoever."* Environmental Finance. https://www.environmental-fin ance.com/content/news/transition-bonds-have-no-future-whatsoever.html

Environmental Finance. (2021d, February 24). *Sustainalytics expects to double size of second-party opinion business in 2021*. Environmental Finance.

Environmental Finance Awards Committee. (2021). *Submit your nomination! Annual market rankings 2021*. Environmental Finance. Email correspondence for subscribers.

EU China Working Group. (2021). *International platform on sustainable finance common ground taxonomy-climate change mitigation instruction report IPSF Taxonomy Working Group Co-chaired by the EU and China*.

European Commission. (2020). *Fossil CO$_2$ and GHG emissions of all world countries*. JRC Publications Repository (Vol. 105, Issue D2). https://doi.org/10. 2760/56420

Ferguson, J. (1994). *The anti-politics machine. Development, depoliticization, and bureaucratic power in Lesotho*. University of Minnesota Press.

Ferrando, T., Junqueira, G. D. O., Prol, F. M., & Coutinho, D. R. (2022). *Debating development: Indebting the green transition: critical notes on green bonds in the South*. EADI Blog.

Frederiksen, T. (2019). Political settlements, the mining industry and corporate social responsibility in developing countries. *Extractive Industries and Society, 6*(1), 162–170. https://doi.org/10.1016/j.exis.2018.07.007

FTSE Russel. (2022). *FTSE/JSE All Bond Index (ALBI) description*. FTSE Russel. https://www.google.com/url?sa=t&rct=j&q=&esrc=s&source=web& cd=&cad=rja&uact=8&ved=2ahUKEwi29MXb3-_1AhXFQ_EDHZI6C08 QFnoECAMQAQ&url=https%3A%2F%2Fresearch.ftserussell.com%2FAnal ytics%2FFactsheets%2FHome%2FDownloadSingleIssue%3FissueName%3DA LBI%26IsManual%3D

Future of Sustainable Data Alliance. (2021). *Taxomania! An international overview*. https://futureofsustainabledata.com/taxomania-an-internati onal-overview/

Gabor, D. (2020, April). *The Wall Street Consensus*, 1–23 (Working Paper). https://doi.org/10.31235/osf.io/wab8m

Gabor, D. (2021). The Wall Street Consensus. *Development and Change, 52*(3), 429–459. https://doi.org/10.1111/dech.12645

Geels, F. W. (2014). Regime resistance against low-carbon transitions: Introducing politics and power into the multi-level perspective. *Theory, Culture & Society, 31*(5), 21–40. https://doi.org/10.1177/0263276414531627

GGKP webinar. (2021, October 1). How green bonds are financing sustainable development in Argentina, Indonesia and South Africa. *Green Growth Knowledge Partnership.* https://www.youtube.com/watch?v=g_1gzD49KaY

Haag, S., & Müller, F. (2019). Finanzplatz Afrika. Grüne Finanzflüsse und afrikanische Energietransitionen [Financial Centre Africa. Green financial flows and african energy transitions]. In *Deutschland und Afrika – Anatomie eines komplexen Verhältnisses* [Germany and Africa—Anatomy of a complex relationship]. Brandes und Apsel.

Hajer, M. (1995). *The politics of environmental discourse.* Oxford University Press.

Hall, S., Roelich, K. E., Davis, M. E., & Holstenkamp, L. (2018, April). Finance and justice in low-carbon energy transitions. *Applied Energy, 222,* 772–780. https://doi.org/10.1016/j.apenergy.2018.04.007

Harrison, C. (2021). *Green bond pricing in the primary market H1.* Climate Bonds Initiative (Vol. 1, Issue March). https://www.climatebonds.net/resources/reports/green-bond-pricing-primary-market-h1-2019

Harrison, C., Partridge, C., & Tripathy, A. (2020). *What's in a Greenium: An analysis of pricing methodologies and discourse in the green bond market.* The Journal of Environmental Investment. http://www.thejei.com/whats-in-a-greenium-an-analysis-of-pricing-methodologies-and-discourse-in-the-green-bond-market/

Hartley, R. (2017). *Ramaphosa—The man who would be king.* Jonathan Ball Publishers.

Henderson, B. R., & Naidoo, P. (2021, November 24). S. *Africa's rising debt is 'major' threat to finance sector.* Bloomberg. https://www.bloomberg.com/news/articles/2020-11-24/south-africa-s-rising-debt-is-major-threat-to-finance-industry

Hickey, S., Abdulai, A. G., Izama, A., & Mohan, G. (2020). Responding to the commodity boom with varieties of resource nationalism: A political economy explanation for the different routes taken by Africa's new oil producers. *Extractive Industries and Society, 7*(4), 1246–1256. https://doi.org/10.1016/j.exis.2020.06.021

Hilbrandt, H., & Grubbauer, M. (2020). Standards and SSOs in the contested widening and deepening of financial markets: The arrival of Green Municipal Bonds in Mexico City. *Environment and Planning A, 52*(7), 1415–1433. https://doi.org/10.1177/0308518X20909391

Holtedahl, P., Farquhar, D., & Briand, R. (2015, April 15). *Unilever's green bond: A difference of opinions.* Environmental Finance. https://www.environmental-finance.com/content/analysis/unilevers-green-bond-a-difference-of-opinions.html

Hugo, R. (2022, March 17). *JSE starts to walk its talk on climate*, 1–4. https://www.businesslive.co.za/bd/opinion/2022-03-17-robyn-hugo-jse-starts-to-walk-its-talk-on-climate/

Hurley, M. (2018, October 8). *Manulife warns of the pitfalls of tighter green bond regulation*. Environmental Finance. https://www.environmental-fin ance.com/content/analysis/manulife-warns-of-the-pitfalls-of-tighter-green-bond-regulation.html

Hurley, M. (2019, September 4). *Green bond comment September: Are stringent standards a good thing?* Environmental Finance. https://www.environme ntal-finance.com/content/analysis/green-bond-comment-september-are-str ingent-standards-a-good-thing.html

Hurley, M. (2021, April 7). *Green bond comment, April 2021: Central banks and a growing "greenium."* Environmental Finance. https://www.environme ntal-finance.com/content/analysis/green-bond-comment-april-2021-central-banks-and-a-growing-greenium.html

IASS/IET/CSIR. (2022). *From coal to renewables in Mpumalanga: Employment effects, opportunities for local value creation, skills requirements, and gender-inclusiveness. Assessing the co- benefits of decarbonising South Africa's power sector* (Issue January).

ICMA. (2020). *Climate transition finance handbook—Guidance for issuers* (Issue December). https://www.icmagroup.org/assets/documents/Regulatory/Green-Bonds/Climate-Transition-Finance-Handbook-December-2020-091 220.pdf

IoDSA. (2022). *Code for Responsible Investing In SA (CRISA)*. Institute of Directors in Southern Africa (IoDSA). http://www.iodsa.co.za/?page=CRI SACode

IPP Office. (2020). *IPP procurement programmes—Evaluation of seller refinancing notices, refinancing protocol/guideline*. https://www.google.com/url?sa=t&rct=j&q=&esrc=s&source=web&cd=&cad=rja&uact=8&ved=2ah UKEwic5Ne56cz1AhUAlP0HHQ8-Cv0QFnoECAgQAQ&url=https%3A% 2F%2Fwww.ipp-projects.co.za%2FPressCentre%2FGetPressRelease%3Ffileid% 3Dce8018fd-fbc1-ea11-9510-2c59e59ac9cd%26fileNa

Janice, K. (2020, March 12). *Inquiry alleges 'substantial impropriety' at South Africa's public investment corporation*. Bloomberg. https://www.bloomberg.com/news/articles/2020-03-12/inquiry-into-south-africa-s-pic-implicates-senior-management

Jones, R., Baker, T., Huet, K., Murphy, L., & Lewis, N. (2020, June). Treating ecological deficit with debt: The practical and political concerns with green bonds. *Geoforum, 114*, 49–58. https://doi.org/10.1016/j.geoforum.2020.05.014

JSE. (2021). *Nedbank lists green residential bond*. JSE News. https://www.jse.co.za/news/news/nedbank-lists-green-residential-bond-jse

JSE. (2022a). *History & company overview*. https://www.jse.co.za/our-bus
iness/history-%26-company-overview
JSE. (2022b). *Leading the way for a better tomorrow—JSE climate change
disclosure guidelines* (Issue February). https://www.jse.co.za/sites/default/
files/media/documents/JSE%20Sustainability%20Disclosure%20Guidance%
20June%202022.pdf
JSE Press. (2020, February 21). *JSE to evolve Green Bond Segment to all-
encompassing Sustainability Segment*. JSE News, 1–2. https://www.jse.co.
za/news/press-releases/jse-evolve-green-bond-segment-all-encompassing-sus
tainability-segment
Kaltenbrunner, A., & Painceira, J. P. (2015). Developing countries' changing
nature of financial integration and new forms of external vulnerability: The
Brazilian experience. *Cambridge Journal of Economics, 39*(5), 1281–1306.
https://doi.org/10.1093/cje/beu038
Karwowski, E. (2019). Towards (de-)financialisation: The role of the state.
Cambridge Journal of Economics, 43(4), 1001–1027. https://doi.org/10.
1093/cje/bez023
Karwowski, E., & Stockhammer, E. (2017). Financialisation in emerging
economies: A systematic overview and comparison with Anglo-Saxon
economies. *Economic and Political Studies, 5*(1), 60–86. https://doi.org/10.
1080/20954816.2016.1274520
Kern, F., & Markard, J. (2016). Analysing energy transitions: Combining insights
from transition studies and international political economy. In T. Van de
Graaf, B. K. Sovacool, A. Ghosh, F. Kern, & M. T. Klare (Eds.), *The
Palgrave handbook of the international political economy of energy* (1st ed.,
pp. 291–318). Palgrave Macmillan. https://doi.org/10.1057/978-1-137-
55631-8
Kew, J. (2020, March 12). Inquiry alleges 'substantial impropriety' at South
Africa's Public Investment Corp. *Bloomberg*. https://www.bloomberg.com/
news/articles/2020-03-12/inquiry-into-south-africa-s-pic-implicates-senior-
management
Kew, J., & Vecchiatto, P. (2021, March 17). Steinhoff new fraud charges near
with police to get report. *Bloomberg*. https://www.bloomberg.com/news/art
icles/2021-03-17/steinhoff-local-charges-nearing-with-new-report-to-help-
police
Kew, J., & Wessels, V. (2019). *South Africa's Public Investment Corporation
scandal risks the country's future*, 1–12.
KfW. (2022). *Invest in the everlasting. Green Bonds—Made by KfW*. https://
www.kfw.de/PDF/Investor-Relations/PFD-Dokumente-Green-Bonds/KfW-
Green-Bond-Presentation.pdf

Khan, M. H. (2010). *Political settlements and the governance of growth-enhancing institutions*. SOAS Research Online (Issue July). http://eprints.soas.ac.uk/9968/1/Political_Settlements_internet.pdf

Kidney, S. (2021). *U.S. green bond review: In run-up to COP, green bonds in high gear*. Email communication.

Knafo, S. (2022). The power of finance in the age of market based banking. *New Political Economy, 27*(1), 33–46. https://doi.org/10.1080/13563467.2021.1910646

Knuth, S. (2018, April). "Breakthroughs" for a green economy? Financialization and clean energy transition. *Energy Research and Social Science, 41*, 220–229. https://doi.org/10.1016/j.erss.2018.04.024

Köhler, J., Geels, F. W., Kern, F., Markard, J., Onsongo, E., Wieczorek, A., Alkemade, F., Avelino, F., Bergek, A., Boons, F., Fünfschilling, L., Hess, D., Holtz, G., Hyysalo, S., Jenkins, K., Kivimaa, P., Martiskainen, M., McMeekin, A., Mühlemeier, M. S., … Wells, P. (2019). An agenda for sustainability transitions research: State of the art and future directions. *Environmental Innovation and Societal Transitions, 31*, 1–32. https://doi.org/10.1016/j.eist.2019.01.004

Kong, L. (2007). Cultural icons and urban development in Asia: Economic imperative, national identity, and global city status. *Political Geography, 26*(4), 383–404. https://doi.org/10.1016/j.polgeo.2006.11.007

Kvangraven, I. H., Koddenbrock, K., & Sylla, N. S. (2020). Financial subordination and uneven financialization in 21st century Africa. *Community Development Journal, 56*, 119–140. https://doi.org/10.1093/cdj/bsaa047

Lehmann, I. (2019, May). When cultural political economy meets 'charismatic carbon' marketing: A gender-sensitive view on the limitations of Gold Standard cookstove offset projects. *Energy Research and Social Science, 55*, 146–154. https://doi.org/10.1016/j.erss.2019.05.001

Lester, A. (2021a, March 15). *"Greenium" for majority of green bond issues in late 2020, says CBI*. Environmental Finance. https://www.environmental-finance.com/content/news/greenium-for-majority-of-green-bond-issues-in-late-2020-says-cbi.html

Lester, A. (2021b, May 5). *Green bond comment, May 2021: Is it the time of consolidation rather than proliferation of bond labels?* Environmental Finance. https://www.environmental-finance.com/content/analysis/green-bond-c...ime-of-consolidation-rather-than-proliferation-of-bond-labels.html

Lester, A. (2021c, July 13). *Sustainability-linked bonds: One year after the principles—Part 1*. Environmental Finance, June 2020. https://www.environmental-finance.com/content/analysis/sustainability...year-after-the-principles-part-1-the-potential-and-the-pitfalls.html

Lester, A. (2022, December 23). *Sustainable bonds in 2022—beyond $ 1trn.* Environmental Finance. https://www.environmental-finance.com/content/ analysis/sustainable-bonds-in-2022-beyond-$1trn.html

Lester, A., & Marchant, C. (2021, April 12). *"Transition" firms preferring sustainability-linked over transition bonds.* Environmental Finance. https:// www.environmental-finance.com/content/analysis/transition-firms-prefer ring-sustainability-linked-over-transition-bonds.html

Lester, A., Rowntree, A., & Cox, T. (2021, July 14). *Bond round-up: Enel, IADB, Mexico, A2A, Banco BPM, Leasys … and more.* Environmental Finance. https://www.environmental-finance.com/content/news/bond-round-u...nel-iadb-mexico-a2a-banco-bpm-leasys-...-and-more.html?pf=print

Lester, A., Rowntree, A., Marchant, C., Cooper, G., Davies, L., Hurley, M., & Cripps, P. (2020, March 30). *Winners revealed in Environmental Finance's Bond Awards 2020.* Environmental Finance. https://www.environmental-fin ance.com/content/news/winners-revealed-in-environmental-finances-bond-awards-2020.html

Ludvigsen, P. (2016, February 22). *Advanced topics in green bonds: Risks.* Environmental Finance. https://www.environmental-finance.com/content/ analysis/advanced-topics-in-green-bonds-risks.html

MacAskill, S., Roca, E., Liu, B., Stewart, R. A., & Sahin, O. (2021). Is there a green premium in the green bond market? Systematic literature review revealing premium determinants. *Journal of Cleaner Production, 280,* 124491. https://doi.org/10.1016/j.jclepro.2020.124491

Maimane, M. (2019, March 28). *Together we can keep the lights on in SA.* Democratic Alliance, 1–4. https://www.da.org.za/2019/03/together-we-can-keep-the-lights-on-in-sa/

Maltais, A., & Nykvist, B. (2020). Understanding the role of green bonds in advancing sustainability. *Journal of Sustainable Finance and Investment, 11,* 233–252. https://doi.org/10.1080/20430795.2020.1724864

Marchant, C. (2019, November 27). *"Rice bonds" could boost climate resilience, say consultants,* 1–2. https://www.environmental-finance.com/con tent/news/rice-bonds-could-boost-climate-resilience-say-consultants.html

McBride, C. M., Kruger, A. C., & Dyson, L. (2022). Trends in probabilities of temperature records in the non-stationary climate of South Africa. *International Journal of Climatology, 42*(3), 1692–1705. https://doi.org/10.1002/ joc.7329

McInerney, C., & Bunn, D. W. (2019, March). Expansion of the investor base for the energy transition. *Energy Policy, 129,* 1240–1244. https://doi.org/ 10.1016/j.enpol.2019.03.035

Michaelsen, J. (2018, June 5). *An underwriter's reflections on green bond pricing.* Environmental Finance. https://www.environmental-finance.com/content/ analysis/an-underwriters-reflections-on-green-bond-pricing.html

Michaelsen, J. (2019, December 6). *In defence of Enel's SDG-linked bond*. Environmental Finance. https://www.environmental-finance.com/content/analysis/in-defence-of-enels-sdg-linked-bond.html

Mihàlovits, Z., & Tapaszti, A. (2018). A new financial tool for renewable energy investments: Green bonds. *Public Finance Quarterly, 63*(3), 303–318.

Mkhize, M., & Radmore, J. (2021). *Utility-scale renewable energy market intelligence report*. https://www.greencape.co.za/assets/Renewable_Energy_MIR_2021_31_3_21.pdf

Monk, A., & Perkins, R. (2020). What explains the emergence and diffusion of green bonds? *Energy Policy, 145*, 111641. https://doi.org/10.1016/j.enpol.2020.111641

Morkoetter, S., Stebler, R., & Westerfeld, S. (2017). Competition in the credit rating industry: Benefits for investors and issuers. *Journal of Banking and Finance, 75*, 235–257. https://doi.org/10.1016/j.jbankfin.2016.09.001

Müller, F., & Claar, S. (2021). Auctioning a 'just energy transition'? South Africa's renewable energy procurement programme and its implications for transition strategies. *Review of African Political Economy, 48*, 333–351. https://doi.org/10.1080/03056244.2021.1932790

Müller, F., Claar, S., Neumann, M., & Elsner, C. (2020). Is green a Pan-African colour? Mapping African renewable energy policies and transitions in 34 countries. *Energy Research and Social Science, 68*(July 2019), 101551. https://doi.org/10.1016/j.erss.2020.101551

Mullin, K. (2018, January 18). *Comment: Assessing Nigeria's sovereign green*. Environmental Finance, 1–5. https://www.environmental-finance.com/content/analysis/comment-assessing-nigerias-sovereign-green-bond.html

Naidoo, P. (2021, August 24). *South Africa unemployment rate rises to highest in the world*. Bloomberg. https://www.bloomberg.com/news/articles/2021-08-24/south-african-unemployment-rate-rises-to-highest-in-the-world

Nanayakkara, M., & Colombage, S. (2019). Do investors in green bond market pay a premium? Global Evidence. *Applied Economics, 51*(40), 4425–4437. https://doi.org/10.1080/00036846.2019.1591611

National Planning Commission. (2019). *Social partner dialogue for a just transition 2050 vision and pathways for a just transition to a low carbon, climate resilient economy and society* (Issue May).

National Treasury. (2011). *Pension Funds Act (24/1956): Amendment of Regulation 28*. Regulation Gazette No. 9485. http://www.treasury.gov.za/publications/other/reg28/Reg%2028%20-%20for%20Budget%202011.pdf

National Treasury. (2020). *Financing a sustainable economy* (Technical Paper 2020 Draft). https://www.treasury.gov.za/publications/other/Sustainability%20technical%20paper%202020.pdf

National Treasury. (2021a). *Government debt and contingent liabilities. 2020 Budget Review.* https://www.treasury.gov.za/documents/national%20b udget/2016/review/chapter%207.pdf

National Treasury. (2021b). *National Treasury publishes Regulation 28 of the Pension Funds Act draft amendments for public comment.* https://www.gov. za/speeches/amendments-regulation-28-pension-funds-act-encourage-invest ment-infrastructure-request

National Treasury. (2021c). *Regulation 28 second draft for comment.pdf.* http://www.treasury.gov.za/publications/other/reg28/Regulation%2028% 20second%20draft%20for%20comment.pdf

National Treasury. (2022a). *Developing a buildings taxonomy entry for South Africa* (Issue March). https://sustainablefinanceinitiative.org.za/wp-con tent/downloads/Briefing-Paper_Developing-a-Buildings-Taxonomy-Entry-for-South-Africa.pdf

National Treasury. (2022b). *Development process for the South African Green Finance Taxonomy—The process and insights from the development of the 1st Edition of the South African green finance taxonomy* (Issue March). https:// sustainablefinanceinitiative.org.za/wp-content/downloads/Briefing-Paper_ Development-Process-for-the-South-African-Green-Finance-Taxonomy.pdf

National Treasury. (2022c). *South Africa sustainable finance initiative—Working groups.* https://sustainablefinanceinitiative.org.za

National Treasury. (2022d). *South African green finance taxonomy* (Issue March). https://sustainablefinanceinitiative.org.za/wp-content/downloads/ SA-Green-Finance-Taxonomy-1st-Edition-Final-01-04-2022.pdf

National Treasury. (2022e, April 1). *Media Statement: South Africa's first national green finance taxonomy launched to assist the financial sector response to climate change and support sustainable development.* https://www.treasury. gov.za/comm_media/press/2022/2022040101%20Media%20statement% 20-%20Green%20Finance%20Taxonomy.pdf

NERSA. (2017). *Monitoring renewable energy performance of power plants* (Issue 10). http://www.nersa.org.za/Admin/Document/Editor/file/Electricity/ Monitor%20of%20Renewable%20Energy%20Performance%20of%20Power% 20Plants%20-%20progress%20in%20the%20first%20half%20of%202018%20-% 20Issue%2012.pdf

NERSA. (2020). *Monitoring renewable energy performance of power plants* (Vol. 2020, Issue 16).

Neumann, M., & Elsner, C. (forthcoming). *Caught between path-dependence and green opportunities – Assessing the impetus for green banking in South Africa.* Working Paper, currently under review.

Ng, T. H., & Tao, J. Y. (2016). Bond financing for renewable energy in Asia. *Energy Policy, 95,* 509–517. https://doi.org/10.1016/j.enpol.2016.03.015

Njini, B. F. (2022, February 1). *South Africa's energy minister rallies behind coal producers*. Bloomberg. https://www.bloomberg.com/news/articles/2022-02-01/south-africa-s-energy-minister-rallies-behind-coal-producers

Pagliari, S., & Young, K. L. (2020). How financialization is reproduced politically. In P. Mader, D. Mertens, & N. van der Zwan (Eds.), *The Routledge international handbook of financialization* (1st ed., pp. 113–124). https://doi.org/10.4324/9781315142876-10

Paterson, M. (2010). Legitimation and accumulation in climate change governance. *New Political Economy, 15*(3), 345–368. https://doi.org/10.1080/13563460903288247

Petry, J. (2020). From national marketplaces to global providers of financial infrastructures: Exchanges, infrastructures and structural power in global finance. *New Political Economy, 26*, 574–597. https://doi.org/10.1080/13563467.2020.1782368

Petry, J., Koddenbrock, K., & Nölke, A. (2021). State capitalism and capital markets: Comparing securities exchanges in emerging markets. *Environment and Planning A: Economy and Space, 55*, 143–164. https://doi.org/10.1177/0308518x211047599

Pilling, D., Cotterill, J., & Hodgson, C. (2022, November 4). South Africa warns $ 8.5bn climate package risks fuelling debt burden. *Financial Times*. https://www.ft.com/content/e6653b1d-2302-4e44-81bb-38dc608d303d

Presidential Climate Commission. (2022). *Framework for a just transition in South Africa. Draft for public comment* (Issue February). https://pccommissionflow.imgix.net/uploads/images/South-Africas-Just-Transition-Framework-for-Stakeholder-Consultation-Feb-2022_2022-02-23-092221_xtvt.pdf

Renewables Now. (2021a, October 29). *Mainstream team dominates S African tender with 1.27 GW of awards*, 1–5. https://renewablesnow.com/news/mainstream-team-dominates-s-african-tender-with-127-gw-of-awards-759071/

Renewables Now. (2021b, October 29). *S Africa unveils 25 preferred bidders in 2.6-GW renewables tender*, 11–14. https://renewablesnow.com/news/s-africa-unveils-25-preferred-bidders-in-26-gw-renewables-tender-759068/

Robinson-Tillett, S. (2014, September 23). *World's NGOs warn UN of 'greenwash' in green bonds market*. Environmental Finance. https://www.environmental-finance.com/content/news/worlds-ngos-warn-un-of-greenwash-in-green-bonds-market.html

Rose, R. (2018, November 14). Steinheist: The inside story behind the Steinhoff scandal. *Daily Maverick*. https://www.dailymaverick.co.za/article/2018-11-14-steinheist-the-inside-story-behind-the-steinhoff-scandal/

Roumpis, N. (2018, January 5). *Nigeria's green bond slightly oversubscribed*. Environmental Finance, 1–2. https://www.environmental-finance.com/content/news/nigerias-green-bond-slightly-oversubscribed.html

Sassen, S. (2005). The global city: Introducing a concept. *The Brown Journal of World Affairs, 11*(2), 27–40. http://eprints.lse.ac.uk/16787/

Schneeweiß, A. (2019). *Große Erwartungen - Glaubwürdigkeit und Zusätzlichkeit von Green Bonds.* https://suedwind-institut.de/files/Suedwind/Pub likationen/2018/2018-39%20Gro%C3%9Fe%20Erwartungen%20%E2%80% 93%20Glaubwuerdigkeit%20und%20Zusaetzlichkeit%20von%20Green%20B onds.pdf

SEB, & GIZ. (2021). *UNCC e-learn: Introduction to sustainable finance.* UNCC:E-Learn. https://uncclearn.org/course/view.php?id=139&page= overview

Sengupta, A. (2002). On the theory and practice of the right to development. *Challenges in International Human Rights Law, 24*(4), 837–899. https:// doi.org/10.4324/9781315095905

Sguazzin, A. (2022, March 24). *Rhino Bond sold by World Bank in first issuance of its kind.* Bloomberg. https://www.bloomberg.com/news/articles/2022-03-24/rhino-bond-is-sold-by-world-bank-in-first-issuance-of-its-kind

Sguazzin, A., & Prinsloo, L. (2022, February 18). *Billions in climate funds face uncertain future in South Africa.* Bloomberg. https://www.bloomberg. com/news/articles/2022-02-18/south-africa-s-8-5-billion-climate-funds-spa rks-battle

Simatele, M. (2015). Market structure and competition in the South African banking sector. *Procedia Economics and Finance, 30*(15), 825–835. https:// doi.org/10.1016/s2212-5671(15)01332-5

Simpson, C., Rathi, A., & Kishan, S. (2021). *The ESG mirage.* https://www. bloomberg.com/graphics/2021-what-is-esg-investing-msci-ratings-focus-on-corporate-bottom-line/

Sinclair, T. J. (2010). Round up the usual suspects: Blame and the subprime crisis. *New Political Economy, 15*(1), 91–107. https://doi.org/10.1080/135 63460903553657

South Africa Sustainable Finance Initiative. (2021). *National treasury publishes updated technical paper on financing a sustainable economy.* South Africa Sustainable Finance Initiative. https://sustainablefinanceinitiative.org.za/

Southall, R. (2016). The coming crisis of Zuma's ANC: The party state confronts fiscal crisis. *Review of African Political Economy, 43*(147), 73–88. https://doi. org/10.1080/03056244.2015.1083970

Sovacool, B. K., Burke, M., Baker, L., Kotikalapudi, C. K., & Wlokas, H. (2017). New frontiers and conceptual frameworks for energy justice. *Energy Policy, 105*, 677–691. https://doi.org/10.1016/j.enpol.2017.03.005

Stoddard, E. (2022, April 3). Moody's upgrades SA's credit outlook on stable debt burden scenario! *Daily Maverick.* https://www.dailymaverick.co.za/ article/2022-04-03-moodys-upgrades-sas-credit-outlook-on-stable-debt-bur den-scenario/

Sullivan, D. (2020). *City of Cape Town green bond.* Water Sewage and Effluent. https://www.google.com/url?sa=t&rct=j&q=&esrc=s&source=web&cd=& cad=rja&uact=8&ved=2ahUKEwiFzd-k9u_1AhWEQvEDHa39BRsQFnoE CAYQAQ&url=https%3A%2F%2Fwww.undrr.org%2Fmedia%2F48285%2Fd ownload&usg=AOvVaw0TOzpbaF5dZApeyagt5LAO

Sum, N.-L. (2009). The production of hegemonic policy discourses: 'Competitiveness' as a knowledge brand and its (re-)contextualizations. *Critical Policy Studies, 3*(2), 184–203. https://doi.org/10.1080/19460170903385668

Sum, N.-L., & Jessop, B. (2013). *Towards a cultural political economy—Putting culture in its place in political economy* (N.-L. Sum & B. Jessop, Eds.; 1st ed.). Edward Elgar.

Swilling, M., & Annecke, E. (2012). *Just transitions—Explorations of sustainability in an unfair world* (1st ed., Vol. 1, Issue 4). United Nations University Press. https://doi.org/10.1080/02652038509373556

Swyngedouw, E. (2017). Unlocking the mind-trap: Politicising urban theory and practice. *Urban Studies, 54*(1), 55–61. https://doi.org/10.1177/004209801 6671475

Takatsuki, Y., & Foll, J. (2019, June 12). *Financing brown to green: Guidelines for transition bonds.* Environmental Finance. https://www.environmental-finance.com/content/analysis/financing-brown-to-green-guidelines-for-transi tion-bonds.html

Talbot, K. M. (2017). What does green really mean: How increased transparency and standardization can grow the green bond market. *Villanova Environmental Law Journal, 28*(1), 127–146. https://tel.archives-ouvertes. fr/tel-01514176

Terazono, E. (2020). *Grieg Seafood takes aim at Cargill through $ 105 million green bond receive free green bonds updates,* 10–12.

Tripathy, A. (2017). Translating to risk: The legibility of climate change and nature in the green bond market. *Economic Anthropology, 4*(2), 239–250. https://doi.org/10.1002/sea2.12091

UNEP FI. (2022a). *About the SSE organizers.* https://sseinitiative.org/about/

UNEP FI. (2022b). *Johannesburg Stock Exchange.* Sustainable Stock Exchanges. https://sseinitiative.org/stock-exchange/jse/

Vecchiatto, P. (2022, February 10). *South Africa in talks with investors on green hydrogen projects.* Bloomberg. https://www.bloomberg.com/news/articles/ 2022-02-10/south-africa-in-talks-with-investors-on-green-hydrogen-projects

Viegas, M. (2017, May 19). *Repsol's green bond: Exploring the controversy.* Environmental Finance. https://www.environmental-finance.com/content/ analysis/repsols-green-bond-exploring-the-controversy.html

Volberding, P. (2021). Leveraging financial markets for development. In *Leveraging financial markets for development.* https://doi.org/10.1007/978-3-030-55008-0

Voss, J., Malcher, M., Puffe, M., Umlauf, F., Urbschat, C., Grundner, C., Kalusa, D., & Euston-Brown, M. (2018). *The electricity distribution industry in Germany and South Africa—A review of policy and regulation*, 1–28 (A discussion paper). https://www.sagen.org.za/publications/energy-policy-reg ulation/79-the-electricity-distribution-in-germany-and-south-africa-a-review- of-policy-and-regulations/file

Waissbein, O., Glemarec, Y., Bayraktar, H., & Schmidt, T. (2013). *Derisking renewable energy investment. A framework to support policy- makers in selecting public instruments to promote renewable energy invest- ment in developing countries.* United Nations Development Programme, 1– 156. http://scholar.google.ch/scholar?q=Derisking+Renewable+Energy+Inv estment+undp&btnG=&hl=en&as_sdt=0,5#0

Wang, E. K. (2018). Financing green: Reforming green bond regulation in the United States. *Brooklyn Journal of Corporate, Financial & Commercial Law, 12*(2), 9.

Wheelan, H. (2020). Day 2 high-level plenary: How to ensure the financial system helps deliver a green recovery (including jobs, low-carbon growth, and environmental resilience)? In Responsible Investor (Ed.), *OECD forum on green finance and investment.* https://oecd-events.org/green-finance-and- investment-2020/onlinesession/a1ce1916-39f3-ea11-96f5-0003ff29803d

World Bank. (2016). *Climate finance online course: Innovative approaches in supporting climate action.* https://knowledge.unccd.int/cbm/climate-fin ance-online-course-innovative-approaches-supporting-climate-action

World Bank. (2020). *Developing a national green taxonomy—A World Bank guide.* https://documents1.worldbank.org/curated/en/95301159341 0423 487/pdf/Developing-a-National-Green-Taxonomy-A-World-Bank-Guide.pdf

Yelland, C., & Lilley, R. (2019, January 17). Paralysis over South Africa's IRP for electricity presents massive economic risk. *Daily Maverick.* https://www. dailymaverick.co.za/article/2019-01-17-paralysis-over-south-africas-irp-for- electricity-presents-massive-economic-risk/

The Limits of Green Finance in Fossil-Based Emerging Economies—Lessons Beyond South Africa

Why have green bonds not taken off in South Africa despite exponential growth rates elsewhere in the world? This book offered seven arguments to shed light on this research puzzle. In this chapter, I situate these main results in the wider context of the theoretical framework that I outlined in Chapter 3. Having situated the findings theoretically, I will zoom out into the wider implications of green bond diffusion in South Africa and beyond. Thereafter, I will discuss potential remedies to green bond. Over the course of this chapter, I, also, point out avenues for further research wherever suitable.

DISCUSSING THE RESULTS IN LIGHT OF THE THEORETICAL FRAMEWORK

As the literature review (Chapter 2) demonstrated, the academic debate has largely focused on the effects of green bonds on other markets as well as the market properties of the instrument. Only little research has dealt with improving the green bond market setup let alone criticized its shortcomings. And with the exception of China, few scholars have dwelled on the track record green bonds achieve in emerging and developing markets. By drawing on three different theoretical strands, I sought to close the gaps in the understanding around green bond diffusion in

M. Neumann, *The Political Economy of Green Bonds in Emerging Markets*, International Political Economy Series, https://doi.org/10.1007/978-3-031-30502-3_6

South Africa. The seven overarching findings I abductively derived in my results chapter variously draw on this theoretical framework.

Cultural Political Economy

A cultural political economy (CPE) approach emphasizes the discursive components that drive the expansion of nascent markets, as is the case with green bonds. This became evident in the discursive frame of a financial sector crisis interpretation of climate change and green bonds as pertinent solutions. Rather than intoning the lack of funds as the key bottleneck to advancing climate-aligned futures, green bond advocates deploy green bonds as bespoke tools to 'untap' institutional investor monies. With a CPE lens, I was able to demonstrate how the burden of action is discursively shifted *from investors* to *issuers*, who are called upon to close the gap in 'bankable' projects. From this argument, green bonds result as the pertinent vehicle to unleash the trillions of US$ 'waiting' in the global capital markets (confer A1).[1]

Secondly, the CPE lens also adds insights into the need for'markets-in-the-making' (Asiyanbi, 2018) to refer to success stories (Lehmann, 2019) as constant reminders of the potency of the instrument. My findings support this relevance of success stories, but also signal its absence in South Africa were it not for the Cape Town bond as its sole exception. By discussing the reception of Nigeria's first sovereign green bond issuance, my research, further, juxtaposes success stories with 'stories of failure', which may equally inhibit market actors to draw on innovative tools, particularly in risk-averse environments as the South African capital markets (confer A2).

My findings, further, underscore that legitimizing strategies applicable in Europe and the USA after the global financial crisis (Monk & Perkins, 2020; Paterson, 2010) have not equivocally gained traction in South Africa. While many bankers in the global North felt the urge to repair their reputation and readily jumped at the opportunity to paint their investments as climate-beneficial, South African financial sector actors emerged from the global financial crisis largely unscathed. To these stakeholders, there are no mistakes to rectify in the aftermath of the global financial crisis which could grant the impetus to go green.

---

[1] Please refer to the box with supplementary questions at the end of Chapter 3.

Furthermore, green finance enthusiasts in South Africa bemoan several additional reasons inhibiting action to mitigate climate change among their colleagues. Relevant arguments include the limited contribution to the climate crisis in terms of CO_2 emission in global comparison,[2] other crises overshadowing climate concerns, and the 'right-to-develop' (Bos & Gupta, 2018; Cheru, 2016; Sengupta, 2002) gaining momentum in defense of the current economic trajectory. CPE helps in linking these discursive arguments to other political economic factors that help in understanding the limited take-up of green bonds in South Africa (confer A3).

Fourthly, CPE is useful to decipher debates around seemingly clear-cut, yet nothing but straightforward definitions of what 'counts' as a green bond (Tripathy, 2017) or an acceptable green bond issuer, respectively. My review of global green bond market debates showed that what is considered green is repeatedly challenged and requires constant re-appraisal and refining. It is a facet of the market so far largely underappreciated in the scholarship on green bond diffusion (see here Monk & Perkins, 2020). My research traced some of the arguments ensuing contested issuances at global stage arguing that innovations in the markets constantly set new precedents for collateral institutions like the Climate Bonds Initiative (CBI) to evaluate and appraise. It, thus, provides a pertinent example of the 'excluding' tendencies of markets (Best & Paterson, 2010) that are better grasped through a cultural political economic understanding (see A4).

Equally important, CPE captures the attempts to rid the transition of its redistributive components by declaring it a 'natural' transition. With view to the energy sector, this term literally naturalizes inherently political questions about the reallocation of benefits and burdens arising from the closure of mines and increased take-up of renewables. Though market rationales as much as environmental rationales favor and support the need to transition, they still do not justify how burden and benefits should be spread across society. CPE helps shine a light on this questionable frame. By problematizing this framing, it simultaneously offers avenues for alternative approaches to handling this predicament (see A5).

Combining CPE with literature on financialization, furthermore, proved fruitful especially when seeking to understand the reproduction

---

[2] That is even though emissions are astonishingly high compared to the mediocre economic output (European Commission, 2020, p. 11).

of the hype (Knuth, 2018) around green bonds. Indeed, not only the discursive frames and key arguments in favor of green bonds are relevant components to its diffusion. CPE also focuses on the interplay between discursive and extra-discursive or material factors (Sum & Jessop, 2013). As I show, it is also the industry dissemination of up-to-date market information through various channels, such as weekly or annual market-updates, the sharing of learnings across competitive divides through best practice handbooks, guidance on issuances, explanation of standards, and the constant recruitment of new members through workshops and webinars which capacitate practitioners and widen the green bond community. My findings, thus, not only corroborate Chiapello's work (2020) on financial practices. They also provide interesting insights into *practices* that grow green capital market-in-the-making (Asiyanbi, 2018) and the self-fulfilling prophecy to which such hypes tend to appeal (Knuth, 2018).

CPE literature often abstracts discursive and extra-discursive political economic findings towards an overarching economic imaginary (Sum & Jessop, 2013). Green bonds embody a trend to reframe inherently political transition endeavors in market-clad guise, driven foremost by notions of bankability. For the reasons inhibiting green bond take-up I delineated in the previous chapter, green bonds can, at best, be considered an 'economic imaginary in-the-making'. Neither has the reframing of the crisis as a lack of investable projects garnered a political majority over labor-driven demands (see especially the just transition section in the previous chapter). Nor have its purported benefits—both discursive and beyond—sedimented beyond those stakeholders *directly* involved in its attempted expansion. These stakeholders, however, do hold powerful sway over the direction of the capital market and the economy more generally. The ongoing regulatory overhaul, especially driven by the green finance taxonomy, may incrementally advance the retention of green bonds as an economic imaginary seeking to trod down a finance-driven transition pathway.

Financialization

The literature on financialization, in turn, offered a diverse toolkit to scrutinize green bond diffusion. The literature on bankability (Baker, 2015; Baker & Sovacool, 2017; Gabor, 2019; Müller et al., 2020) meticulously delineates efforts of turning transition endeavors into marketable investment opportunities. My research on green bonds in South Africa seconds this trajectory. It adds important insights into bankability as a non-negotiable component of enlisting institutional investors for low-carbon transitions. With development banks increasingly bridging the risk divides in project finance (Griffith-Jones et al., 2021; Volberding, 2021), green bonds serve as a vehicle to drive the 'billions to trillions' agenda of the SDGs (Mawdsley, 2018). They, thus, contribute to restructuring transition endeavors towards the needs of financial markets (confer B1).

Secondly, my research provided a more nuanced picture regarding the purported benefits of green bond issuances. Especially in an emerging market context, the so-called *greenium*, which enables the issuer to raise capital below conventional market rates (MacAskill et al., 2021), only anecdotally transpires. In some instances in South Africa, the capital raised through green bonds turned out as costly if not more expensive than conventional debt. With risk-return matrices hardly outmaneuvered, this finding underscores the limited benefits the instrument can generate for emerging economies with fundamentally subordinate financial markets (Kaltenbrunner & Painceira, 2015; Kvangraven et al., 2020). Therein, rating agencies represent key gatekeepers for accessing international capital markets. A downgrade of a country's credit rating effectively curtails the state's ability to cheaply borrow capital for infrastructural transformation. By assessing the state's ability to repay its debts, these credit rating agencies support structural reforms that invariably favor austerity measures to avoid additional strain on public coffers. Moody's improved credit outlook following the South African government reprioritizing fiscal consolidation (Stoddard, 2022) is one such case in point. Still, in challenging fiscal contexts like South Africa, attracting investments into the local capital market remains a challenge that even a green label cannot solve in the short term (confer B2).

Thirdly, my findings lend additional credence to concerns about green bond reliance on market metrics deepening structural inequalities (Bigger, 2017; Bigger & Millington, 2019; Caprotti et al., 2020). This is most evident in the requirement for issuers to dispose of a functioning balance sheet that could serve as a reference if not collateral for the bond. This sharpens divisions—whether between big multinationals and up-and-coming firms with limited track record or well-endowed first-tier municipalities as opposed to smaller marginal ones—as only the economically well-endowed can reap the benefits of the bond. In the case of municipal actors, for example, only the wealthier municipalities have been able to issue green bonds and benefit from its proceeds. In this light, green bonds hardly appear as an emancipatory let alone transformational tool.

My research on green bonds, furthermore, provides important insights in Bracking's observation of green financial innovations separating environmental from economic returns (Bracking, 2015; Jones et al., 2020). This separation enables an assessment of the motivations driving the decision to purchase a green bond. My interviews demonstrated that economic considerations, or more specifically anticipated returns, take precedence for institutional investors and regulatory authorities. For the former, this is evident in the demands for bankability on the part of the investors and the struggle of South African issuers to generate bankable climate-aligned projects specifically and economically viable projects for investors more generally. For the JSE as an example of the latter, it is evident in the absence of mechanisms to sanction issuers in case of a green default. The 'green' or sustainable component of the bond can, at best, be considered a positive byproduct in the decision-making process. This heightens the risk of greenwashing practices, which adversely affect both markets (loss of credibility and integrity) and the climate (missing positive impact). For climate considerations to weigh more heavily on decision-making processes of institutional investors, demand-side regulation will have to be significantly tightened and more investment opportunities generated on the supply side (confer B3).

Lastly and though largely from a pessimistic premise (Volberding, 2021), financialization literature offers insights in de-risking practices and their interference in bank—versus market—based lending (Gabor, 2020a; Karwowski & Stockhammer, 2017; Knafo, 2022). My discussion of the conflict over refinancing loans of the energy tender program which would enable capital market actors to gobble up and securitize banking sector loans sheds new light on the competing interests in these nascent and heavily de-risked spaces. The interviewees demonstrated that opening up markets to private investors and simultaneously offering state guarantees to backstop said investments can create unintended winners and losers. In the renewable energy tender, the de-risking state (Gabor, 2020b, 2021) actively produced winners that did not contribute to meeting the state's socio-economic objectives, thus disclosing the limits of the de-risking toolbox. With a largely oligopolist setup, the commercial banks were able to set loan conditions and, thus, reaped tremendous profits for investments wherein risks were displaced to the sovereign and, ultimately, taxpayers. Without possibilities for refinancing, developers foot the bill of inflated capital costs. Financializing the energy transition in South Africa through public guarantees for private investments, thus, also unearths interesting fault lines between domestic and foreign capital as much as the public and private risk distribution (Christophers et al., 2020).

The guidelines which the IPP office ultimately imposed, further, disclose the myriad of underlying and at times mutually incompatible interests that constrain green bond diffusion. They also underscore that political economic questions around distribution and its externalities fundamentally drive behavior, even in market-inducing institutional innovations like the IPP office. These findings, thus, provide an interesting addition to the emerging literature on de-risking low-carbon transition endeavors (Elsner et al., 2021; Gabor, 2020b; Geddes et al., 2018). Furthermore, they provide insights into the policy tools of a state deploying austerity measures to rehabilitate increasingly empty fiscal coffers. The growing contingent liabilities resulting from backstopping private investments serve as one such work-around. They need to be closely monitored given their potency to destabilize the sovereign's ability to meet its debt obligations. The refinancing conundrum demonstrated the tension between public and private sectors. As Mariana Mazzucato (2011) argued in her seminal work, a main apple of discord is rewarding entities that take the risks for climate-aligned projects to take place. In this tradition, Griffith-Jones et al (2021) raise concerns about development banks taking on excessive risks to crowd in private finance—at least in comparison with the rewards reaped upon successful completion. This question over the distribution of risks and returns is at the heart of contemporary development finance and leaves plenty of room for further scholarship and debate (see B4).

Transition Studies

Adding important facets to the previous two literature strands, some strands within Transition Studies analyze vested political interests (Geels, 2014, 2019; Kern & Markard, 2016) and fossil path dependence (Baker et al., 2021; Burton et al., 2019; Unruh, 2000) that sway transition trajectories. My findings suggest that fossil path dependence heavily confines green bond diffusion in South Africa. The lack of bankable projects that would live up to green bond standards certainly exemplifies the lock-in that the energy-intensive South African economy has maneuvered itself into. Efforts to reverse the course and drive structural transformations

(Swilling & Annecke, 2012) are largely absent in the financial market. As per current trajectory, sustainability labeled bonds would likely result in regime reconfiguration (Geels & Schot, 2007; Köhler et al., 2019), especially with view to ongoing discussions to fund the decarbonization of the country's main emitters, Eskom and Sasol. Both are at the core of the minerals-energy complex that has increasingly financialized in order to retain its dominance in the country (Baker, 2015; Baker et al., 2021). Regardless of their current financial situation or green credentials, the oil parastatal and energy utility will be key actors in South Africa's transition. The two entities account for more than half the country's CO_2 emissions (CBI & Agora Energiewende, 2021, p. 10). Given the present disposition of the energy sector, a green overhaul of the sector without these two players seems highly unlikely. How green financial instruments, whether green, transition, KPI-linked bonds, or other forms of funding incentives can pave the way to reconfigure the energy regime in line with climate needs is one of the major questions South Africa will have to answer sooner than later (see C1).

The country's green finance taxonomy could become a key enabler for these institutions to revamp their operations towards greater climate alignment. It is the key development at the landscape level. But it remains to be seen, how appealing this dual lane of transition and green taxonomy will be to foreign investors and whether the interoperability of taxonomies across the globe will yield more foreign long-term investment in the country (Dafermos et al., 2021; Hilbrandt & Grubbauer, 2020; Hyun et al., 2020; Tripathy, 2017). This holds true especially in light of greenwashing being the most salient concern among practitioners (Mihàlovits & Tapaszti, 2018; Talbot, 2017; Wang, 2018). The 'flexible' domestic green finance taxonomy can certainly be viewed as an attempt to incorporate domestic market actors that would otherwise not be able to list any green assets—potentially at the detriment of climate alignment (see C2). This ties in nicely with the financialization literature discussing capital market deepening and demonstrates that the re-engineering of domestic markets in the global image (Gabor, 2020b) comes with strings attached, which safeguard domestic market contexts.

As Transition Studies scholarship oftentimes concludes, transition endeavors require *comprehensive* policy mixes (Müller et al., 2020, 2021) to ensure a timely, orderly, and fair transition. A financial innovation like green bonds cannot do the trick on its own. It is too narrow an instrument with limited applicability in the emerging market context. My findings underscore the lack of supportive regulatory framework policies to scale up low-carbon investment opportunities. Given the myriad of crises befalling the country, it comes as no surprise that the current administration struggles to prioritize a green structural overhaul. So far, green bonds have not emerged out of its niche to become a powerful financing vehicle for South Africa's low-carbon transition.

In the academic just transition discourse, redistributive and participatory elements are foregrounded to avoid focusing on technical fixes blind to these elements. Against the backdrop of rampant social crises evident in record levels of unemployment and unparalleled (racial) inequality (Chancel et al., 2022; Koomson & Awaworyi Churchill, 2022; P. Naidoo, 2021; UNDP, 2020), it comes as no surprise that green bonds have not taken off more readily in South Africa. Due to their deliberately simple design, they hardly incorporate these concerns. Market actors, more generally, pursue narrower objectives of profitability in comparison with publicly accountable actors (Karwowski, 2019; Kennedy, 2018), who need to balance vested interests and reallocate burdens and benefits fairly. Bankability merely ensures the division of proceeds between issuers and investors. So far, there is not enough socio-economic participation enshrined in the process as those procedures likely inhibit the very investments the instrument seeks to unlock. When considering the setup of the green finance taxonomy as a governing framework, civil society organizations could merely comment on the process. They have played no part in the steering group largely consisting of financial industry players and consequently do not weigh in on decision-making processes. The same holds true for the JSE's green segment which predominantly consulted investors during its setup. And despite its social criteria, the renewable energy tender program has been unable to create enough jobs and absorb a substantial share of workers currently stuck in (fossil) industries eventually rendered obsolete in the medium run. A green bond-led transition approach that ignores existing inequalities would, indeed, amount to what Swilling and Annecke (2012, p. xviii) consider an "unjust transition". As things stand, the needs of affected workers and communities are not sufficiently recognized. It comes as no surprise, that just transition demands clash with those of a green-finance-led transition. Transition studies is apt in raising exactly these questions about job security, participation, and co-ownership, shining a light on the trade-offs between investment and social needs (see C3 and C4).

As the refinancing conundrum exemplifies, non-financial logics exert pressure on the regulatory environment within which green bonds maneuver, at times preventing the siphoning of profits. In combination with the depoliticizing elements of CPE, the just transition literature helps understand diametrically opposed efforts to either depoliticize or repoliticize transition trajectories as efforts to safeguard the status quo or benefit in the redistribution arising from socio-technical transitions.

These complex dynamics of evolving transition pathways cannot be understood in disciplinary isolation. Each literature strand provided useful lenses to understand the political economic predicaments on which green bond expansion rests. Combining these various literature strands proved very vital to better understand the stalling take-off of green bonds in South Africa. It pointed out blind spots inherent to fin-tech-driven efforts to transition the country's economy. Not only did it demonstrate the limited leverage of the instrument itself. First and foremost, my work needs to be understood as a plea for interdisciplinary approaches to studying and making sense of transition endeavors—approaches informed by political economic and critical finance scholarship that untangle the conflicts around transition trajectories. Only multiple theoretical angles help address the literature gaps identified in Chapter 2. I provided a comprehensive assessment of green bond market developments that offer takeaways across camps, whether insights into investor decision-making and the oft-missing greenium (marketeers), I shed light on the political economy around green regulation and expanded the conceptual criticism of green bonds (reformists) and offered new insights into limits of financializing transition trajectories (critics). By foregrounding discursive elements, I contributed important qualitative research towards these green markets-in-the-making and deepened our understanding of a still very young market. In delving into an emerging market like South Africa, I digressed from mainstream research that largely focuses on the global North and off-late China. Yet how can the findings be interpreted in light of the South Africa's political economy and beyond?

Insights on Green Bonds in South Africa and Beyond

The hypotheses on South Africa's political economy, which I delineated in the context chapter (Chapter 4), were significantly substantiated. My results underscored the diverse but unanimously adverse influence of the fossil path dependence onto green bond diffusion, some of which were summarized in the section directly above. To speak of a green overhaul of the South Africa's capital markets has so far been premature. Green bonds still make up only a marginal share of bonds traded on the JSE. According to Sarah McPhrail, applying the nascent green finance taxonomy would yield roughly five percent of current bond listings as eligible for the green label (Author's Notes at Green Taxonomy Launch, 2022). That the country's fossil path dependence influences the trajectory of the labeled bond market is evident in the country's current green finance taxonomy draft, which seeks to accommodate both international investors' preference for credible green assets as much as energy-intensive industry players through a transition taxonomy. The country's fossil path dependence, thus, remains the biggest obstacle to overcome in advancing climate alignment.

My findings also second the government's legitimacy and capacity crisis. Many interviewees bemoaned the inaction of the government in driving the transition, whether that is because of the corruption tarnishing key state-owned institutions, the inability to agree on and chart out more ambitious renewable energy targets or the delays in implementation. Despite increased efforts to restructure the energy sector along market rationales, however, public institutions retain strong foothold on governing the sector, whether regarding regulation energy generation or on questions of privatization. The governing party's continued grasp on energy sector is evident in both, the stalling reforms as much as in the refinancing struggle. The latter, also, disclosed the preliminary limits to further financializing the transition endeavors. The refinancing stalemate did slow the issuance of green bonds as refinancing vehicles in the renewable energy space. Had the refinancing standoff been resolved favorably for developers and institutional investors, it would have likely resulted in significantly more green bond issuances. That the office insists on its prerogative of granting approval demonstrates its resolve to keep a say in how benefits arising from investment into the transition are divided. It also underscores the government's unwavering need to make positive headlines. Unfortunately, this resolute position of the Department of Energy has not resulted in more consistent or cheaper service delivery for its citizens. It, nonetheless, shows that the government needs to work harder to regain legitimacy so carelessly wasted, ensuing 'state capture' under the Zuma administrations.

The aftermath of the global financial crisis proved very uneven. It seems that if the global financial crisis taught financial sector actors in South Africa something, it is to not veer from how they conducted business before the crisis. As things stand at least, they have not shown tremendous risk appetite to embark on new financial tools like green bonds. Business as usual seems to prevail. Against the charge of green projects being perceived as elitist and coupled with a widespread fear among financial practitioners around popular unrest, many financial practitioners opt for a quiet profile to not fan the simmering unrest and already tense debates around inequality. My findings, thus, provide an ambivalent picture regarding the hypothesis that financial actors emerged emboldened from the global financial crisis. Financial practitioners seem emboldened to stick to the status quo and simultaneously hesitant to venture into semi-chartered 'green' territories. Whether climate change will prompt financial practitioners to act before the livelihoods of poorer segments in society are further eroded remains to be seen. Ironically, many financial practitioners see the onus to pave the way for climate alignment on the side of the government which quite a few of them seem to perceive as largely uncapable.

The crises of unemployment and inequality, of eroding public service provision, and of energy provide unparalleled challenges, chiefly for the government, but, as argued above, also for market actors. Magnified during the Covid-19 pandemic, demonstrations against government decisions have gained momentum in the last two years; unemployment and inequality have reached new heights (Chancel et al., 2022; P. Naidoo, 2021). Load shedding continues to cost the country dearly (B. P. Naidoo & Prinsloo, 2022), both in terms of forgone profits for businesses and social ramifications around services and livelihoods dependent on continuous supply of energy. The structural overhaul of the energy sector around the unbundling of Eskom into separate entities has been fiercely opposed by trade unions. The limited job creation springing from the renewable energy tender program (though this is arguably due to the lack of ambitious rollout of renewables) further complicates policy-making. Add to that the significant fiscal constraints and one starts getting a vague idea about the competing policy options the government needs to counterweigh. My findings are certainly consistent with concerns around competing policy trajectories. Whether the Presidential Climate Committee and investments under the green recovery banner can chart out common ground for socio-economic and climate concerns will be an interesting space to watch.

More generally, the brief exercise into South Africa's turbulent political economic history has proven worthwhile in understanding the continued relevance of the country's Apartheid past on its present policy-making—i.e. in the absence of prescribed 'green' assets, and the deep rootedness of South Africa's capital markets in the Minerals-Energy Complex (Baker, 2015; Fine & Rustomjee, 1996). Without a chapter on South Africa's political economy, reasons as to why green bonds do not expand in South Africa in line with global markets would have been left underexposed and improperly contextualized. More tangible than in most other countries on this planet, South Africa's history of fossil extraction (see Chapter 4) is tied so directly to its persisting racial inequalities. The book demonstrated that charting out a way forward cannot ignore these grievances by defining it in narrow technical terms. Future research may delve into these racial divides to advance ways to combine questions of financing the transition with bottom-up inclusion.

South Africa's struggle with scaling-up green bonds likely applies in analogous country contexts as well. Emerging markets will be increasingly at the center of the attention, given the anticipated higher yields. As per current projections, labeled bond issuances are expected to reach US$ 100 billion by 2023, up from US$ 40 billion in 2020 (Lester, 2021). Beyond South Africa and China, members of the BRICS like Brazil and India and emerging hydrogen markets like Namibia, Morocco will be interesting spaces to watch. Research that accompanies these growth expectations is certainly in order.

Scrutinizing opportunities to fund transitions of other countries steeped in fossil dependence will be interesting options, if not for green bonds than definitely for transition or KPI-linked debt securities. This holds true especially since South Africa's pursuit of a transition taxonomy (National Treasury, 2022). Accompanying these transition endeavors steeped so deeply in fossil dependence from a scholarly rather than industry perspective will be vital.

Simultaneously, my conceptual critique of green bonds in the context of emerging economies carries wider implications. For green bonds as a tool, my findings affirm its limited leverage in emerging markets. To upend structural hurdles prevailing in contemporary capital markets, the tool has not diversified enough from conventional financial tools without climate change components. This begs the question of reforming the instrument to alleviate some of its shortcomings. Yet what are the latest ideas that have been debated?

BEYOND GREEN BONDS—FINANCIAL TOOLS TO ADDRESS CLIMATE CHANGE?

Beyond efforts to improve the green bond concept by specifying standardization for sub-sectors, there have been interesting developments in the sustainable debt realm. In this subsection, I comment on some of these developments to offer interesting avenues for further research.

Within the labeled bond community, several developments will be interesting to watch, ranging from emerging national standards and their interoperability to new types of actors in the market and conceptual innovations.

Firstly, the governing standards like the green taxonomies currently negotiated, drafted, and adopted across the globe will remain a fascinating space to accompany as a researcher. Local needs already politicize these standardizing processes and will eventually balance them against the need to attract foreign investment, which requires commensurability and interoperability. Safeguarding these domestic industrial interests will be an overriding theme accompanying the standardization of investment criteria fueling transition endeavors whether to the benefit or detriment of climate-aligned futures.

Central banks have become more active in the green bond space, both as issuers and investors. While the Bank of International Settlements (BIS) set up two sizable green bond funds, the European Central Bank invested in said BIS green bond funds (Hurley, 2021). The latter also signaled sustainability-linked bonds to be eligible for its pandemic emergency purchasing program 'PEPP'. Given their political mandates, central banks could play an even more central role in driving climate finance in the future.

Conceptually, several innovations have succeeded green bonds, some of which I have already discussed in the results chapter, namely transition and KPI-linked bonds. While ESG-linked catastrophe bonds will likely see their first issuance soon (Perrot & Lester, 2021), research focus should turn to quickly expanding markets on KPI-linked bonds. The latter also feature innovative ways to tie investor return to the conservation of nature, as in the case in the World Bank maiden Wildlife Conservation Bond (WCB) which aims at supporting the conservation of rhinos in South Africa (Daily Maverick/Reuters, 2022; World Bank, 2022). If this 'pay-for-success' bond structure proves successful in foregrounding impact, it will likely be replicated in other regions such as Kenya (Sguazzin, 2022). Against the backdrop of South Africa's transition taxonomy, it also remains to be seen whether transition bond issuances will pick up at the JSE or whether KPI-linked bonds, the more successful variant on a global level can leave a mark. A key challenge will be aligning economic with environmental or climate-related returns to avoid Bracking's criticism (2015) of separating and prioritizing economic returns over other considerations. Not every new label has strong arguments to offer for the sustainable bond market. In comparison with transition bonds, KPI-linked bonds more readily tie return to impact by demanding clearcut targets followed by pecuniary sanctions in case the issuer misses them. More innovations along these lines will likely appear in this space. From a Transition Studies and financialization perspective, it remains to be seen whether these innovations can extend beyond temporary capital fixes (Castree & Christophers, 2015) to drive economic alignment with climate and environmental needs. These new bond structures and regulatory ideas do not upend market mechanisms. They, thus, do not fundamentally transform ownership structures. But, with innovative ideas like these, at least climate and environmental benefits can more closely align with economic returns.

In contrast to these technical fixes that mainly revolve around the idea of pricing in as many externalities as possible to avoid market failure, other programs focus on funding decarbonization across a North-South divide and, thus, foreground redistributive negotiations. COP26 emphasized the 'right to develop' is a potent argument rallying developing and emerging countries under a united banner. COP27, in turn, was the first of its kind to open the floor for a debate 'loss and damage' (*The Guardian*, 2022) and conclude with the setup of a fund the details of which will be agreed upon by next year's COP (*The Economist*, 2022b). The negotiated US$ 8.5 in development finance earmarked for South Africa's coal phase-out has the potential for a redistributive compromise in return for forgoing further coal exploitation across the North-South divide. More voluminous agreements with similar setups have been forged between Indonesia, the USA, and Japan among others, for a green transition in Indonesia (*The Economist*, 2022a). With its current composition of just 4% in grants and the rest in hard-currency-denominated loans and guarantees, however, it rather fuels South Africa's debt burden (Pilling et al.,

2022). Though the Just Energy Transition Fund is already touted as a blueprint for other emerging and developing economies at COP 27, it cannot become a starting point for reparations for climate coloniality (Perry, 2021; Sultana, 2022), unless the grant component outweighs its loan and credit guarantee counterparts. The funding modalities for a just transition across North-South divides are a key space to watch the attempts at incorporating political economic concerns into climate governance.

Similarly, debt relief for developing and emerging economies has regained discursive currency amid rising inflation (mainly due to appreciation of fossil fuel and food prices through Russia's invasion of Ukraine) and a hawkish Federal Reserve that successively increased its base lending rate to 1.50–1.75% (Pollard, 2022; Richter, 2022; Rockeman & Miller, 2022; Torres, 2022) that stoke the fear of another Volcker Shock that exacerbated the debt crisis across Latin America in the late 1970–80 (Sommer, 2022). In his op-ed intervention with the Financial Times, Gallagher (2022) argues for debt relief to be linked to climate and development targets. This form of debt for climate alignment is not without precedent. Seychelles exchanged sovereign debt in return for marine conservation by creating new marine parks (Carrington, 2018; Cassola, 2018; Gerretsen, 2020). Essentially, the Nature Conservancy bought US$ 22 million of national debt owed to the UK, France, Belgium, and Italy at a discount (ibid.). Similar to previous initiatives that forgo outstanding demands on debt, this form of debt forgiveness in return for nature conservation will likely be exclusively emulated in public debt contexts. It nonetheless offers an alternative to green bonds following an inverse logic and foregrounds distributional concerns that are too often swept under the carpet when gearing up for a finance-led transition. These examples demonstrate the need to expand research not only on the generational, but more so on the geographical divides characterizing the nexus between green finance solutions and calls for a just transition across global South and North.

My research underscores the relevance of institutional investor mandates as promising precursors for low-carbon investments. Indeed, the overarching outlook on safeguarding returns arguably includes preventing climate change from leaving assets stranded. How political pressure can be mobilized to better align mandates with climate targets will be a core concern of corporate governance and could significantly support the scale-up of climate-aligned solutions like green bonds for the capital markets. At the meso- and macro-level, green bond regulation could also be tightened. Practical questions come in readily: How can regulations be devised as stringent as possible to not sacrifice climate impact in favor of industry benefits? Could climate thresholds, for example, be incrementally increased to set incentives for more thorough greening? What are ways to straddle the trade-off between environmental and social concerns, i.e. through domestic communities co-owning and co-benefiting from project returns.

This brief juxtaposition of current developments both within technical and redistributive channels of financing demonstrates interesting prospects for scholarly inquiry that extend beyond the scope of this book.

Concluding Remarks

By way of summarizing this book, climate change has developed into a paramount crisis that needs to be urgently addressed. My research scrutinized the political economy of transition endeavors driven by financial sector innovations. By critically evaluating 'green' innovations in the financial realm, this work ties in with scholarship advancing pathways to addressing climate change from an international political economy (IPE) vantage point (Paterson, 2020b) thereby contributing to closing a "blind spot" within IPE (Paterson, 2020a, p. 2; see also LeBaron et al., 2020). My work disclosed the political trade-offs guiding seemingly technical endeavors and, thus, enriches socio-technical transition scholarship (i.e. Geels, 2014; Köhler et al., 2019). It, also, adds to the debate around financing low-carbon transitions by demonstrating both the potential and—more so—the limits of green bonds. It thus provides insights for critical finance scholarship (i.e. Christophers, 2021; Gabor, 2021) as much as reform-oriented finance scholars (i.e. Banga, 2019; Monk & Perkins, 2020). By deploying a qualitative methodology, lastly, I contributed important empirical findings to a field otherwise dominated by quantitative analyses. Though at times very extensive interviews, I was able to foreground the discursive logics and practices driving and inhibiting finance-led transition endeavors. My work on green bonds added various new facets to these literature strands and provides a comprehensive assessment for some of the reasons behind the limited take-up of green bonds in South Africa.

On this premise, green bonds can be summarized as an incomplete instrument. They can certainly play a role in directing funding towards climate alignment and offer a fascinating valve for climate-aligned profit-making. The instrument embodies the attempt to price in climate externalities, confers visibility to issuers pursuing low-carbon solutions, and lifts capital market engagement with climate change and decarbonization onto new heights. But green bonds fall short of ambition in several ways, each yielding reasons for the limited take-up of green bonds in South Africa.

First and foremost, they do not upend market rationales. Like other market instruments, green bonds do not overcome the very limitations the market accords to these instruments. Green bonds require profitable returns to be attractive for investors. This dependence on market metrics directly impedes a successful expansion in emerging markets. Profitable projects—whether green or any other color—are hard to find in South African context, putting off investors. The oft-touted advantage of a *greenium* or lower capital costs for issuers neither materializes consistently in subordinate financial markets. The instrument, thus, carries no transformational potential to overcome structural limitations of capital markets.

Secondly, their record on creating additionality and, thus, climate-aligned outcomes can be questioned. Globally, it is predominantly used to refinance *existing* projects rather than financing new developments. Due to the risk divide in the project finance context, hardly any institutional investor is ready to take the risks associated with construction. Transition and KPI-linked bonds can be read as attempts to tackle this shortcoming and so are efforts at pooling projects for a portfolio play with diversified risks.

It is, again, due to its underlying logic of profitability that green bonds offer limited clout in a political economic environment fraught with fossil path-dependency and socio-economic crises. It essentially lacks the characteristics to accommodate concerns beyond a simple risk-return logic and carries limited participatory or re-distributional potential. For an economy locked in fossil dependence, green investment opportunities are scarce, providing a structural explanation for the instrument's limited success. The (necessarily) cumbersome procedures accompanying environmental and climate due diligence actively discourage some investors from entering this space, disclosing the immediate trade-offs between climate alignment and a just transition, on the one hand, and rent-seeking, on the other. That is why green bonds face opposition as an instrument orchestrated mainly by the business elite in top-down fashion.

By turning a blind eye on the political economic ramifications, a climate-aligned overhaul will have on the rest of the South African economy, the instrument unveils its narrow technical recipe. Beyond offering financial leverage and promising trickle-down effects of pension fund returns to its retired members, the instrument does little to advance a just transition. Rather than transforming unequal socio-economic structures, the tool presents, at best, an opportunity for economic reconfiguration towards closer climate alignment. Its limited take-up in South Africa comes as no surprise given this politically charged terrain of the transition trajectory.

What is more, the hype around this instrument is driven out of the green bond community itself and is, therefore, partially engineered. Notwithstanding the global growth rates, we are far from a green overhaul of the capital markets, not least in the South African context. The missing take-up in South Africa demonstrates the limited resonance and success rate it yields in an emerging market context.

There is very little time left to address the climate crisis. Finding ways to finance mitigation and adaptation endeavors is an integral question of our generation. My work on green bonds offered a glimpse into contemporary efforts to align capital markets with climate goals. Climate change can only be tackled through comprehensive and concerted action endowed with the necessary political will. Green bonds represent a small cog in the machinery whose trajectory has yet to properly incorporate just transition components in order to garner the necessary political support. There are more financial innovations to ensue and, thus, plenty of more research to conduct to advance climate alignment. An implementation addressing the political economic contexts through fair and participatory mechanisms will likely get us there faster.

References

Asiyanbi, A. P. (2018). Financialisation in the green economy: Material connections, markets-in-the-making and Foucauldian organising actions. *Environment and Planning A, 50*(3), 531–548. https://doi.org/10.1177/030851 8X17708787

Author's notes at Green Taxonomy Launch. (2022). *Launch of the green finance taxonomy for South Africa* (pp. 1–9). via Zoom.

Baker, L. (2015, July). The evolving role of finance in South Africa's renewable energy sector. *Geoforum, 64*, 146–156. https://doi.org/10.1016/j.geo forum.2015.06.01

Baker, L., Hook, A., & Sovacool, B. K. (2021, July). Power struggles: Governing renewable electricity in a time of technological disruption. *Geoforum, 118,* 93–105. https://doi.org/10.1016/j.geoforum.2020.12.006

Baker, L., & Sovacool, B. K. (2017). The political economy of technological capabilities and global production networks in South Africa's wind and solar photovoltaic (PV) industries. *Political Geography, 60,* 1–12. https://doi.org/10.1016/j.polgeo.2017.03.003

Banga, J. (2019). The green bond market: A potential source of climate finance for developing countries. *Journal of Sustainable Finance and Investment, 9*(1), 17–32. https://doi.org/10.1080/20430795.2018.1498617

Best, J., & Paterson, M. (2010). *Cultural political economy* (J. Best & M. Paterson, Eds., 1st ed.). Routledge.

Bigger, P. (2017). Measurement and the circulation of risk in green bonds. *Journal of Environmental Investing, 8*(1), 273–287.

Bigger, P., & Millington, N. (2019). *Getting soaked? Climate crisis, adaptation finance, and racialized austerity* (Working Paper). https://www.uam.es/gru posinv/meva/publicacionesjesus/capitulos_espanyol_jesus/2005_motivacion paraelaprendizajePerspectivaalumnos.pdf and https://www.researchgate.net/ profile/Juan_Aparicio7/publication/253571379_Los_estudios_sobre_el_cam bio_conceptual_

Bos, K., & Gupta, J. (2018). Climate change: The risks of stranded fossil fuel assets and resources to the developing world. *Third World Quarterly, 39*(3), 436–453. https://doi.org/10.1080/01436597.2017.1387477

Bracking, S. (2015). Performativity in the Green Economy: How far does climate finance create a fictive economy? *Third World Quarterly, 36*(12), 2337–2357. https://doi.org/10.1080/01436597.2015.1086263

Burton, J., Marquard, A., & McCall, B. (2019, July). *Socio-economic considerations for a Paris Agreement-compatible coal transition in South Africa* (pp. 1–24). www.climate-transparency.org

Caprotti, F., Essex, S., Phillips, J., de Groot, J., & Baker, L. (2020, April). Scales of governance: Translating multiscalar transitional pathways in South Africa's energy landscape. *Energy Research and Social Science, 70,* 101700. https://doi.org/10.1016/j.erss.2020.101700

Carrington, D. (2018, February 22). Debt for dolphins: Seychelles creates huge marine parks in world first finance scheme. *The Guardian.* https://www.the guardian.com/environment/2018/feb/22/debt-for-dolphins-seychelles-cre ate-huge-new-marine-parks-in-world-first-finance-scheme

Cassola, G. (2018). *Case study: Debt-for-nature-finance swap.* https://seyccat. org/wp-content/uploads/2019/07/SSCOE-Debt-for-Nature-Seychelles-Case-Study-final.pdf

Castree, N., & Christophers, B. (2015). Banking spatially on the future: Capital switching, infrastructure, and the ecological fix. *Annals of the Association of American Geographers, 105*(2), 378–386. https://doi.org/10.1080/000 45608.2014.985622

CBI & Agora Energiewende. (2021). *Green bonds in South Africa: How green bonds can support South Africa's energy transition.* https://www.climatebonds. net/files/reports/cbio_sa_energytrans_03d.pdf

Chancel, L., Piketty, T., Saez, E., & Zucman, G. (2022). *World Inquality Report.* https://wir2022.wid.world/www-site/uploads/2021/12/ WorldInequalityReport2022_Full_Report.pdf

Cheru, F. (2016). Developing countries and the right to development: A retrospective and prospective African view. *Third World Quarterly, 37*(7), 1268–1283. https://doi.org/10.1080/01436597.2016.1154439

Chiapello, E. (2020). Financialization as a socio-technical process. In P. Mader, D. Mertens, & N. van der Zwan (Eds.), *The Routledge international handbook of financialization* (1st ed., pp. 81–91). https://doi.org/10.4324/978131 5142876-7

Christophers, B. (2021). Fossilised capital: Price and profit in the energy transition. *New Political Economy, 27*(1), 146–159. https://doi.org/10.1080/135 63467.2021.1926957

Christophers, B., Bigger, P., & Johnson, L. (2020). Stretching scales? Risk and sociality in climate finance. *Environment and Planning A, 52*(1), 88–110. https://doi.org/10.1177/0308518X18819004

Dafermos, Y., Gabor, D., & Michell, J. (2021). The Wall Street Consensus in pandemic times: What does it mean for climate-aligned development? *Canadian Journal of Development Studies / Revue Canadienne d'études Du Développement, 42*(1–2), 238–251. https://doi.org/10.1080/02255189. 2020.1865137

Daily Maverick/Reuters. (2022, March 24). *World Bank sells first 'rhino' bond to help South Africa's conservation efforts.* https://www.dailymaverick.co.za/art icle/2022-03-24-world-bank-sells-first-rhino-bond-to-help-south-africas-con servation-efforts/?utm_term=Autofeed&utm_medium=Social&utm_source= Facebook&fbclid=IwAR2FTCSFLtvM55KpfnVyxt8cDUZhmMwqVkY-751 DyBNmMu7bZmqdgQrprBs#E

Elsner, C., Neumann, M., Müller, F., & Claar, S. (2021). Room for money or manoeuvre? How green financialization and de-risking shape Zambia's renewable energy transition. *Canadian Journal of Development Studies, 43*(2), 276–295. https://doi.org/10.1080/02255189.2021.1973971

European Commission. (2020). Fossil CO_2 and GHG emissions of all world countries. In *JRC Publications Repository* (Vol. 105, Issue D2). https://doi. org/10.2760/56420

Fine, B., & Rustomjee, Z. (1996). The political economy of South Africa: Introduction. In *Poverty and governance in South Asia* (pp. viii–16). https://doi. org/10.4324/9781315741932-8

Gabor, D. (2019). *Securitization for sustainability—Does it help achieve the sustainable development goals.* https://us.boell.org/sites/default/files/gabor_finalized.pdf

Gabor, D. (2020a). Critical macro-finance: A theoretical lens. *Finance and Society, 6*(1), 45–55. https://doi.org/10.2218/finsoc.v6i1.4408

Gabor, D. (2020b, April). *The Wall Street Consensus* (Working Paper, pp. 1–23). https://doi.org/10.31235/osf.io/wab8m

Gabor, D. (2021). The Wall Street Consensus. *Development and Change, 52*(3), 429–459. https://doi.org/10.1111/dech.12645

Gallagher, K. (2022, April 12). Letter: Linking debt relief to climate change is way to go. *Financial Times.* http://www.rhumb-line.com/pdf/BorgersonForeignAffairsarticle.pdf

Geddes, A., Schmidt, T. S., & Steffen, B. (2018). The multiple roles of state investment banks in low-carbon energy finance: An analysis of Australia, the UK and Germany. *Energy Policy, 115*, 158–170. https://doi.org/10.1016/j.enpol.2018.01.009

Geels, F. W. (2014). Regime resistance against low-carbon transitions: Introducing politics and power into the multi-level perspective. *Theory, Culture & Society, 31*(5), 21–40. https://doi.org/10.1177/0263276414531627

Geels, F. W. (2019). Socio-technical transitions to sustainability: A review of criticisms and elaborations of the multi-level perspective. *Current Opinion in Environmental Sustainability, 39*, 187–201. https://doi.org/10.1016/j.cosust.2019.06.009

Geels, F. W., & Schot, J. (2007). Typology of sociotechnical transition pathways. *Research Policy, 36*(3), 399–417. https://doi.org/10.1016/j.respol.2007.01.003

Gerretsen, I. (2020, August 3). *The deal that saved Seychelles' troubled waters* (pp. 1–8). https://www.bbc.com/future/article/20200803-the-deal-that-saved-seychelles-troubled-waters

Griffith-Jones, S., Spiegel, S., Xu, J., Carreras, M., & Naqvi, N. (2021). Matching risks with instruments in development banks. *Review of Political Economy.* https://doi.org/10.1080/09538259.2021.1978229

Hilbrandt, H., & Grubbauer, M. (2020). Standards and SSOs in the contested widening and deepening of financial markets: The arrival of Green Municipal Bonds in Mexico City. *Environment and Planning A, 52*(7), 1415–1433. https://doi.org/10.1177/0308518X20909391

Hurley, M. (2021, April 7). Green bond comment, April 2021: Central banks and a growing "greenium." *Environmental Finance.* https://www.environmental-finance.com/content/analysis/green-bond-comment-april-2021-central-banks-and-a-growing-greenium.html

Hyun, S., Park, D., & Tian, S. (2020). The price of going green: The role of greenness in green bond markets. *Accounting and Finance, 60*(1), 73–95. https://doi.org/10.1111/acfi.12515

Jones, R., Baker, T., Huet, K., Murphy, L., & Lewis, N. (2020, June). Treating ecological deficit with debt: The practical and political concerns with green bonds. *Geoforum, 114*, 49–58. https://doi.org/10.1016/j.geoforum.2020.05.014

Kaltenbrunner, A., & Painceira, J. P. (2015). Developing countries' changing nature of financial integration and new forms of external vulnerability: The Brazilian experience. *Cambridge Journal of Economics, 39*(5), 1281–1306. https://doi.org/10.1093/cje/beu038

Karwowski, E. (2019). How Financialization undermines democracy. *Development and Change, 50*(5), 1466–1481. https://doi.org/10.1111/dech.12537

Karwowski, E., & Stockhammer, E. (2017). Financialisation in emerging economies: A systematic overview and comparison with Anglo-Saxon economies. *Economic and Political Studies, 5*(1), 60–86. https://doi.org/10.1080/20954816.2016.1274520

Kennedy, S. F. (2018). Indonesia's energy transition and its contradictions: Emerging geographies of energy and finance. *Energy Research and Social Science, 41*(June 2017), 230–237. https://doi.org/10.1016/j.erss.2018.04.023

Kern, F., & Markard, J. (2016). Analysing energy transitions: Combining insights from transition studies and international political economy. In T. Van de Graaf, B. K. Sovacool, A. Ghosh, F. Kern, & M. T. Klare (Eds.), *The Palgrave handbook of the international political economy of energy* (1st ed., pp. 291–318). Palgrave Macmillan. https://doi.org/10.1057/978-1-137-55631-8

Knafo, S. (2022). The power of finance in the age of market based banking. *New Political Economy, 27*(1), 33–46. https://doi.org/10.1080/13563467.2021.1910646

Knuth, S. (2018, April). "Breakthroughs" for a green economy? Financialization and clean energy transition. *Energy Research and Social Science, 41*, 220–229. https://doi.org/10.1016/j.erss.2018.04.024

Köhler, J., Geels, F. W., Kern, F., Markard, J., Onsongo, E., Wieczorek, A., Alkemade, F., Avelino, F., Bergek, A., Boons, F., Fünfschilling, L., Hess, D., Holtz, G., Hyysalo, S., Jenkins, K., Kivimaa, P., Martiskainen, M., McMeekin, A., Mühlemeier, M. S., ... Wells, P. (2019). An agenda for sustainability transitions research: State of the art and future directions. *Environmental Innovation and Societal Transitions, 31*, 1–32. https://doi.org/10.1016/j.eist.2019.01.004

Koomson, I., & Awaworyi Churchill, S. (2022, June). Employment precarity and energy poverty in post-apartheid South Africa: Exploring the racial and ethnic dimensions. *Energy Economics, 110*, 1–3. https://doi.org/10.1016/j.eneco. 2022.106026

Kvangraven, I. H., Koddenbrock, K., & Sylla, N. S. (2020). Financial subordination and uneven financialization in 21st century Africa. *Community Development Journal*, 1–22. https://doi.org/10.1093/cdj/bsaa047

LeBaron, G., Mügge, D., Best, J., & Hay, C. (2020). Blind spots in IPE: Marginalized perspectives and neglected trends in contemporary capitalism. *Review of International Political Economy, 28*(2), 283–294. https://doi.org/10.1080/09692290.2020.1830835

Lehmann, I. (2019, May). When cultural political economy meets 'charismatic carbon' marketing: A gender-sensitive view on the limitations of Gold Standard cookstove offset projects. *Energy Research and Social Science, 55*, 146–154. https://doi.org/10.1016/j.erss.2019.05.001

Lester, A. (2021, April 26). Emerging market sustainable bonds deliver "more impact." *Environmental Finance*. https://www.environmental-finance.com/content/analysis/emerging-market-sustainable-bonds-deliver-more-impact.html

MacAskill, S., Roca, E., Liu, B., Stewart, R. A., & Sahin, O. (2021). Is there a green premium in the green bond market? Systematic literature review revealing premium determinants. *Journal of Cleaner Production, 280*, 124491. https://doi.org/10.1016/j.jclepro.2020.124491

Mawdsley, E. (2018). From billions to trillions': Financing the SDGs in a world 'beyond aid.' *Dialogues in Human Geography, 8*(2), 191–195. https://doi.org/10.1177/2043820618780789

Mazzucato, M. (2011). The entrepreneurial state. *Soundings, 49*(49). Demos. https://doi.org/10.3898/136266211798411183

Mihàlovits, Z., & Tapaszti, A. (2018). A new financial tool for renewable energy investments: Green bonds. *Public Finance Quarterly, 63*(3), 303–318.

Monk, A., & Perkins, R. (2020). What explains the emergence and diffusion of green bonds? *Energy Policy, 145*, 111641. https://doi.org/10.1016/j.enpol. 2020.111641

Müller, F., Claar, S., Neumann, M., & Elsner, C. (2020). Is green a Pan-African colour? Mapping African renewable energy policies and transitions in 34 countries. *Energy Research and Social Science, 68*(July 2019), 101551. https://doi.org/10.1016/j.erss.2020.101551

Müller, F., Neumann, M., Elsner, C., & Claar, S. (2021). Assessing African energy transitions: Renewable energy policies, energy justice, and SDG 7. *Politics and Governance, 9*(1), 119–130. https://doi.org/10.17645/pag.v9i1.3615

Naidoo, B. P., & Prinsloo, L. (2022, April 19). South Africa Is poised for 101 days of power outages this year. *Bloomberg*. https://www.bloomberg.com/news/articles/2022-04-19/power-plant-breakdowns-force-eskom-to-widen-south-africa-outages?utm_source=google&utm_medium=bd&cmpId=google

Naidoo, P. (2021, August 24). South Africa unemployment rate rises to highest in the world. *Bloomberg*. https://www.bloomberg.com/news/articles/2021-08-24/south-african-unemployment-rate-rises-to-highest-in-the-world

National Treasury. (2022). *Development process for the South African green finance taxonomy—The process and insights from the development of the 1st edition of the South African green finance taxonomy* (Issue March). https://sustainablefinanceinitiative.org.za/wp-content/downloads/Briefing-Paper_Development-Process-for-the-South-African-Green-Finance-Taxonomy.pdf

Paterson, M. (2010). Legitimation and accumulation in climate change governance. *New Political Economy, 15*(3), 345–368. https://doi.org/10.1080/13563460903288247

Paterson, M. (2020a). Climate change and international political economy: between collapse and transformation. *Review of International Political Economy, 28*(2), 394–405. https://doi.org/10.1080/09692290.2020.1830829

Paterson, M. (2020b). SS-03 'the end of the fossil fuel age'? Discourse politics and climate change political economy. *New Political Economy, 26*(6), 923–936. https://doi.org/10.1080/13563467.2020.1810218

Perrot, Q., & Lester, A. (2021, May 10). ESG "rapidly evolving" in cat bond market despite lack of deals. *Environmental Finance*. https://www.environmental-finance.com/content/analysis/esg-rapidly-evolving-in-cat-bond-market-despite-lack-of-deals.html

Perry, K. K. (2021, February). The new 'bond-age', climate crisis and the case for climate reparations: Unpicking old/new colonialities of finance for development within the SDGs. *Geoforum, 126*, 361–371. https://doi.org/10.1016/j.geoforum.2021.09.003

Pilling, D., Cotterill, J., & Hodgson, C. (2022, November 4). South Africa warns $ 8. 5bn climate package risks fuelling debt burden. *Financial Times*. https://www.ft.com/content/e6653b1d-2302-4e44-81bb-38dc608d303d

Pollard, A. (2022, April 21). South African Rand pummeled by floods and Covid amid hawkish fed. *Bloomberg*. https://www.bloomberg.com/news/articles/2022-04-21/south-african-rand-pummeled-by-floods-and-covid-amid-hawkish-fed

Richter, F. (2022, June 22). US makes most aggressive interest rate hike since 1994. *World Economic Forum*, 1–6. https://www.weforum.org/agenda/2022/06/rates-inflation-federal-reserve-united-states

Rockeman, O., & Miller, R. (2022, March 16). Fed lifts rates a quarter point and signals more hikes to come. *Bloomberg*. https://www.bloomberg.com/news/articles/2022-03-16/fed-lifts-rates-a-quarter-point-in-opening-bid-to-curb-inflation

Sengupta, A. (2002). On the theory and practice of the right to development. *Challenges in International Human Rights Law, 24*(4), 837–899. https://doi.org/10.4324/9781315095905

Sguazzin, A. (2022, March 24). Rhino bond sold by World Bank in first issuance of its kind. *Bloomberg*. https://www.bloomberg.com/news/articles/2022-03-24/rhino-bond-is-sold-by-world-bank-in-first-issuance-of-its-kind

Sommer, J. (2022, September 22). Bad news from the fed? We've been here before. *The New York Times* (pp. 1–7). https://www.nytimes.com/2022/09/22/business/fed-rate-inflation-volcker.html

Stoddard, E. (2022, April 3). Moody's upgrades SA's credit outlook on stable debt burden scenario! *Daily Maverick*. https://www.dailymaverick.co.za/article/2022-04-03-moodys-upgrades-sas-credit-outlook-on-stable-debt-burden-scenario/

Sultana, F. (2022). The unbearable heaviness of climate coloniality. *Political Geography, 99*, 102638. https://doi.org/10.1016/j.polgeo.2022.102638

Sum, N.-L., & Jessop, B. (2013). *Towards a cultural political economy—Putting culture in its place in political economy* (N.-L. Sum & B. Jessop, Eds., 1st ed.). Edward Elgar Publishing Limited.

Swilling, M., & Annecke, E. (2012). *Just transitions—Explorations of sustainability in an unfair world* (1st ed., Vol. 1, Issue 4). United Nations University Press. https://doi.org/10.1080/02652038509373556

Talbot, K. M. (2017). What does green really mean: How increased transparency and standardization can grow the green bond market. *Villanova Environmental Law Journal, 28*(1), 127–146. https://tel.archives-ouvertes.fr/tel-01514176

The Economist. (2022a, November 16). Indonesia's tilt at King Coal. *The Economist*.

The Economist. (2022b, November 20). A new UN fund for "loss and damage" emerges from COP27. *The Economist*. www.economist.com/international/2022/11/20/a-new-un-fund-for-loss-and-damage-emerges-from-cop27

The Guardian. (2022, November 7). Loss and damage issue keeps us Cop27 negotiators wrangling late into the night. *The Guardian*. https://www.theguardian.com/environment/2022/nov/07/loss-and-damage-issue-keeps-us-cop27-negotiators-wrangling-late-into-the-night

Torres, C. (2022, April 21). Powell hardens hawkish pivot toward half-point fed rate hikes. *Bloomberg*. https://www.bloomberg.com/news/articles/2022-04-21/powell-hardens-hawkish-pivot-toward-half-point-fed-rate-hikes

Tripathy, A. (2017). Translating to risk: The legibility of climate change and nature in the green bond market. *Economic Anthropology, 4*(2), 239–250. https://doi.org/10.1002/sea2.12091

UNDP. (2020). *Human Development Report 2020: The next frontier human development and the anthropocene: South Africa*. UNDP. http://hdr.undp.org/sites/all/themes/hdr_theme/country-notes/ZAF.pdf

Unruh, G. C. (2000). Understanding carbon lock-in. *Energy Policy, 28*(12), 817–830. https://doi.org/10.1016/S0301-4215(00)00070-7

Volberding, P. (2021). *Leveraging financial markets for development*. https://doi.org/10.1007/978-3-030-55008-0

Wang, E. K. (2018). Financing green: Reforming green bond regulation in the United States. *Brooklyn Journal of Corporate, Financial & Commercial Law, 12*(2), 9.

World Bank. (2022, March 23). *Wildlife conservation bond boosts South Africa's efforts to protect black rhinos and support local communities*. *3*, 0–3. https://www.worldbank.org/en/news/press-release/2022/03/23/wildlife-conservation-bond-boosts-south-africa-s-efforts-to-protect-black-rhinos-and-support-local-communities

Index

© The Author(s), under exclusive license to Springer Nature
Switzerland AG 2023
M. Neumann, *The Political Economy of Green Bonds in
Emerging Markets*, International Political Economy Series,
https://doi.org/10.1007/978-3-031-30502-3

Printed by Printforce, the Netherlands